Public Adminis...
A case study approach

Bob Mitchell and John Harrison

Mitch, Bob
Von Bell, Bob
Public administration... ...
I. Title. II. Harrison, John.
351

ISBN 0 273 03485

All rights reserved; no part of this
be reproduced, stored in a retrieval system, or
transmitted in any form or by any means, me-
electronic, mechanical, photocopying, recording, or
otherwise, without either the prior written permission
of the Publishers or a licence permitting restricted
copying in the United Kingdom issued by the
Copyright Licensing Agency Ltd, 90 Tottenham
Court Road, London W1P 9HE. This book may not
be lent, resold, hired out or otherwise disposed of by
way of trade in any form of binding or cover other
than that in which it is published, without the prior
consent of the Publishers.

Typeset by P. TEK Art Ltd,
Addscombe, Croydon, Surrey
Printed and bound in Great Britain.

PITMAN PUBLISHING
128 Long Acre, London, WC2E 9AN

A Division of Longman Group UK Limited

© Bob Mitchell and John Harrison 1991

First published in Great Britain 1991

British Library Cataloguing in Publication Data
Mitchell, Bob
  Public administration: A case study approach.
  I. Title   II. Harrison, John
  351

ISBN 0 273 034855

Typeset by ⊼ Tek Art Ltd,
Addiscombe, Croydon, Surrey
Printed and bound in Great Britain

Contents

Preface

Contents

Decisions made in the Town Hall and in the British and European Parliaments have far-reaching effects on our lives from the cradle to the grave. We ignore them at our peril! We can and should influence what they do by using our vote at the ballot box and making our voices heard. In order to exercise this duty wisely we need to know what they do and understand the policies they advocate. With this in mind, we have written *Public Administration* to help bring about an awareness and stimulate an interest in current political and governmental issues. In examining these issues we have also drawn attention to the day-to-day responsibilities and problems encountered by administrative staff working in public sector organisations. With the increasing influence of the European Community in many aspects of business and public administration, we have included a chapter and a case study based on its organisation and functions.

The content and approach of this book is appropriate for those studying for:

1   BTEC National in Public Administration
    • Public Administration 1 and 2
    • Integrated Core Units
2   BTEC National in Business and Finance
    • Aspects of the Organisation in its Environment
    • Option Unit Business and Government
    • Integrated Core Units
3   GCE 'A' Level in Politics and Government.

We have taken account of the anticipated changes in assessment which will be made in future to provide for NVQ competences and we are confident that the realistic and high-quality simulations provided in this book will meet this need.

Key facts of politics and government are given in the chapters, together with selected current topics for class discussion or homework purposes. Whilst these provide useful guidance and information, students should be encouraged to refer to other information sources and the relevant statutes which are listed on p 183.

The case studies are contributed by staff at work and are, therefore, drawn from current administrative practices, reflecting as they do today's office scenario and the problems involved in everyday public administration situations. We have included a cross-section of public sector organisations which complement the content of the chapters.

The case studies contain:

• background information about the organisation
• organisation charts
• relevant statistical data
• job descriptions of specific personnel roles
• problems and situations associated with administrative procedures
• student activities.

Each case study has a number of integrated and problem-solving activities to develop work skills and to contribute towards the achievement of the BTEC National objectives. One section of the activities is designed for students working on their own and another section for students working in groups. These tasks are intended to develop skills of recall, research, analysis, use of initiative, team-work and an understanding of modern administrative practices. As a result, the student is encouraged to learn through association with an organisation and it is hoped that this experience will prove to be both rewarding and thought-provoking.

The case studies are comprehensive and provide a realistic setting for the activities but they are not intended to supply all of the answers. Students should be encouraged to develop their own ideas and find out information for themselves by turning to books, journals, newspapers, radio and television and other sources. The material on which these case studies are based was supplied at the time of the authors' visits to the organisations and it does not take account of any changes that may have taken place subsequently. Also, the information in the chapters must be viewed in the light of any recent developments and changes in legislation which may have taken place since the book was written.

We would wish to reiterate our thanks to all the staff we were privileged to meet when we called on them to discuss their work. They were all most helpful and keen to contribute their experiences for the benefit of others. We also wish to thank their managers for allowing us to visit their offices and for the valuable information they supplied for the case studies.

Acknowledgements

We would like to thank the following for their advice and valuable contributions to the case studies:

Richard Ashworth — British Gas Southern
Richard Bates — Southampton Labour Party
Dipti Bhayani — BBC
Patricia Church — Audit Commission
Michael Dempsey — NALGO
Tony Ford — Cantell School
Wendy Gardiner — Southampton City
  Council
Gordon Ifill — ACAS
Rod Leafe — Eastleigh College of Further
  Education
Lorna Leverett — Hampshire County Council
Vaughan Lindsay — Shelter

Helen McAvoy — European Parliament
Ellie Man — Wessex Regional Health
  Authority
Dorota Mosowicz — Shelter
Beverley Pearce — British Gas Southern
Sir David Price, MP
Linda Ronaldson — BBC
Maggie Smart — House of Commons
Isabel Ward — House of Commons
Sally Woodford — Wessex Regional Health
  Authority
Staff of the Southampton Reference Library

Part A

Introduction

1 The meaning of public administration

Public administration has been defined as 'the action part of government; the means by which the purposes and goals of government are realised' (Corson and Harris, '*Public Administration in Modern Society*', McGraw Hill (1969)). Traditional constitutional theory states that governments, i.e. the elected politicians, make policy and the administrators carry it out. With the growing complexity of government this clear distinction has become blurred at the edges. As we shall see later, administrators in both central and local government often have a considerable influence on policy-making. Indeed, it is no longer possible to clearly distinguish between policy and administration.

Public administration versus Private administration

It is usually argued that public administration is primarily concerned with producing a service to the public. It must take account of social and environmental costs as well as financial costs and it has to balance conflicting social interests. In theory it should always act in the public interest and be subject to continuing public criticism. Unfortunately the public interest is usually coloured by the policies and practices of the particular political party in power nationally or locally at any given time. Similarly the complexities of the modern governmental administrative machine are often too great for the individual citizen to comprehend. How often have we heard the plaintive cry: 'It doesn't matter what I say or do — no one in authority will take any notice' or 'Why should I bother to vote — nothing will change'. One side effect of this attitude has been

the growth of pressure groups either on a national or local basis. We shall return to the role of pressure groups in Chapter 6. Since 1979 the Conservative Government has had as one of its major objectives the control of public expenditure. Both central and local government have had to pay much more attention than hitherto to efficiency and minimising costs, sometimes at the expense of services. Performance targets have been set in most public institutions. The threat of privatisation and competitive tendering has compelled public administration to be more cost-conscious and to act in a more business-like way.

It is generally the case that administrators in the private sector are primarily concerned with maximising profits on behalf of their shareholders. However, this is not always so. Sometimes managers are more concerned with the growth and expansion of their company than with the short-term maximisation of profits. In the past shareholders have been content to let the managers manage and only intervene when things went seriously wrong. In recent years, however, the institutional investors have largely replaced individual shareholders and they tend to keep a closer check on the progress of the company. Also, even the largest companies, such as BAT plc, may be subject to take-over bids if their profit ratios are not considered adequate. On the other hand, the private sector has been forced to pay some attention to social costs. In recent years the environment has become a major political issue. Private industry has begun to realise that it cannot ignore the social consequences of its production. People are concerned about pollution of the atmosphere, our rivers and the sea. The threat of legislation, primarily from the European Community (EC), is compelling private and public industry to spend considerable sums of money to reduce or prevent pollution. This inevitably reduces their overall profit.

The public sector

In financial terms the public sector is defined as all those organisations and activities which need to be financed from public funds. They can conveniently be divided into five groups:

- central administration — the Civil Service
- local administration — local government service
- directly financed organisations, e.g. the National Health Service
- quasi non-governmental organisations — quangos, e.g. Health and Safety Commission and Executive, Monopolies and Mergers Commission, Race Relations Board, etc.
- public corporations — nationalised industries, e.g. British Rail, Post Office, etc.

We shall deal with each of these groups in later chapters.

The size of the public sector

It is the declared aim of the Conservative Government to 'roll back the frontiers of the state'. The reasons given for this are political and economic, as follows:

1 There is a belief that people should be encouraged to 'stand on their own feet' and not be too reliant on the all powerful machine of government. This, it is argued, increases individual freedom and choice.
2 The strongly held view that in general the private sector inspired by the profit motive is more efficient than the public sector. This is illustrated in Case Study 1 on British Gas plc which is an example of a state industry that has been privatised. A discussion of the arguments for and against privatisation are given in Chapter 9.
3 A desire to reduce both taxation and government borrowing. The latter is seen as an essential element in the fight against inflation. To achieve these twin objectives public expenditure must be reduced as a proportion of total expenditure as must the public sector

borrowing requirement (PSBR), i.e. the difference between the government's income from taxation and what it spends.

As we shall see in later chapters the 1980s brought forth a reduction in the number of civil servants; restrictions on local government and health service spending; a requirement for competitive tendering for parts of the functions of local authorities and health authorities; a reduction in the number of quangoes; privatisation of a large part of the nationalised industry sector with the consequent reduction in the number of people employed in the public sector; and a substantial reduction of public expenditure as a proportion of gross domestic product (GDP). Much of the political controversy in the 1980s was about the role of the state and the amount it spent. This argument will undoubtedly continue into the 1990s.

In this brief introduction we have used such terms as 'state' and 'government'. Before proceeding to a more detailed analysis we need to define these terms and account for the development of the British Constitution.

Discussion questions

1 What are the essential differences between public administration and private administration?
2 Is private administration more efficient than public administration and, if so, why?
3 Is there a case for increasing taxation in order to provide better public services?

Written questions

4 List the organisations which have been transferred from the public sector to the private sector since 1979.
5 Contact one of the organisations you have included in (4) in your area and write a report showing any changes in their organisation that have occurred since privatisation.

CASE STUDY 1 British Gas plc

Company background

'This is the story of British Gas. It begins under the sea and ends with its customers in their homes, offices, public buildings and factories' — the introduction to British Gas 'Energy is our Business' pamphlet.

We have deliberately included British Gas in our book of public administration case studies as it is a good example of a privatised public service company. In 1986 British Gas became a public limited company with nearly 2.7 million shareholders, many owning shares for the first time. Up until this date British Gas had been a public corporation with its assets in public ownership and with a board of management appointed by the Secretary of State for Energy, and accountable through its annual report to Parliament.

Gas is of great importance to Britain's economy. More than half the gas sold in Britain is used by households, mostly for heating and hot water. Against competition from other fuels, British Gas provides almost 60 per cent of the energy supplied to our homes. In 1976 13.4 million households used gas and by 1987 this figure had increased to almost 16.5 million. This increase results from the policy of investing in extensions to the mains and making gas more widely available. In addition, an important contribution has been made by marketing. British Gas has collaborated with manufacturers in developing and promoting appliances and their 750 showrooms provide an opportunity for customers to see the latest appliances for heating and cooking. The increased sales of gas and appliances have helped to create wealth and the profits generated over the last five years have enabled the company to invest some £3500 million to improve service and expand business.

In addition to the domestic market, British Gas has around half a million commercial customers including offices, hotels, shops, restaurants, schools and government buildings and it supplies about a third of industry's heat energy.

The advice of British Gas as a leader in gas technology is sought by overseas gas companies. Technology pioneered by British Gas engineers has been adopted in many countries, including the USA, Japan and West Germany.

The company not only supplies gas through an extensive pipeline grid but, unlike most overseas gas companies, its activities include exploring for gas and operating offshore gas fields, as well as selling and servicing gas-burning appliances.

Until the 1960s gas in Britain was essentially a manufactured fuel derived mainly from coal, but today's gas is a clean, naturally-occurring fuel, consisting largely of methane. For the most part it is extracted from undersea fields off the coasts of Britain and Norway. The gas fields are generally operated by oil companies including Amoco, BP, Conoco, Phillips, Shell and Total, but British Gas has a stake in two developed gas fields and owns two others outright.

British Gas has contracts to buy gas with over 60 different companies. These contracts specify the maximum and minimum amounts of gas that can be taken from the field each year, the price and the quality. The purchasing of gas is of crucial importance to the business. Unless it buys gas efficiently British Gas cannot ensure that it makes a return on its massive investments, and that there is enough gas to meet demand. Very large sums are involved in gas purchase, for example, in 1987 gas worth more than £3000 million was bought. In negotiating each contract the interests of all concerned must be taken into account, i.e. the customers for gas, the owners of the gas fields, as well as British Gas itself.

The company's aims embodied in its charter for staff are:

- to enhance the long-term profitability of the company in the best interests of shareholders
- to meet the company's regulatory responsibilities as a public gas supplier
- to provide a gas supply that is safe, secure, reliable, economical and supported by high standards of service
- to manage the business in the most effective manner, with clear policy direction from the Board of Directors
- to manage the supporting activities of appliance selling, installation and contracting, and exploration and production so that each

makes the best contribution to the company's profitability
- to foster good relations with shareholders, customers, employees, suppliers and the community.

British Gas prides itself on being a good neighbour and caring for the communities it serves. The arts, sport, education, community projects and youth programmes all benefit each year from the company's financial assistance.

Nearly 80 000 people work directly for British Gas at its headquarters in London and at the 12 regions. The headquarters co-ordinates the regional operations and formulates broad policy for the industry. It also obtains bulk supplies of gas and distributes them to the regions and manages an annual £70 million research and development programme. Each of the regions is a substantial

business in its own right, with a degree of autonomy which ensures that within the framework of the overall organisation, it can develop and sustain its own identity. The regions manage all day-to-day customer-related activities. The administrative tasks facing the regions are formidable. They include issuing nearly 80 million accounts each year. An investment of over £100 million in information technology plays an integral part in helping to run the business more efficiently.

Case study situation

Beverley Pearce, the subject of this case study, works at the Southern Regional headquarters as an Administrative Assistant in the Customer Accounting Department — 5300 people are employed by British Gas Southern, 500 of whom are engaged in customer accounting. Beverley has been one of their employees since she left the local sixth form college and, prior to her present job, she worked as a Junior Clerk in the debt collection section. Whilst she has been employed Beverley has continued her education by attending a BTEC National Certificate day-release course at the local technical college, gaining a distinction.

Figures 1.2 and 1.3 show the management structure for the regional headquarters and the structure of the Customer Accounting Planning Department containing Beverley Pearce's position. She works under the direction of the Supervisor of the Administration Section and is a member of a team reporting to the Special Services Officer.

Job description

Beverley assists in the development of customer accounting mainframe systems and procedures and in the development and maintenance of micro-computer systems. Her duties consist of the following:

1 Assisting in the development of mainframe systems in operation in customer accounting from feasibility through systems specification, testing, training and implementation.
2 Developing end-user computer applications

Fig 1.1 Beverley Pearce, Administrative Assistant in the Customer Accounting Department of British Gas Southern

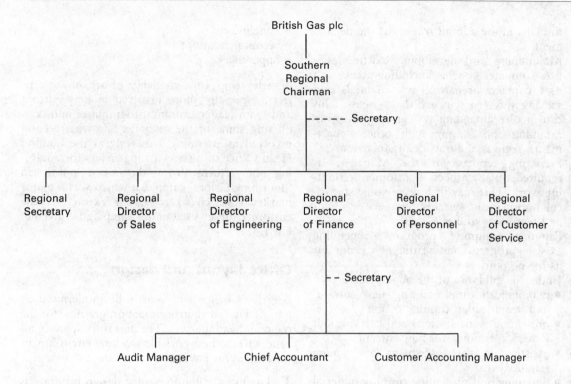

Fig 1.2 Organisation chart for British Gas plc Regional Management Structure

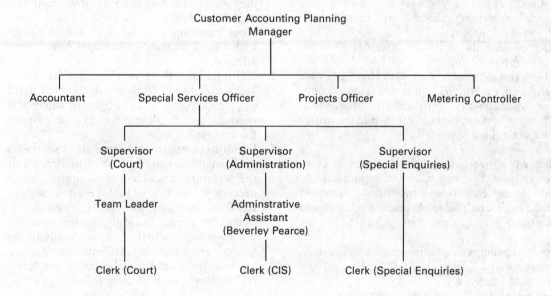

Fig 1.3 Organisation chart for British Gas plc Customer Accounting Planning Department

to assist in the administration of the department.

3 Maintaining and developing existing end-user computer systems, including acting as a user contact, preparing user manuals and seeking ways to improve the systems. This can involve amending system designs, programming and liaising with other departments, regions and outside organisations.

4 Preparing reports for the Manager, as required, on any aspect of customer accounting work. This may include periodic statistical information, systems reference manuals and feasibility studies.

5 Running computer programs, amending existing programs and writing new programs as the need arises.

6 Under the guidance of the Supervisor:
- planning and implementing 'new entrant' and 'team leader' training courses
- presenting some sessions and carrying out induction training for new entrants
- assisting in the assessment of training requirements
- designing and presenting training material for courses, staff briefings and policy changes to meet specific needs for the Customer Accounting Department, other departments and external agencies
- analysing effectiveness of courses and recommending changes to management where appropriate.

7 Supervising the customer information services support team;

8 Undertaking general administrative duties for the department, including ordering stationery, recruitment administration and organisation of special events, e.g. seminars, office moves, school visits, etc.

In her work involving the development of computer systems, Beverley has to communicate the results of her enquiries in the form of a report and she finds it helpful to present the information using the following categories:

- report headings, i.e. recipient(s), sender, date, reference and subject
- terms of reference
- procedure, i.e. the steps taken to conduct the enquiry
- findings

- conclusions
- recommendations
- appendices.

Beverley enjoys the challenge of organising projects, especially those involved in new entrant and team leader training programmes and conducting some of the sessions. She was recently involved in attending a meeting at the London Head Office to discuss arrangements for analysing the returns from the much publicised 'Banishing Gripes' campaign which was a major market research exercise. An extract of the customer survey used in this campaign is given in Fig 1.4.

Office layout and design

Beverley's office will shortly be modernised as part of a major refurbishment programme for the regional headquarters. The aim is to upgrade all offices to the best possible working environment for employees having regard to the following:

1 **Layout:** a computer-aided design program is used to provide an open-plan layout with screens and cabinets to identify work areas.

2 **Working relationships:** attention is paid to the needs of individuals and groups and how they interrelate with the idea of developing a 'team' concept.

3 **Floor covering:** carpets of a modern design with hard-wearing qualities have been selected.

4 **Lighting:** here there is a trial in the use of local 'uplighting' from stands close to desks to provide more efficient lighting where it is needed, as an alternative to the existing fluorescent lighting.

5 **Furniture:** systems furniture is used with cable management, i.e. cables hidden inside the furniture. Each desk is equipped, where necessary, with a double electric socket. Laminate furniture has been selected in preference to veneer not only for its durability but to be sympathetic with the needs of the 'green' environment. Systems furniture is ergonomically and socially better for integrating people with modern technology.

In re-designing the offices at the Southern Region Headquarters Richard Ashworth, the Project

Customer Survey

I would like you to think about the total service that we offer, and let me know how you feel by answering the questions below.

Please indicate how you feel by giving us a score out of 10 (10 = excellent, 1 = very poor). If you don't know please leave blank.

Attending to gas leaks	☐	Laying gas pipes	☐
Repairing appliances	☐	Repairing gas pipes	☐
Installing appliances	☐	Gas bills	☐
Servicing appliances	☐	Selling appliances	☐
Telephone enquiries	☐	Bill payment options	☐
Meter reading	☐	Maintaining your gas supply	☐

What most pleases you about the service we offer?

____

What most irritates you about the service we offer?

____

If you had to pick one thing which we could do which would most improve your view of our service, what would it be?

____

If you wish to make any further comments please put them on the reverse then return the completed survey in the envelope attached.

British Gas

Detach here and place in envelope.

Fig 1.4 British Gas plc Customer Survey

Controller, has also incorporated such features as the use of green plants with attractive foliage, co-ordinated colour schemes, a variety of layout to provide interest and, of course, the requirements for the health and safety of employees.

Communications

In a large organisation, such as British Gas Southern, it is important to provide regular communications with staff and this is achieved by means of monthly newspapers, regular newsletters and quarterly administration meetings for the staff of each section. Staff are also encouraged to make suggestions by means of the official suggestion scheme in which staff may qualify for cash awards. In the suggestion scheme form it states: 'No management claims to have the monopoly of ideas — and your idea may be the very one to improve efficiency:

- it may save money (and time is also money!)
- it may increase sales
- it may improve service to customers
- it may improve equipment or appliances
- it may cut down waste
- it may prevent accidents or fire hazards
- it may simply improve the way we go about things.

In presenting your suggestion it would help if you were able to quantify certain information such as:

- estimated cost savings
- cost of implementation
- benefits to staff or company'

Staff appraisal

A staff appraisal scheme operates throughout British Gas Southern in which each member of staff has an interview once a year with their immediate supervisor. The forms illustrated below are completed and agreed between both parties to establish the employee's performance during the past year and to fix targets for the following year.

BRITISH GAS plc Southern   **Strictly confidential**

Management appraisal

Review date ....

Name ....   Pay no. ....

Job title ....   Date of birth ....

Department ....   Grade ....

....   Date of present appointment ....

Review completed by:

   Name ....

   Job title ....

   Department ....

Reviewed approved by:

   Name ....

   Job title ....

   Department ....

Part 1 *Key result areas*

A *Objectives for period under review*

Objective	Details of standard of performance achieved for each objective

Part I

B *Key skill areas*

In the performance category column please indicate which of the following categories is appropriate.

- **strength** : this is an area where the individual demonstrates high ability and performance

- **satisfactory** : this is an area where the individual shows performance and ability adequate to the needs of the job role

- **needs improvement** : this is an area where the individual is below the required standard and must make efforts to improve

- **not applicable** : this key skill area is not a part of the job role.

Skill area	Performance category	Supporting comments
Job knowledge		
Planning		
Control		
Problem solving		
Decision making		
Technical ability		
Cost control		
Attitude to change		

Skill area	Performance category	Supporting comments
Leadership		
Team building		
Delegation		
Communication (oral)		
Communication (written)		

C *Overall assessment* – please tick

Outstanding ( ) A performance which is consistently characterised by exceptionally high quality work, intellectual ability and leadership.

Highly commendable ( ) High quality and quantity of work together with marked initiative and leadership.

Commendable ( ) Sound judgement and mastery of appointment. At times produces work of a quality that exceeds that of 'fully proficient' for the appointment.

Fully proficient ( ) Fully acceptable performance. Objectives met and assignments properly handled.

Marginal ( ) Performance does not fully meet requirements of position. Some objectives and assignments are not met. Above normal supervision required.

Unsatisfactory ( ) Clearly below minimum standard. Objectives not normally met nor work completed. Deficient in most major aspects.

Comments
(Indicate the areas of activity that have led to the above assessment.)

Part II   *Future key result areas*

A   *Objectives for forthcoming year*

Objective	Required standards of performance against each objective

Part II   *Future key result areas*

B   *Action plan*

Please indicate what actions need to be taken to:

(a) improve performance in the appropriate skill areas, and
(b) meet the objectives for the forthcoming year.

(i)   General

(ii) Coaching and counselling

(iii) Training courses

(iv) Attachments/transfers
     – within the directorate
     – across directorates
     – to provide customer contact

(v) Personal

Appraisee's comments

Signature .... Date ....

Second Appraiser's comments

Signature .... Date ....

Strictly confidential   *Development review*

Name .... Pay no. ....

Job title .... Date of birth ....

Date of start in industry .... Grade ....

Date of present appointment ....

---

1 **Career potential**

    1.1 What are his/her personal career ambitions?

    1.2 What are his/her abilities and are they being fully utilised in his/her present job?

    1.3 Is he/she promotable?   yes / no / undetermined

    1.4 Is he/she mobile   at present / in the next   years/ no

---

2 **Appropriate moves within the next three years** (take account of personal preferences)

    2.1 Development of lateral assignments (positions and possible dates)

    2.2 Promotional possibilities (positions and possible dates)

---

3 **Long-term potential** (please give a realistic assessment based on current performance/progress being maintained)

---

4 **Training/experience needed to fit him/her for future moves**

Courses:

Projects/Assignments:

Other:

Review completed by .... *Position* ....

Date ....

Review approved by .... *Position* ....

Date ....

Privatisation

What have been the effects of privatisation at British Gas? Beverley Pearce was of the opinion that more attention was now being given to providing customer satisfaction as well as promoting a 'caring' image, such as their involvement with conservation. For example, British Gas recently sponsored the opera *A Small Green Space* which tells the story of how a young boy inspires his neighbours and friends to fight against apathy, cynicism and bureaucracy so that a plot of land can be left undeveloped. Other British Gas sponsorships include Cathedral Classics, Bobby Charlton's Sports Day and the Central Ballet.

STUDENT ACTIVITIES FOR INDIVIDUALS

1 Examine an 'off-the-shelf' computer applications package and report on its suitability for your purpose. Use the report format suggested by Beverley Pearce.

2 Why do you think British Gas conducted its 'Banishing Gripes' campaign? Design a customer survey form which could be used by your organisation.

3 Contribute an idea for your organisation's suggestion scheme, quantifying the information requested in the British Gas scheme.

4 Your employer intends to introduce a staff appraisal scheme in the near future. Who should be involved in arranging it? What procedures would you recommend, and what benefits would be gained from such a scheme?

5 You have been asked for your views on re-designing and re-furbishing the open-plan office in which you work. Research modern methods of layout and design for offices equipped with new technology and write a memo to your Office Manager with your findings.

STUDENT ACTIVITIES FOR GROUP WORK

1 Discuss the social and economic implications of privatising a public service industry.

2 The gas, electricity, water and telephone authorities are all involved in digging holes to lay cables. Discuss the means by which this work should be co-ordinated to avoid unnecessary work and disturbance.

3 Obtain the published reports from British Gas plc, another well known public limited company and a nationalised industry and prepare a presentation comparing the three organisations under the following headings:
(a) aims
(b) profitability
(c) organisational structure
(d) impact on the community
(e) environmental issues
(f) international links.

4 Working in groups of five, conduct a survey of 100 of your friends, relatives, teachers and colleagues at work (20 each) to find out how many of them have purchased shares in British Gas or any of the other privatised industries. Make sure that all age groups over the age of 21 are represented in your survey.

Find out how many of those who did purchase shares still possess them and their reasons for holding on to them.

Using the results of your survey write a short report indicating whether you consider the government has been successful in its policy of encouraging wider share ownership.

2 The constitutional background

Ever since man began to live in communities there has been a need for rules to regulate relationships between individuals in the group and some method of enforcing those rules. The rules form the basis for a **constitution** which may be defined as 'the system or body of fundamental principles by which a nation, state or other organisation is constituted and governed'. As Professor Dicey, an eminent constitutional lawyer, wrote 'the constitution determines the exercise of the sovereign power within that political society or state'. The sovereign power is in effect the government. It may, in a dictatorship, be an individual, e.g. Stalin in the USSR in the 1930s, a small group, e.g. the former military junta in Argentina or it may be an elected parliament or congress.

What is a state?

It is common to refer to the whole apparatus of government as 'the state' but this is not strictly accurate. Statehood is really a concept of international law. To qualify as a state there must be:

- defined territorial limits
- a people
- organised government controlling both internal and external affairs.

For example, Antarctica is not a state nor is a colony such as Hong Kong.

Historically the three main functions of a state were:

- to maintain law and order within its boundaries
- to provide the means to repel external aggression
- to raise the money to achieve the two points above.

Today, in most modern societies, the state performs many other functions, e.g. education, provision of welfare services, etc.

What is a nation?

The word **nation** may be used in two different ways. It can be defined as 'a body of people marked off by common descent, language, culture or historical descent'. In this context a nation may not be a state. Scotland is a nation by this definition but it is not a state as it does not have its own government. The aim of the Scottish National Party (SNP) is to obtain separate statehood for Scotland and Plaid Cymru in Wales has a similar aim. Many current political problems in the world today revolve around this issue. The Palestinians are demanding an independent state, as are many of the national groupings in the USSR, e.g. Lithuania.

Alternatively, the word nation may be used as a synonym for state. In this case the binding factor is the territorial boundary. Mrs Thatcher constantly referred to 'the nation state' when discussing the future of the EC. Should the EC become a supra-national state or should it remain as a grouping of sovereign nation states? In this context a nation may have several different languages, e.g. Switzerland, and a variety of cultures.

19

Types of state

There are two main type of state:

- federal
- unitary.

A **federal state** is one in which power is divided between a central body and a number of local bodies. Each body has the power to make its own laws within its sphere. Usually such matters as defence, foreign policy and international trade are reserved for the central body. The main examples of federal states are the United States of America, Canada, Australia, West Germany and Switzerland.

A **unitary state** is where power is concentrated in one body. The United Kingdom (UK) is a unitary state in which all power, i.e. sovereignty, resides in Parliament. The central body may delegate certain matters to other bodies as a matter of administrative convenience but overall control remains with the central body. For example, in the UK certain matters are delegated to local government but Parliament could, if it wished, abolish all local councils.

Types of constitution

Most countries now have some form of written constitution. There is a document or series of documents which can be referred to as 'the constitution'. These may be detailed as in the case of the USA or merely contain a set of basic rules which regulate the principal institutions of government. The UK is one of the few states without any form of written constitution.

Constitutions may be divided into two classes:

- rigid
- flexible.

A **rigid constitution** is one that cannot be easily amended. There is a special procedure needed to change certain laws within the constitution. Usually this requires more than a simple majority. The procedure for amending the American Constitution is very complicated and can take a long time, for example, even though the Prohibition Amendment was repealed in 1933, some states continued to operate prohibition until 1966.

A **flexible constitution** is one that can be amended without special procedure. The British Constitution is flexible. It can be amended at any time by a simple majority in Parliament. No Parliament can bind its successors.

There is a current argument as to whether Britain should adopt a formal Bill of Rights setting out a system of basic rights, e.g. freedom of speech, freedom of association, which cannot be amended by a subsequent Parliament. (Further discussion of this topic is contained in Chapter 13.)

A written constitution need not be rigid. New Zealand has a written constitution but it can be amended by a simple majority in Parliament.

Government

Government may be defined as those functions concerned with the organisation and running of a state's affairs. These functions can be divided into three categories:

- legislative
- executive
- judicial.

The **legislative function** is concerned with the making of laws and is carried out in the UK by Parliament.

The **executive function** is concerned with the shaping of policy — both domestic and foreign — and the administration of the laws laid down by the legislature. In the UK the responsible body is the Cabinet and the various government departments.

The **judicial function** is to ensure that the law as laid down by legislation and judicial precedent (*see* Chapter 11) is adhered to; to punish those who break the law; and to settle disputes between individual subjects.

The separation of powers

In 1748 the French Philosopher Montesquieu published a book entitled *L'Esprit des Lois* which had a great influence on political thought. He argued that the three functions of government (legislative, executive and judicial) should be carried out by three separate institutions and each should be a check on the others. If two or more of the functions were exercised by the same body then tyranny would result.

Montesquieu's writings had a great influence on those who wrote the American Constitution. Legislative power is vested in the Congress (Senate and House of Representatives); executive power in the President who must be elected every four years; and judicial power in the Supreme Court. No member of one branch of government may be a member of either of the others, with the exception of the Vice-President who presides over the Senate in an *ex officio* capacity. There is also a system of checks and balances. For example, the President may veto legislation by Congress but the veto can be overturned by a two-thirds majority in the Senate. The Supreme Court can rule as unconstitutional any law passed by Congress or any action of the President. However, members of the Supreme Court are appointed by the President who may, when vacancies occur, appoint people in tune with his own way of thinking.

In the UK the separation of powers is less rigid. Government Ministers are also Members of Parliament (MPs). The Monarch is an integral part of all three branches of government. The Lord Chancellor is a member of the Cabinet, Chairman of the House of Lords and Head of the Judiciary. As there is no written constitution judges can only interpret the law and cannot declare a law unconstitutional. However, the independence of the judiciary is an essential part of the conventions of the constitution.

Supremacy of Parliament

Only Parliament has the right to make laws. It can pass any law that it likes; repeal a law made by a previous Parliament; and override, by passing a new law, any judicial interpretation of an existing law. This means that, as long as it retains a majority in Parliament, a British Government can do virtually what it likes. This led Lord Hailsham, a former Lord Chancellor, to describe our system as an 'elective dictatorship'. Of course, any government has to be responsive to public opinion but as general elections are usually only held every four or five years this is not as severe a limitation as it seems. Occasionally MPs rebel against their own party as in the

case of Sunday trading but not often in sufficient numbers to defeat the government.

Some restrictions on the sovereignty of Parliament are involved in our adherence to treaties and our membership of international organisations, particularly the EC. It is now recognised that EC law transcends national law but in the last resort Parliament could vote to take Britain out of the EC or to withdraw from any of its other treaty obligations. Thus the limitation on our sovereignty only applies so long as Parliament is willing to allow that limitation to take place.

Constitutional conventions

As we have seen Britain does not have a written constitution but there are unwritten rules known as constitutional conventions. These are practices which have been in existence for some time and are now accepted as the normal thing to do. It will take time for a practice to become a convention and similarly a long-standing convention will not lightly be discarded.

It is a convention that the Monarch will choose the leader of the majority party in the House of Commons to be Prime Minister. This is a twentieth century convention — Queen Victoria sometimes had different ideas — and is made simpler now that all political parties have a procedure for electing their leader. Indeed the existence of a Prime Minister and a Cabinet is a convention. There is no legislation which refers to either.

Other conventions are:

1   A government must resign if it loses a vote of confidence in the House of Commons (the Callaghan Government in 1979).
2   Parliamentary committees are appointed with a party representation equivalent to that in the House of Commons.
3   The House of Lords will not defeat a bill if it has appeared in the government party's election manifesto.
4   The Chairman of the Public Accounts Committee shall be a member of the opposition.
5   Parliament shall meet at least once a year — if it did not, certain Acts of Parliament which have to be renewed annually would have no legal foundation, e.g. the act which permits

us to have a standing army or the Finance Act which allows the collection of revenue.

Is Britain a democracy?

The word 'democracy' literally means rule by the people. It originated in the city states of Ancient Greece and enabled everyone, or at least those allowed to vote, to take part in the process of government through a system of plebiscites. A modern equivalent is the referendum used to test popular opinion on such issues as whether we should remain a member of the EEC (1975) and whether there should be devolution for Scotland and Wales (1979). However, Parliament only allowed consultative referenda and despite many requests has refused to extend referenda to other issues, such as capital punishment.

In Britain we are said to have **representative democracy**. At regular intervals we vote for our MPs and entrust them to carry on the work of government. As Abraham Lincoln said 'Government of the people, by the people and for the people'. Many countries in Eastern Europe describe themselves as 'people's democracies' even though, until the momentous events of 1989, they operated single-party systems with no official opposition to the party in power.

A number of tests may be applied in judging whether a state is a democracy. For example:

1 Are the individual rights of citizens protected?
2 What choice do citizens have in electing their representatives? Is there a plural system, i.e. more than one choice of party?
3 Are all citizens allowed to vote?
4 Is there adequate opportunity for calling representatives to account once they have been elected?
5 Are citizens free to criticise the activities of their elected representatives?
6 Do those in power reveal the information necessary for the electorate to make an informed judgement on their activities?
7 Are ordinary people encouraged to take an active part in the political process?

Discussion questions

1 What is a state? What are its main functions?
2 What is the difference between a federal state and a unitary state? In which category would you place the Soviet Union?
3 What is meant by the division of powers?
4 What are the main differences between the British Constitution and the American Constitution? Which do you think gives most protection to the individual citizen?
5 Is the British system of government really democratic?

Written question

6 Divide into groups of five or six. Each group should assume that it is forming a new local voluntary organisation, such as a youth club, sports club or residents' association. Write a constitution for that organisation.

Part B

Central government

3 The institutional framework

Parliament

As we saw in Chapter 2 under the British Constitution Parliament is supreme. It is usually referred to as the doctrine of the Sovereignty of Parliament. Parliament consists of the Monarch, the House of Commons and the House of Lords and is the supreme legislative authority in the UK.

The Monarchy

Britain has a hereditary Head of State who reigns but does not rule. The Monarch has to act within the bounds of the constitution. Today the powers of the Monarchy known as the royal prerogative are almost always exercised on the advice of the Prime Minister and the Government. Prerogative powers are important because they do not need the formal consent of Parliament. An Order in Council can be made and approved by the Privy Council which usually means a small group of senior Ministers who are Privy Councillors.

The main prerogative powers are:

- to open and close Parliament
- to dissolve and summon Parliament
- to appoint the Prime Minister and other Ministers
- to make treaties and enter into diplomatic relations with other states
- to declare war and make peace
- to control the armed forces
- to appoint judges and Church of England bishops
- to pardon offenders
- to award honours.

Parliament decides on the opening and closing dates of each annual session of Parliament. The Queen attends the formal opening of each session of Parliament. She makes the speech from the throne in the House of Lords. This speech is prepared by the Prime Minister and Cabinet and normally consists of the government's proposals for new legislation in the ensuing session. The House of Commons is summoned to the House of Lords to hear the speech. By convention — based on Charles I attempt to arrest MPs — the Monarch is not permitted to enter the House of Commons.

If Parliament has run for five years then there must be a dissolution and a general election held although this rule can be waived in exceptional circumstances, as during the war in 1940. However, the Prime Minister can recommend a dissolution at any time and the Monarch has no constitutional right to refuse such a request. If the government is defeated in the House of Commons on a vote of confidence, as happened in 1979, then there will usually be a dissolution.

The appointment of a Prime Minister is normally straightforward: it is the leader of the political party with a majority in the House of Commons. In the past there have been some difficulties when a Prime Minister has resigned, e.g. Anthony Eden in 1956 and Harold MacMillan in 1963, but today all the political parties have a mechanism for rapidly electing a new leader if one dies or retires. Other Ministers are appointed on the recommendation of the Prime Minister.

The Prime Minister is usually involved in the appointment of the senior judges whilst the rest are appointed on the advice of the Lord Chancellor. The Prime Minister is also involved in the appointment of the Archbishops of Canterbury and York.

In pardoning convicted offenders the Queen acts on the advice of the Home Secretary. Most honours are awarded by the Queen on the advice of the Prime Minister but there are a few honours which are within the personal gift of the Monarch.

The Monarch also has a very important role as Head of the Commonwealth. In many cases former British Colonies which have become independent are only linked together by an allegiance to the Crown. In recent years Queen Elizabeth II has paid particular attention to this role and has worked hard to keep the Commonwealth together. In this role she has a greater responsibility than in her role as Head of State where all major decisions are taken by Ministers.

No Act of Parliament can become law until it has been signed by the Monarch. The last Monarch to refuse to do so was Queen Anne in the early part of the eighteenth century. There are constitutional arguments concerning in what circumstances, if any, the Monarch could refuse to sign a bill that had passed through all its stages in the Commons and Lords. One possibility is if, without any exceptional circumstances, e.g. war or economic collapse, a government sought to extend the life of the existing Parliament beyond the five-year period.

The Queen meets the Prime Minister every week and may often offer impartial advice based on her experience. The Monarch provides continuity whilst Prime Ministers and Governments come and go. Queen Elizabeth II has had nine Prime Ministers and considerable experience of affairs of state. She travels widely and knows personally many Heads of State in both the Commonwealth and the rest of the world. In the last resort, however, the Monarch acts on the advice of the Prime Minister who is directly responsible to Parliament and the people.

About 85 per cent of the cost of the Monarchy is funded by an allocation from Parliament called the Civil List. Allowances are made to other members of the Royal Family who perform ceremonial duties. The Civil List for the financial year 1990–1 is estimated at £5.9 million.

Discussion question

1 Do you think the Monarchy still has a useful role to play?

The Prime Minister

The Prime Minister is the leader of the political party which has a majority in the House of Commons. Today all the major parties elect their leaders so the Prime Minister has to retain the confidence of the back-bench MPs. It is a modern convention that the Prime Minister shall be a member of the House of Commons. This has not always been so. In the nineteenth century many prime ministers came from the House of Lords. However, in 1963 when Alec Douglas Home was chosen to replace Harold MacMillan he had to renounce his peerage and seek election to the House of Commons. In his classic book *The English Constitution*, Walter Bagehot described the Prime Minister as *primus inter pares* or the leading member of a team of equals. In recent times this has no longer tended to be true. Many political commentators argue that cabinet government has been replaced by prime ministerial government. A strong Prime Minister, such as Mrs Thatcher, may dominate her Cabinet but this may not always be so. The office of Prime Minister rests mainly on convention rather than law and with different personalities the position could easily change. Much of the Prime Minister's power rests on the power of patronage, e.g. the Prime Minister appoints all other Ministers in the government and also has considerable influence in the appointment of the top civil servants.

The Prime Minister may appoint a team of personal policy advisers. In 1970 Edward Heath set up a 'think-tank' known as the Central Policy Review Staff but it was disbanded by Mrs Thatcher in 1983. As an alternative she established a No 10 Policy Unit. It is often alleged that some of her non-elected policy advisers had more influence than senior Ministers. It was a dispute between a Minister and a policy adviser that led to the resignation of Nigel Lawson as Chancellor of the Exchequer in 1989.

The Cabinet

The word 'cabinet' means private room and was where the Kings and Queens of England met with their close personal advisers. Today the Cabinet consists of the top 20–25 Ministers, most of whom are MPs but a few come from the House of Lords.

The Major Cabinet in November 1990 consisted of:

Prime Minister and First Lord of the Treasury:	John Major
Leader of the House of Commons and Lord President of the Council:	John MacGregor
Lord Chancellor	Lord Mackay
Secretary of State for Foreign and Commonwealth Affairs	Douglas Hurd
Home Secretary	Kenneth Baker
Chancellor of the Exchequer	Norman Lamont
Secretary of State for Education and Science	Kenneth Clarke
Secretary of State for Northern Ireland	Peter Brooke
Secretary of State for Defence	Tom King
Secretary of State for Scotland	Ian Lang
Secretary of State for Wales	David Hunt
Secretary of State for the Environment	Michael Heseltine
Secretary of State for Energy	John Wakeham
Secretary of State for Health	William Waldegrave
Secretary of State for Social Security	Anthony Newton
Secretary of State for Transport	Malcolm Rifkind
Secretary of State for Trade and Industry	Peter Lilley
Minister of Agriculture, Fisheries and Food	John Gummer
Secretary of State for Employment	Michael Howard
Chief Secretary to the Treasury	David Mellor
Lord Privy Seal and Leader of the House of Lords	David Waddington
Chancellor of the Duchy of Lancaster*	Chris Patten

*This post is unpaid as he is also Chairman of the Conservative Party and paid out of Party funds.

The Cabinet meets at least once a week usually on Thursday mornings. Minutes are kept of the meetings and they are kept secret for 30 years. It is not usual for votes to be taken at Cabinet meetings. It is impossible for all important matters to be discussed at full Cabinet meetings so a system of Cabinet committees has been instituted. There are over 20 of these (including sub-committees) organised on a permanent basis and several more created on an *ad hoc* basis to deal with particular issues. Other Ministers attend the Cabinet committees and sub-committees but it is rare for a non-Cabinet Minister to attend a Cabinet meeting. Some Cabinet sub-committees may consist only of civil servants.

To support the Cabinet there is a Cabinet Office consisting of civil servants headed by the Secretary of the Cabinet. The Cabinet Office organises meetings, prepares agendas, distributes Cabinet papers and takes minutes. The Secretary of the Cabinet is one of the two most senior civil servants and has close contact with the Prime Minister. The Cabinet Office also includes the Management and Personnel Office dealing with Civil Service training and recruitment and the Central Statistical Office.

A convention of the modern Cabinet is that of collective responsibility. Once a decision has been taken by the Cabinet it must be supported by all its members. In 1986 Michael Heseltine, then Secretary of State for Defence, resigned because he could not support a Cabinet decision over the future of the Westland Helicopter.

In 1975 Harold Wilson suspended Cabinet collective responsibility over the issue of the EEC and allowed Cabinet Ministers to campaign on either side of the referendum on whether Britain should remain a member of the EEC.

Discussion question

2   It is often said that Cabinet government has given way to prime ministerial government. What, if any, are the checks on the power of the Prime Minister? Do you think there should be fixed-term Parliaments?

Departmental Ministers

Most Cabinet Ministers are responsible for a central department of state. They will be supported by Junior Ministers (Ministers of State and Parliamentary Secretaries). Some lesser departments are headed by non-cabinet Ministers. Each department will have a full complement of civil servants headed by a Permanent Secretary (*see* Chapter 4).

Each Minister has a private office which is their own secretariat. This is headed by the Principal Private Secretary who is the Minister's closest aide and usually accompanies him/her on outside visits. They are often potential 'high flyers' and may serve more than one Minister during their stay in the private office. Many Principal Private Secretaries have eventually risen to the top ranks in the Civil Service.

The Minister usually also has one or more advisers who are not civil servants and a Parliamentary Private Secretary (PPS) who is an MP and whose job it is to maintain a liaison between the Minister and their back-bench colleagues. The PPS may also arrange for sympathetic colleagues to put down parliamentary questions which the Minister particularly wants to answer. Bob Mitchell was Parliamentary Private Secretary to Tony Crosland when he was Secretary of State for Education.

Another important convention is that Ministers are responsible for the actions of their civil servants whether or not they have personal knowledge of their actions. In 1954 the Minister of Agriculture, Sir Thomas Dugdale, resigned when one of his civil servants had acted improperly over the sale of land at Crichel Down. Similarly, Lord Carrington resigned as Foreign Secretary in 1982 when the Foreign Office failed to predict the invasion of the Falkland Islands, but more recently there have been cases where the convention has been breached and the Minister has not resigned. *See* Case Study 3 for further details of the administration of the Foreign Office.

House of Commons

At present the House of Commons has 650 MPs as follows:

England	523
Wales	38
Scotland	72
Northern Ireland	17

Each MP represents a constituency. There are periodic reviews of constituency boundaries to take account of population changes. This is carried out by the independent Boundary Commission. The objective is to have roughly the same number of voters in each constituency but account has to be taken of the area and size of the constituency. If an MP dies or resigns then a by-election will be held in their constituency.

The maximum length of a Parliament is five years but the Prime Minister can at any time ask the Queen to dissolve Parliament and hold a general election. This gives the Prime Minister the power to call a general election at a time of

his/her choosing. Some other Parliaments have fixed terms and elections are only held at regular intervals, usually every four or five years.

Any British subject over the age of 21 may be an MP except aliens, i.e. non-British subjects; mental patients; bankrupts; persons serving a sentence of one year or more; clergymen of the Churches of England, Scotland and Ireland and the Roman Catholic Church; persons convicted of corrupt practices at parliamentary elections; persons holding an office of profit under the Crown (e.g. judges, civil servants, members of the armed services, police officers and members of public corporations) and members of the House of Lords.

The House of Commons usually sits about 160 days per year. From Monday to Thursday it starts at 2.30 pm and rarely finishes before 10.30 pm and sometimes continues well into the night. On Friday the House of Commons sits from 9.30 am to 3.00 pm. However, in very exceptional circumstances this can be extended and there can also be Saturday sittings.

The proceedings are presided over by the Speaker. The first Speaker was in the Model Parliament of 1295. In Tudor and Stuart times he was regarded as the agent of the King. However, since 1689 it has been clearly established that the Speaker is the spokesman for the House of Commons in dealing with the Crown, the House of Lords and other bodies.

The Speaker has complete control over debate in the House. If an MP refuses to obey his ruling the Speaker has power to 'name' the MP and to have them removed from the chamber. He can also insist that an MP withdraw a remark if he holds it to be 'unparliamentary language' and can suspend the sitting if there is serious disorder either in the chamber or in the public gallery. The Speaker must be seen to be impartial and after his election as Speaker he gives up all his political party activities.

On Monday to Thursday the first hour of the sitting is taken up with Question Time where Ministers in turn answer oral questions put down (two weeks previously) by MPs. Normally an MP will be allowed to ask a supplementary question in addition to their original one. The Prime Minister answers questions on Tuesdays and Thursdays from 3.15 to 3.30 pm.

The last half hour of each day's sitting is taken up by an adjournment debate where an MP can raise issues relating to individuals or to their constituency. When a vote is taken bells ring and MPs have eight minutes to get into one of the two division lobbies (an 'aye' lobby and a 'no' lobby). As they leave the division lobbies they are counted by tellers and the results of the vote are given to the Speaker who reads them out.

A typical day's proceedings is as follows:

2.30 pm — 2.40 pm	Prayers followed by private business dealing with Private Bills, e.g. British Railways Bill
2.40 pm — 3.15 pm	Questions to the Secretary of State for Education and Science
3.15 pm — 3.30 pm	Questions to the Prime Minister
3.30 pm — 10.00 pm	Second reading of a Public Bill
10.00 pm — 10.15 pm	Vote on second reading
10.15 pm — 11.45 pm	Debate on statutory instrument
11.45 pm — 12.15 am	Adjournment debate

All debate in the House of Commons is taken down verbatim and published in *Hansard* which is issued daily. Members are protected by parliamentary privilege against any action for slander or defamation in relation to remarks made in Parliament. MPs are also protected by privilege against threats of intimidation from people outside.

MPs are paid a salary and receive allowances for secretarial help and for extra expenses involved in living in London. They also have free postage and free travel between London and their constituencies. However, their salaries and expenses compare unfavourably with most other European Parliaments. Very few MPs have their own office and, in general, facilities for MPs leave much to be desired.

Many MPs have additional sources of income. Some are directors of companies whilst others receive financial help from trade unions. Every MP has to declare his/her interests which are published annually in a Register of Interests. When an MP becomes a Minister they must give up all their outside interests. Members of Parlia-

ment have many duties both inside and outside Parliament. As well as attending debates in the chamber they also sit on committees (*see* p.31) which mostly meet in the mornings. At weekends they have many constituency duties. Most MPs hold regular constituency 'surgeries' where members of the public can bring their individual problems. They will also be expected to open bazaars and attend meetings of constituency organisations. In addition, they have their political party work, addressing public meetings and local party meetings.

The average MP receives 100–200 letters a week — many more if there is a particular current issue or constituency problem.

Members of Parliament have several loyalties: to their own consciences; to those who elected them; to their local political party who selected them as a candidate; and to their parliamentary party. Sometimes these loyalties conflict. The MP may be conscientiously opposed to capital punishment but know that most of their constituents are in favour of it. It may be in the national interest to place new naval shipbuilding orders in areas of high unemployment but this could result in loss of jobs in the MP's own constituency. The government, which the MP supports, has called for restrictions on public expenditure but this is strongly opposed by the local party. The MP's own government may propose to use a site in their constituency to store nuclear waste. These are typical conflicting loyalties that every MP will face from time to time.

Case Study 2 relates to the House of Commons and the secretarial and administrative services of an MP.

Discussion question

3 Where do you think an MP's first allegiance should be? On what occasions should an MP defy the Party Whip when voting in Parliament?

House of Lords

There are about 1200 peers who have the right to sit in the House of Lords. There are:

- 26 Lords Spiritual — the Archbishops of Canterbury and York and 24 senior bishops of the Church of England

- 20 Lords of Appeal in Ordinary — the Law Lords who perform the judicial work of the House of Lords when it is sitting as the final Court of Appeal
- approximately 800 hereditary peers who have inherited their title
- approximately 350 life peers created under the Life Peerages Act 1958. Their titles do not pass on to their heirs.

Peers are not paid a salary but may claim attendance allowances. Since 1963 it is possible for a peer who inherits a title to disclaim it and remain as a commoner. The next heir upon the death of his/her father can choose whether he/she wishes to assume the peerage or disclaim it. If he/she does disclaim it then the peerage is extinguished.

Aliens, bankrupts or those under 21 cannot sit in the House of Lords. Those convicted of a serious crime can only sit once their sentence has been served. Civil servants who are peers may sit but cannot speak or vote.

The Lord Chancellor presides over the House of Lords. Unlike the Speaker he retains his political affiliations and is a member of the Cabinet.

Average daily attendance by peers in the House of Lords is only about 300. Many of these are the life peers. Many hereditary peers take little interest in the proceedings and some never attend at all. Life peers are in the main former MPs and people who have had a distinguished career, e.g. in industry or the professions. They are very able people but tend to be drawn from the older age group. Debates in the House of Lords tend to be of a higher standard than those in the Commons. Although many peers have political affiliations they are inclined to be less partisan than MPs. There are over 200 peers who do not have direct party affiliations. They are known as cross-benchers as they occupy the seats (non-existent in the Commons) facing the Lord Chancellor on the Woolsack.

Since the Parliament Acts of 1911 and 1947 the House of Lords has only limited powers. It can delay bills, other than Money Bills, for a year but very rarely uses this power. Its main function is to scrutinise legislation at a more leisurely pace than is possible in the Commons. By convention the House of Lords will not oppose any bill which has formed part of the manifesto of the political party controlling the government. However, it will very often amend bills. In the 1980s the House of Lords often passed amendments against the wishes of the government. In contrast the government only suffered one major defeat in the House of Commons on the Sunday Trading Bill.

Reform of the House of Lords

The main criticisms levelled against the House of Lords are:

1 It is impossible to defend the hereditary principle and in any case many hereditary peers play little part in its proceedings.
2 The average age is too high.
3 It has an inbuilt Conservative Party majority but this is probably less true today than in previous times.

Various attempts have been made to reform the House of Lords. In 1969 the Labour Government introduced a bill to this end but had to withdraw it following opposition from back-benchers of all parties who saw the reforms as either too radical or too moderate.

Suggestions that have been made are:

1 Abolish it altogether and have single chamber government.
2 Have a wholly elected second chamber.
3 Have it partly elected and partly appointed.

There is general agreement that the hereditary principle is indefensible and most would agree that a second chamber is necessary and that it should be complementary to and not rival the House of Commons. There is, however, very little agreement on the details of how the second chamber should be constituted. It is because of this that the House of Lords has continued to exist in its present form for so long and it may well be some time before any major reform takes place.

Discussion question

4 Does Britain need a second chamber? If so, what form do you think it should take?

The legislative procedure

An Act of Parliament starts life as a bill drafted by expert lawyers known as Parliamentary Counsel. It is usually arranged in clauses and sub-clauses. When important new legislation is proposed the government may issue a Green Paper. This is a discussion document and may set out the various options. Individuals and interested organisations are invited to send in their comments. These are considered by the government who may then issue a White Paper. This states the government's intentions and it may be debated in Parliament. Then the government asks Parliamentary Counsel to draft a bill. There are four types of Parliamentary Bill:

1 Public Bills which alter the law of the land and are usually introduced by the government.
2 Private Members' Bills which are similar to Public Bills but are introduced by an MP. A ballot is held at the beginning of each session and 20 members have the opportunity to introduce a Bill on successive Fridays. The time allocated to Private Members' Bills is limited and if they are too controversial or are opposed by the government they have little chance of success. Some important pieces of legislation have, however, started in this way, e.g. Murder (Abolition of Death Penalty) Act 1965, the Abortion Law Reform Act 1967 and the Chronically Sick and Disabled Persons Act 1970.
3 Private Bills which give extra powers to organisations, e.g. local authorities. If opponents wish to challenge a Private Bill then it will be sent to a Private Bill Committee consisting of four MPs. Proceedings are similar to a court of law with both the promoters and the opponents being legally represented. The committee can reject the bill but not amend it. It is then reported to the House of Commons and follows the normal procedure.
4 Hybrid Bills which alter the general law but have a particular effect on certain individuals or organisations, e.g. the British Museum Act 1964. They are usually sent to a select committee for examination and then return to the House as a normal Public Bill.

Public Bill procedure

Most Public Bills start in the House of Commons but some less controversial ones, particularly where there is a strong legal content, may start in the House of Lords. If a bill is declared by the Speaker to be a Money Bill then the House of Lords cannot delay it.

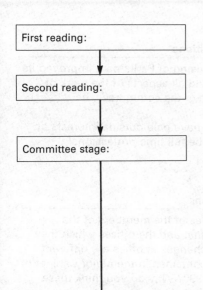

First reading:

Second reading:

Committee stage:

A formal reading of the bill's title. It is then printed and distributed to MPs.

The Minister introduces the bill and there is usually a day's debate where the principles of the bill can be discussed. There is often a vote at the end of the debate. If the government wins the vote the bill proceeds to the committee stage.

It is sent to a Standing Committee of between 16 and 50 MPs selected in proportion to the party strengths in the House of Commons. Here the bill is examined clause by clause. Amendments may be moved and voted upon. If the bill is very controversial the opposition may use delaying tactics at this stage. Large numbers of amendments will be moved and long speeches made. To ensure it obtains its legislation, the government may then propose a guillotine motion which sets out a timetable for the remaining stages of the bill. If the bill is very important, e.g. a constitutional matter, it may be considered by a committee of the whole house where all MPs can participate.

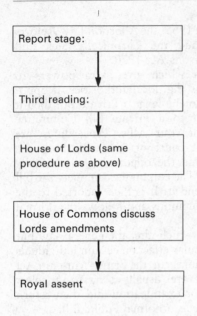

The report stage is where any amendments made in committee are considered by the whole House. MPs who were not on the committee have the opportunity to table their own amendments.

Finally, the bill receives a third reading which is usually formal with only a short debate. There can be another vote at this stage.

Having passed all its stages in the House of Commons the bill has to go through the same procedure in the House of Lords. If amendments are made there these have to be returned to the House of Commons for further discussion. The Lords have the power to delay a bill (except a Money Bill) for one year but rarely use this power. However, in 1990 they did reject the War Crimes Bill even though it had passed through all its stages in the House of Commons.

Finally, the bill is sent to the Monarch to receive the Royal Assent. It then becomes the law of the land.

Normally this whole procedure takes several months but in case of emergency all the stages in both houses can be completed in one day, e.g. Emergency Powers Act 1939.

Delegated legislation

Acts of Parliament often lay down general principles but leave the detailed application to regulations and orders made by Ministers. The Act delegates to the Minister this power and the regulations and orders when issued have the force of law. A good example is the Health and Safety at Work Act 1974.

The regulations and orders are submitted to Parliament in the form of statutory instruments. They are scrutinised by the Statutory Instruments Committee and in some cases may be subject to a short debate in Parliament. There are also judicial checks on delegated legislation.

As long ago as 1929 Lord Hewart in his book *The New Despotism* complained at the growth of delegated legislation saying that it gave too much power to Ministers and was not sufficiently subject to parliamentary control. Since then the amount of delegated legislation has increased enormously. Parliament does not have the time or ability to consider all the technical details. It is, therefore, important that the courts

should have a role in ensuring that Ministers do not abuse their power. There have been attempts in some Acts of Parliament to exclude the power of the courts to declare the regulations void on the grounds that they are 'ultra vires'.

Over 2000 statutory instruments are issued annually. There is a need for more publicity as these regulations do have the force of law and it is no defence in a court of law for a citizen to plead ignorance.

Discussion questions

5   Has the televising of Parliament improved its image? Should all aspects of the work of Parliament, e.g. the committees, be televised?
6   Should MPs have paid outside interests or should they be full-time professional members?

Written questions

7   List the names of the members of the present Cabinet and the offices which they hold. What changes in office are different from those contained in the Major Cabinet of November 1990? Why do you think these changes were made?

8 Take any recent Act of Parliament and examine any orders or regulations made under the Act by the relevant Minister. Do you think Ministers have too much power in dealing with delegated legislation and, if so, how would you seek to control that power?

9 Find out as much as you can about the background and work of your local MP. Write a profile of him or her suitable for inclusion in your college newspaper. *See* Case Study 2 which includes an account of the parliamentary career of Sir David Price.

CASE STUDY 2 The House of Commons

Case study situation

In this case study we take a glimpse inside the 'corridors of power' of the Houses of Parliament to study the administrative and secretarial services provided for MPs. The information is based on the experience of Isabel Ward who is Private Secretary to Sir David Price.

Sir David Price, a Conservative, has been an MP since 1955 and represents Eastleigh in Hampshire. He is a senior member of the all-party Health Select Committee and during his parliamentary career has served in the following capacities:

- Parliamentary Secretary to the Board of Trade 1962–4
- Member of the Select Committee on Science and Technology 1965–70
- Joint Parliamentary Secretary to the Minister of Technology 1970
- Parliamentary Secretary to the Minister of Aviation 1970–1
- Parliamentary Under-Secretary for Aerospace 1970–2
- Chairman of the Parliamentary and Scientific Committee 1973–5 and 1979–82
- Member of the Public Accounts Committee 1974–5
- Member of the Select Committee on Transport 1979–83
- Vice-Chairman of the Conservative Arts and Heritage Committee 1979–87
- Chairman of the Conservative Shipping and Shipbuilding Committee 1979 to present

Isabel Ward has been Sir David Price's Private Secretary since 1980 and before taking up this position she had been a secretary at the Clark's Shoe Factory in Street, Somerset. She trained for secretarial work at the Langham Secretarial College and later qualified for a Diploma in Theology.

Isabel is employed directly by Sir David Price who pays her salary from the office costs allowance which all MPs receive. Payment of MP's

Fig 3.1 Isabel Ward, Private Secretary to Sir David Price MP

salaries is administered from the Fees Office (*see* below).

Administration of the House of Commons

The offices and departments for the administration of the House of Commons are as follows:

Office/Department	Function
Department of the Clerk of the House	Clerks to the House and Committees Registrar of Members' interests
Fees Office	Payment of MP's salaries, allowances and issue of travel warrants, etc.
Serjeant-at-Arms Office	Security of Parliament
Department of the Library	Library and information services
Department of the Official Report	Publication of *Hansard*
Vote Office	Distributes copies of *Hansard* and Reports
Refreshment Department	Catering

These facilities are provided for the 650 MPs. (523 from England, 72 from Scotland, 38 from Wales and 17 from Northern Ireland)

Secretary's job description

A typical job description for a Private Secretary to an MP is as follows:

1   Purpose of job: to provide the MP with a shorthand/typewriting service and provide administrative support ensuring that standards of confidentiality are maintained.

2   Main duties:
   - take down in shorthand and transcribe various letters and reports
   - maintain a filing system, associating previous papers with current correspondence, and extracting documents on request

- answer the telephone and take and pass on messages
- sort incoming post into priority order and prepare draft replies to routine correspondence
- investigate issues raised in constituency correspondence and follow up such cases, ensuring their timely resolution
- receive visitors and make arrangements for groups of constituents to visit Parliament
- make travel arrangements.
- maintain an appointments diary for the Member, arranging and cancelling appointments (as required).

At first sight this may appear to be like any other secretary's job but it is in the application of these duties and the total involvement of the Secretary in the running of the office where the differences occur. The major tasks are concerned with providing efficient and effective communication with all of the interested parties. These are illustrated in Fig 3.2.

The MP's mailbag from these various sources is considerable. Sir David Price replies to every letter he receives from his constituents. Some are dictated but others are prepared by Isabel for Sir David's approval. Parliamentary headed paper is supplied by HMSO and overprinted with the member's name. Isabel uses an electronic typewriter and has access to an office copier. If she has an excessive amount of typing to do she may call upon the services of the typing agency which is based in Parliament. At the time of our visit Isabel had been particularly busy replying to a vast number of letters received from constituents complaining about the community charge. The letters, which are sent in official paid envelopes, are despatched from the House of Commons Post Office. Mail for parliament and government departments are sorted and distributed by an internal mail service. In addition to typing letters, Isabel is required to type Sir David's speeches, usually from his handwritten notes.

Constituent's cases

Some of the cases taken up on behalf of MPs may be prolonged and extend over several years as in the case of one lady who lived in an old house which she bought before a motorway was built.

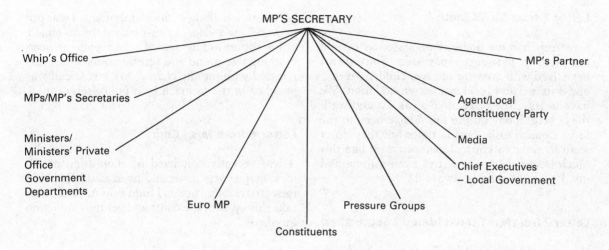

Fig 3.2 Communication links of an MP's Secretary

Immediately the traffic started to use the motorway she noticed cracks appearing in her house. She is convinced that they are caused by the construction of the motorway and the vibration from the volume of traffic using it. She spent thousands of pounds on repairs and is seeking compensation from the Department of Transport. Sir David Price has been involved in presenting his constituent's claim for compensation to the Department of Transport (DoT), but the Minister does not accept that his department is liable. This case has involved local councillors, local authority officials, DoT at regional and national level, Inspectors' investigations and reports and several ministerial representations, as in the following course of events:

1   Letter received from constituent.
2   MP wrote to DoT.
3   MP advised constituent of action taken.
4   MP received reply from Minister.
5   MP sent Minister's reply to constituent.
6   Constituent replied, she did not agree with contents.
7   MP wrote to Minister again expressing constituent's disappointment.
8   Minister confirms DoT is not liable.
9   MP sent Minister's reply to constituent.
10 Constituent replied, she insists that DoT Inspectors should visit her property and see for themselves.
11 HM Inspectors visit the property.

12 Inspectors confirm that damage is not due to motorway construction.
13 Minister suggests that constituent should have meter readings taken of traffic vibrations.
14 Local authority offer to take meter readings.
15 Readings taken at low period of traffic flow and not over 24 hours, to which constituent objects . . .

Some of the individual cases taken up by MPs involve delicate personal and human relations, as in the case of the constituent who joined a foreign dating agency and began an exchange with a Chinese girl. He went to China, met her, fell in love and they became engaged. He wanted to marry her and live in the UK. He was advised that he would stand a better chance if he went to China and married her, so that he could bring his wife back to the UK. He arranged the marriage in China and his wife then applied for entry to the UK. She was refused entry by the Home Office on the grounds that her intentions were not honourable, but she could appeal. She appealed and was again refused entry. The constituent now has a wife he cannot live with. He cannot live in China and his wife is not permitted to enter the UK. In this case Sir David Price has been in communication with his constituent, the Home Office and the Foreign Office to try to resolve this difficult situation.

The following letters are extracted from some typical mail received by MPs.

Letter 1 from Mr W Smith

'I recently had my house re-possessed as I could not meet the mortgage repayments. Since then I have lived with my wife and two children aged 5 and 3 in bed and breakfast accommodation. We have to leave the place after breakfast and walk the streets all day until 6 pm. I have been to the local Council Office many times but they don't seem to want to know. I cannot go on like this much longer. My wife suffers from asthma and my 3 year old child is always ill.'

Letter 2 from Mrs T Davis (dated 2 September)

'My son and his friend left England on July 20th to go on a climbing holiday in the Pyrénées. They should have returned on August 20th. I had a card from him from Perpignan postmarked July 27th but have heard nothing since. I am worried sick as is his friend's mother who has also heard nothing. I have been in touch with the police but nothing seems to have happened.'

Letter 3 from Mr J Brown

'I worked for 10 years as a sheet-metal worker for XYZ Ltd. Six months ago the firm went into liquidation and I was made redundant. I have not yet received any redundancy money. I do not belong to a trade union.'

Letter 4 from Mr R Williams

'I retired in December 1989. I was before that a self-employed bricklayer. I have just received a letter dated 1 April 1990 from the Inland Revenue saying that they had made a mistake in my tax assessment for the years 1987–8 and 1988–9 and that I owed them £635 tax. I am now living on the old age pension and cannot possibly pay that amount. In any case it was their mistake so I don't see why I should have to pay.'

Letter 5 from Miss J Carter

'I was in a night club with my boy friend when it was raided by the police. I was taken to the police station along with several others. I was put in a cell and later strip-searched by a female police officer in full view of a male police officer. Nothing was found and several hours later I was released without any charge. My boy friend was punched in the stomach by a police sergeant.'

Letter 6 from Mrs I Court

'I was recently convicted of shoplifting at the local magistrates court and fined £200. This is a miscarriage of justice as I didn't do it. Could you take this up with the court and get the conviction quashed?'

Letter from Miss G Harris

'Four weeks ago I left my job and applied for unemployment benefit. This was refused on the grounds that I had left the job voluntarily. I applied for social security but despite several visits and phone calls have not yet had any money. I don't know what to do next. I have had to borrow from a friend to buy food.'

Letter 8 from Annette Parsons

'My son recently had his raincoat stolen at school. The Headmaster tells me that there is nothing he can do and that pupils leaving clothes in the school cloakroom do so at their own risk. I am a one-parent family with two younger children so I cannot afford to buy him another one.'

Appointments

The Private Secretary manages the Member's diary and makes appointments according to their wishes. Visitors to Parliament may request an appointment with their MP. If the appointment has not been pre-arranged a green card is completed giving the name of the MP and the reason for the visit. The attendant of the Serjeant-at-Arms Office notifies the MP's Secretary that a green card has been received and, if possible, the Secretary arranges the appointment. She will arrange to interview the visitor herself if the MP is not available.

Sources of information

When investigating the issues raised in consti-tuency correspondence Isabel has to know where to look for information. She has access to *Who's Who*, a useful source of information about eminent people, and has the following books in her office for reference:

Vacher's Parliamentary Companion
The Diplomatic Corps Guide
The Parliamentary Internal Directory
List of Ministerial Responsibilities
Electoral Roll for the Constituency
List of Conservative Party Officers for the Constituency
Local Authority Year Books
Hansard

The following books also contain useful informa-tion for public administration offices:

Whitaker's Almanack
The Statesmen's Year Book
Dod's Parliamentary Companion

STUDENT ACTIVITIES FOR INDIVIDUALS

1 What action would you expect an MP to take with the letters received on p. 36?
2 Draft letters for the MP to reply to two of the correspondents (as in 1 above).
3 Refer to relevant reference books to find the answers to the following questions:
   (a) the name of your local MP, his/her political party and the date when they were first elected to Parliament
   (b) the name and address of your Euro MP
   (c) the name of the Speaker of the House of Commons
   (d) the name and official title of the Deputy Speaker of the House of Commons
   (e) the name of the Secretary of State for the Environment
   (f) two of the main issues discussed in Parliament last week
   (g) the name and telephone number of the Chief Executive of your district council
   (h) the name and telephone number of the Chief Executive of your county council.

STUDENT ACTIVITIES FOR GROUP WORK

1 Discuss:
   (a) in what ways an MP's Private Secretary could benefit from new technology in their office
   (b) the communication links set up by the MP's Secretary (p. 35) and suggest why each is important for the MP
   (c) has the televising of Parliament made you more aware of the work of MPs? Should it continue in its present form or would you like to see changes?
   (d) why are there so few women MPs (what proportion of MPs are women)?
2 Using appropriate reference sources selected from those given above carry out a survey of MPs and use illustrative diagrams to show:
   (a) the number of MPs elected from England, Scotland, Wales and Northern Ireland.
   (b) the political representation for each of these areas (each group to work on a different area).
The groups should then report back to the class to compare results and finally prepare a diagram to show the political representation for the whole of the UK.

4 The Civil Service

History

Until the middle of the nineteenth century appointment to the Civil Service was by patronage and often depended on knowing the right people. Posts were often given as a reward for political service and were in fact sinecures with the appointee receiving a salary but doing no real work. This led to inefficiency and often corruption. In 1852 Parliament asked Sir Charles Trevelyan and Sir Stafford Northcote to prepare a report on the future of the Civil Service.

Northcote-Trevelyan Report 1854

The report made five recommendations which laid the foundation of the present Civil Service:

1 Recruitment should be by competitive examination.
2 Promotion should be by merit and not seniority.
3 The Civil Service should be politically neutral.
4 The 'intellectual' side of administration should be separated from the mechanical or routine side.
5 Recruitment should be unified with the possibility of inter-departmental promotion.

In 1855 the Civil Service Commission was set up as an independent body to control the recruitment of civil servants. Since 1870 open competition has been the only method of recruitment to the Civil Service except for the Foreign Office. The Treasury answered in Parliament for the work of the Civil Service Commission. Recruitment was established on a rather rigid system based on educational qualifications. There were three classes:

- Administrative Class with graduate entry at 22
- Executive Class with GCE 'A' level entry at 18
- Clerical Class with GCE 'O' level entry at 16

There was very little opportunity of promotion between the classes.

In the twentieth century the scope of government increased dramatically and with it the number of civil servants. By 1960 there were almost one million. Criticism of the Civil Service structure came from many quarters. The main criticisms were:

1 Treasury control was more concerned with saving money than improving quality.
2 The top civil servants came from too narrow a base: most were Public School educated and Oxbridge graduates.
3 The top civil servants were generalist administrators often with classics degrees and had insufficient knowledge of industry and trade.
4 The specialists in the Civil Service, e.g. scientists, lawyers and accountants rarely occupied senior positions.
5 There were very few opportunities for civil servants to obtain managerial skills.
6 The administrative, executive, clerical grading system was too rigid and prevented able staff from receiving deserved promotion.

In response to these criticisms a committee was set up in 1966 under the chairmanship of Lord Fulton, Vice-Chancellor of Sussex University to 'examine the structure, recruitment and management including training of the Home Civil Service'.

Fulton Report 1968

The committee accepted many of the criticisms listed above and came forward with the following recommendations:

1 A new Civil Service Department should be set up to take over the Treasury's former role. This department should be under the control of the Prime Minister who should be assisted by another Minister of Cabinet rank.
2 The Permanent Secretary of the Civil Service Department should be designated as Head of the Home Civil Service and the Civil Service Commission should be part of this new department.
3 All classes should be abolished and replaced by a single unified structure covering all non-industrial civil servants. The grading of each post should be by job evaluation.
4 Employing departments should have a greater role in recruitment and more attention should be paid to the relevance of the university course to the post they are being recruited to.
5 Both specialists and general administrators should have more training in management.
6 A Civil Service College should be established to provide this training. A proportion of the places on these courses should be set aside for non-civil servants, e.g. industrialists and local government officers.
7 More emphasis should be placed on the career development of civil servants and there should be greater mobility between the Civil Service and industry, e.g. secondments both ways.
8 The principles of accountable management should be applied to the work of every department. Each department should establish a planning unit under the control of a senior policy adviser. The adviser's main role is to ensure that possible future developments are taken into account when present policy decisions are made.
9 A Minister should be allowed to employ on a temporary basis a number of experts to assist him.
10 Further investigation should be made into removing unnecessary secrecy in policy making and administration.

Since 1966 many but not all of these recommendations have been put into effect. A Civil Service Department was created in 1968 but abolished in 1981 when control of the service was divided between the Treasury and the Cabinet Office. A Civil Service College was opened at Sunningdale in Berkshire in 1970 but has disappointed many of its supporters.

The movement towards a unified grading structure has been slow but there are now greater opportunities for internal promotion between one group and another. A 'fast stream' promotion channel was established, including a Higher Executive Officer (A) grade. Those appointed to this grade will take up posts designed to give them a broad picture of the work of the Civil Service, perhaps in the Cabinet Office or a Minister's Private Office. Figure 4.1 shows the entry and promotion paths.

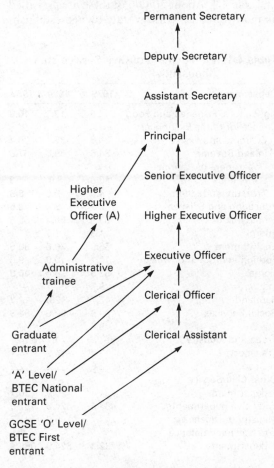

Fig 4.1 Civil Service entry and promotion paths

Attempts have been made to introduce accountable management and to make greater use of specialists but most top level civil servants are still generalist administrators. In 1979 the new Conservative Prime Minister appointed Sir Derek Raynor, a former executive with Marks and Spencers as an Efficiency Adviser with the role of reducing waste and inefficiency in the Civil Service. Other Ministers have appointed specialist advisers. Very little has been done about excessive secrecy and as the Westland affair shows the reverse seems to have happened in some cases.

The Civil Service today

There are about 570 000 civil servants in Britain employed in the various departments, as shown in Table 4.1. About 70 000 of these are classified as industrial and work in state-owned establish-

Table 4.1 Employment of Civil Service staff (thousands)

Department	1979	1984	1989
Agriculture, Fisheries and Food	14.5	12.1	10.9
Chancellor of the Exchequer:			
Customs and Excise	28.8	25.1	26.4
Inland Revenue	84.6	69.8	67.0
Department of National			
Savings	10.8	8.0	7.3
Treasury and others	4.0	9.5	8.3
Education and Science	3.7	2.4	2.5
Employment	53.6	56.4	55.0
Energy	1.3	1.1	1.1
Environment	56.0	36.6	30.6
Foreign and Commonwealth	12.1	10.0	9.6
Home	33.5	36.4	40.8
Industry	9.5	–	–
Scotland	13.7	12.8	12.3
Social Services	100.9	92.6	94.3
Trade	9.6	–	–
Trade and Industry	–	14.7	14.7
Transport	13.9	14.2	14.1
Wales	2.6	2.2	2.2
Other Civil Service			
departments	31.4	20.9	30.7
Total civil departments	484.6	424.8	427.9
Ministry of Defence	247.7	199.2	141.3
Total civil and defence			
departments	732.3	624.0	569.2

(Source: *HMSO Annual Digest of Statistics*)

ments. The numbers of industrial civil servants have been reduced as a result of the privatisation of the Royal Ordnance Factories and part of the Royal Dockyards. Of the remainder about 230 000 form the Administration Group of which 1800 are classified as senior civil servants with a rank of principal or above. Of the total about 60 per cent are women but in the senior positions this falls to under 10 per cent. The departments employing most civil servants are the Ministry of Defence, the Department of Social Services, the Department of Employment, the Inland Revenue and the Prison Service.

Civil servants are defined as 'servants of the Crown, other than holders of political and judicial offices, who are employed in a civil capacity, and whose remuneration is paid wholly and directly out of monies voted by Parliament'. They are covered by the Official Secrets Act. In 1985 Clive Ponting, a senior civil servant in the Ministry of Defence, was prosecuted under the Official Secrets Act. He argued that a civil servant must ultimately place his loyalty to Parliament and the public interest above his obligation to the government of the day. He was acquitted. Soon after Sir Robert Armstrong, Head of the Home Civil Service, issued instructions to all civil servants which said:

> 'Civil servants are under an obligation to keep the confidences to which they become privy in the course of their official duties; not only the maintenance of trust between Ministers and civil servants but also the efficiency of government depends on their doing so . . . . Civil servants are servants of the Crown. For all practical purposes the Crown in this context means and is represented by the government of the day'.

It is clear that some civil servants do not accept this definition and since 1985 there have been a series of leaks of official documents to opposition MPs.

Discussion question

1 Where do you think a civil servant's first loyalty should be? What should a senior civil servant do if he or she knows that the Minister is deliberately misleading Parliament?

The role of the Civil Service

As we saw in Chapter 1 the theory is that governments make policy and the administrators carry it out. This view has been challenged by many observers who argue that Governments and Ministers come and go whilst the Civil Service goes on for ever. It is this continuity plus the detailed knowledge that they possess which give civil servants an important role in policy making. How crucial that role is may depend on the strengths and weaknesses of individual governments and Ministers.

The British Civil Service has a very high reputation. It contains some of the best brains in the country, is incorruptible and is politically neutral. However, this neutrality and the desire to protect their Minister from criticism in Parliament or elsewhere often leads to excessive caution and resistance to change. Shirley Williams once described the Civil Service as 'a beautifully designed and effective braking mechanism. It produces a hundred well-argued answers against initiative and change' (1) and from the opposite end of the political spectrum Sir John Nott said 'Whitehall is the ultimate monster to stop governments changing things' (2).

Business people constantly complain of the 'dead-hand of government' and to meet this criticism Lord Young when Secretary of State for Trade and Industry said 'my department should spend far more of its time finding ways to help industry to trade than it should do inventing and enforcing rules and regulations to stop industry trading' (3).

Despite these criticisms most Ministers agree that once they have made a decision their civil servants will loyally carry it out. Most civil servants concede that they prefer strong Ministers willing to make decisions and to fight for their policies in Cabinet and elsewhere.

The future

We live in a highly competitive world. Britain's economic record over the last 25 years has not been good. We have fallen behind many of our major competitors. It would be wrong to make the Civil Service the scapegoat for this but if the decline is to be halted we need to re-think our political and administrative structures. Some of the Fulton recommendations have not been fully implemented. Insufficient attention has been paid to managerial accountability. Government departments deal with an equivalent amount of money to many of the largest companies in this country. For example, the Scottish Office spends as much (£8 billion) as Shell UK earns. It is, therefore, important to have people with proven managerial ability running these departments.

Peter Hennessey in his excellent book *Whitehall* posed the fundamental political question for the 1990s and into the twenty-first century 'Are the executive functions of central government to be treated as big business and staffed accordingly?' If so, the public administrator will become the public manager. This has already happened in the National Health Service and to some extent in local government.

References

(1) Shirley Williams, 'The Decision Makers' in *Policy and Practice: the Experience of Government*, RIPA (1980).
(2) Quoted in 'Thatcher's 3000 Days', BBC1 Panorama (4 January 1988).
(3) Lord Young's Speech to the Conservative Party Conference (1987).

Discussion questions

2 Outline the present procedures for recruitment to the Civil Service. What changes will be needed if public administrators are to be public managers?
3 What is the role of the Minister's Private Office? *See* Case Study 3 which gives an outline of the Foreign Office with a detailed breakdown of the staff in the Secretary of State's Private Office.

Written questions

4 Find out and list all the government departments and draw up an organisation chart for the Treasury and the Department of the Environment. What are the purposes of an organisation chart?
5 Find out the total number of Permanent Secretaries and Deputy Secretaries. In each

case discover how many of them are women. What steps are needed to ensure that more women rise to the top positions in the Civil Service?

6 Referring to Table 4.1:
   (a) illustrate these figures in graphical form
   (b) work out which government departments had the largest percentage fall in manpower between 1979 and 1989 and suggest the reasons why
   (c) give reasons why the Department of Employment and the Home Office have shown increases in the number of civil servants employed
   (d) explain why the number of Customs and Excise Officers have increased since 1984.

7 You have recently obtained your BTEC National Award. In response to your application to join the Civil Service you have been called for an interview. A friend who has been through the selection procedure tells you that one of the questions is likely to be 'What qualities are essential in a good civil servant?' Prepare notes for the answer you would give to this question.

CASE STUDY 3 The Foreign Office

Case study situation

As an example of the role and organisation of a government department we have selected one of the major offices of state, the Foreign and Commonwealth Office, and to illustrate the secretarial and administrative support required by a senior government Minister, we have drawn upon the experiences of Maggie Smart. Maggie is well qualified to do this as a result of her distinguished career in the Civil Service where she served as Secretary to Peter Walker, Sir Geoffrey Rippon and Tony Crosland when they were successively Secretaries of State for the Environment. When Tony Crosland became Foreign Secretary she moved with him to the Foreign Office as 'Diary' Secretary in his private office. On the death of Tony Crosland, Dr David Owen, who had been a Minister of State at the Foreign Office, became Foreign Secretary and Maggie continued to work for him in the same capacity. When the Conservative Party won the general election in 1979, Lord Carrington was appointed Foreign Secretary and Maggie remained in his Private Office for a short while before rejoining Dr David Owen as his Private Secretary. The organisation chart in Fig 4.2 gives an outline of the organisation of the Foreign Office with a detailed breakdown of the staff in the Secretary of State's Private Office, including the position occupied by Maggie Smart.

Overseas relations and responsibilities of the Foreign Office

The major role of the Foreign and Commonwealth Office is to provide a means of communication between the UK Government and Foreign Governments and international organisations for discussing and negotiating international relations. The Foreign Office is responsible for:

- alerting the government to the implications of developments abroad
- protecting British interests overseas
- protecting British citizens abroad
- disseminating and explaining British policies and cultivating friendly relations with governments abroad
- discharging British responsibilities to dependent territories.

These responsibilities and services are administered by the Foreign Office through the following departments:

- Aid Policy
- Arms Control and Disarmament
- Central African
- Claims
- Commercial Management and Exports
- Commonwealth Co-ordination

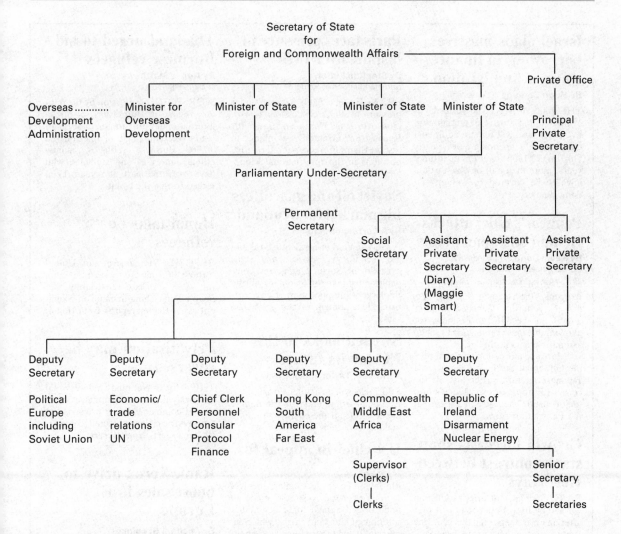

Fig 4.2 Organisation chart for the Foreign and Commonwealth Office

- Communications:
    Administration
    Engineering
    Operations
    Planning Staff
- Consular
- Cultural Relations
- Defence
- East African
- Eastern European
- Economic Relations
- European Community
- Falkland Islands
- Far Eastern

- Finance
- Government Hospitality
- Home Estate and Services
- Information
- Information Technology
- Internal Audit
- Library and Records
- Maritime, Aviation and Environment
- Mexico and Central America
- Middle East
- Migration and Visa
- Narcotics Control and Aids
- Nationality and Treaty
- Near East and North Africa

Israel plans massive borrowing to finance wave of immigration

By Hugh Carnegy in Jerusalem

THE Bank of Israel said yesterday it estimated that a wave of immigration by Soviet Jews will require additional Government spending of nearly Shk7bn (£2.13bn) over the next three years, more than half of which would have to be covered by foreign and domestic borrowing.

Peugeot's chief attacks Britain on Japan plants

By Kevin Done, Motor Industry Correspondent, in Paris

MR JACQUES Calvet, chairman of Peugeot, the leading French carmaker, yesterday launched a bitter attack on the UK government for allowing Japanese car makers to set up assembly plants in the UK.

"More and more, don't we hear people talk about the UK as if it were a Japanese aircraft carrier just off the coast of Europe, or even Japan's fifth major island?" he asked in a speech at the Paris motor show.

Growth forecasts show stark contrast between Germanys

EAST German industrial production will fall by 10 to 15 per cent next year after an even steeper fall this year, the Bonn finance ministry said yesterday, highlighting the stark contrast with West German growth.

EC agrees draft statutes for a European central bank

By Peter Norman, Economics Correspondent

CENTRAL BANK governors of the 12 European Community states yesterday agreed the draft statutes of a future European central bank, although Britain expressed reservations about the project.

Paris faces pressure in dispute over IMF

By Stephen Fidler, Euromarkets Correspondent

FRANCE seems likely to come under pressure to make concessions to Britain over the European Bank for Reconstruction and Development to resolve their differences about relative positions in the International Monetary Fund.

Soviet oil and gas 'offers big market for Scotland'

By A Correspondent

A HUGE market for Scottish oil and gas technology, services and skills exists in the Soviet Union, and companies must take the lead in capturing this largely untapped market, the Scottish Development Agency (SDA) says.

Sweden looks to the EC for its future

By Robert Taylor in Stockholm

SWEDEN will be a full member of the European Community by the middle of the 1990's, if the country's opinion makers have their way.

UN chief in appeal for peace

Mr Javier Pérez de Cuéllar, the UN secretary general, yesterday made an impassioned appeal for a negotiated solution of the Gulf crisis, which he said could end otherwise in "a tremendous conflagration", **Michael Littlejohns writes from the UN, New York.** Addressing a pre-General Assembly lunch, he said he was discouraged because he had not heard the words "dialogue", "peace" and "justice" mentioned in the search for a resolution of the problem. "Please don't forget that we have to avoid war."

Visa deal reached

Hungary, Britain, Belgium, the Netherlands and Luxembourg have agreed that visas will not be necessary for short-term travellers between their countries.

Thailand urged to aid Burmese refugees

By Roger Matthews in Bangkok

WORSENING repression by the military regime in Burma has set off an international effort to persuade Thailand to ease the plight of an estimated 40,000 Burmese refugees, mainly ethnic minorities and students, who have over the past two years been forced to flee the country.

Hanoi talks on refugees

BRITISH, Vietnamese and United Nations officials are to meet in Hanoi this week to discuss repatriating boat people languishing in camps throughout Asia, **Reuter reports from Hanoi.**

Privatisation may be reversed

THE African National Congress said yesterday it might renationalise state-owned companies being privatised in South Africa if it was elected to power, **Reuter reports from Harare.**

Rank Xerox drive to boost sales in E Europe

By Michael Skapinker

RANK Xerox, the office machinery manufacturer, said yesterday that greater freedom of information in eastern Europe and the introduction of a market economy would result in a four-fold increase in the number of photocopiers sold in the region by 1995.

The company, jointly owned by Xerox Corporation of the US and the UK's Rank Organisation, said it expected to increase its sales to the Soviet Union and other eastern European countries by 300 per cent over the next five years. Rank Xerox's sales to eastern Europe were about £50m in 1989.

(Reproduced by permission of the *Financial Times*)

Fig 4.3 Extracts from articles published in the *Financial Times*

- News
- North America
- Overseas Estate
- Personnel:
    Operations
    Policy
    Services
- Protocol
- Republic of Ireland
- Research
- Resource Management
- Science, Energy and Nuclear
- Security:
    Co-ordination
    Policy
- South America
- South Asian
- South East Asian
- South African
- Southern European
- South Pacific
- Soviet
- Technical Security
- Training
- United Nations
- West African
- Western European
- West Indian and Atlantic

The newspaper cuttings in Fig 4.3 are typical of the wide ranging issues reported on daily from around the world and which the Foreign Office will be involved in or will wish to monitor.

Overseas Missions

The Foreign Office is represented abroad by embassies and high commissions in nearly 130 countries as well as subordinate consulates general and consulates and missions at eight multilateral organisations. These are staffed by members of the Diplomatic Service and local people. An embassy is involved in the following main areas of work:

- political and economic;
- export promotion and commercial development;
- consular and immigration;
- aid administration;
- information and communications;
- cultural relations.

Overseas Development Administration

A separate division of the Foreign Office, headed by the Minister for Overseas Development, the Overseas Development Association (ODA) is responsible for administering Britain's aid programme for developing countries and other countries in need. The assistance provided includes financial aid on concessionary terms and technical support, i.e. engaging specialist staff and supplying training facilities either directly to the countries concerned or through multilateral aid organisations, such as the UN and its specialised agencies.

The British Council

The British Council, a quango (as referred to in Chapter 9), is appointed and mostly financed by the Foreign Office to promote a wider knowledge of Britain and the English Language abroad and the development of closer cultural relations between Britain and other countries. Its staff serve as education advisers to diplomatic missions and provide educational assistance to developing countries in association with the ODA.

Relations with other government departments

Figure 4.4 illustrates the involvement of other government departments and quangoes in overseas relations and the co-ordinating role of the Foreign Office. Policy matters concerning the EC are co-ordinated by the Cabinet Office (*see also* Chapter 10 which deals with the EC, NATO, UN and other treaty obligations).

Secretarial support services

Much of Maggie Smart's work as a member of the Foreign Secretary's team of Private Secretaries involved organising his daily schedule. This entailed:

- controlling the Foreign Secretary's appointments diary

Overseas Development Administration

British Council

Ministry of Defence

FOREIGN OFFICE

CABINET OFFICE
(EC Policy)

Treasury

Department of Trade
and Industry
(British Overseas Trade Board)
(Export Credit Guarantee Department)

Fig 4.4 The co-ordinating role of the Foreign Office

0830	Meeting with Private Secretaries
0900	Meeting with Junior Ministers
0945	Office meeting on Rhodesia
1030	Cabinet meeting at 10 Downing Street
1300	Draft speech over sandwich lunch
1400	Meeting at Foreign Office to finalise questions
1430	Foreign affairs questions in the House of Commons
1530	Meeting with Foreign Ambassador at Foreign Office
1630	Meeting with Constituency Secretary in House of Commons
1830	Heathrow Airport to meet US Secretary of State
2000	Public meeting in London Constituency
2200	Vote in House of Commons
2230	Meeting with group of MPs

(Depart next day at 0700 for EC meeting in Brussels)

Fig 4.5 Specimen appointments card for the Foreign Secretary

- co-ordinating all the necessary briefing for the Foreign Secretary for each meeting
- co-ordinating detailed arrangements for overseas visits by the Foreign Secretary, sometimes accompanying him
- preparing a daily appointments card — this is prepared on the previous day and placed in the Foreign Secretary's overnight red box with the necessary briefing papers. The appointments card shown in Fig 4.5 gives details of appointments, meetings, visits, as well as a note of what is happening in the House of Commons
- anticipating and reacting quickly when circumstances change to readjust the diary and schedule of appointments
- searching through the telegrams — some 50/60 were received each day from all over the world — in order to be up to date on events as well as noting any dates of meetings, such as NATO, state visits, etc. which could involve the Foreign Secretary
- briefing all staff involved with the Foreign Secretary's appointments
- issuing the detectives and driver with full details every day of the Foreign Secretary's movements (two detectives escort him at all times) and discussing with the detectives the security arrangements for the Foreign Secretary's advance programme
- handling general correspondence

- replying to invitations
- communicating with the Prime Minister's Private Secretaries concerning appointments which also involve the Prime Minister
- answering telephone queries from other government Ministers' Offices and the Cabinet Office
- liaising with the Secretaries of Foreign Ambassadors concerning visits and arranging for newly appointed ambassadors to meet the Foreign Secretary
- communicating with the Party Agent concerning appointments in the constituency
- carrying out weekend duty involving liaison with the Foreign Office Resident Clerk.

There was enormous scope for personal initiative in planning the Foreign Secretary's day. Maggie always tried to allow some slack in the diary to allow for any unforeseen changes in plans, as the best made plans could so easily be turned upside down with an unexpected item of news. She had to anticipate how long meetings would take place, always keeping an eye on the parliamentary programme, state visits, etc. It was vital to allocate her time and effort wisely to complete tasks in order of priority.

Much of Maggie's day was spent dealing with people, either on the telephone or when they visited the Foreign Secretary. She was required to make the necessary introductions, having regard to the correct protocol. Her work was highly confidential and strict security measures were of the utmost importance.

STUDENT ACTIVITIES FOR INDIVIDUALS

1 Read the foreign affairs news in a current newspaper and prepare a digest of each item as it would be given to brief the Foreign Secretary.
2 For each item of news in (1) find out:
  (a) which department(s) of the Foreign Office would be involved or would be required to monitor it
  (b) the name of the Head of State of the country concerned and the name and address of its Embassy/High Commission in London
  (c) the international organisations of which the country is a member, e.g. EC, UN, Commonwealth
  (d) the system of government in that country
  (e) its principal imports and exports and details of Britain's trade with the country.

3 How would you suggest Maggie Smart should introduce the Ambassador of one of the countries featured in your news items in (1) when visiting the Foreign Secretary?

STUDENTS ACTIVITIES FOR GROUP WORK

1 Using the newspaper cuttings in Fig 4.3:
  (a) locate the countries concerned on a world map to ascertain which countries have common borders with them
  (b) find out who are the major trading partners of each country
  (c) identify which department(s) of the Foreign Office would be involved or would require to monitor each item of news, say whether any other government departments would be involved and, if so, which ones
  (d) discuss the implications for Britain of each of these items of news.
2 Each member of the group to give a five-minute talk on a foreign country, based on their research (see activities for individuals).
3 Discuss whether foreign aid is organised better by government or by voluntary agencies? How can you ensure that money for aid benefits the people who need it most? What form of aid is most effective?

5 Central government finance

All governments need money to carry out their essential functions. The money is raised through taxation. The earliest Parliaments were set up to approve taxes levied by the King on his subjects. They established a principle which still exists today, i.e. 'grievances before supply'. In other words, Parliament as representative of the people insisted that the King should listen to their complaints before granting him the money that he needed. Since the Bill of Rights 1689 taxation cannot be imposed by the Monarch but must have the approval of Parliament. The main slogan in the American War of Independence which resulted in Britain losing her American colonies was 'no taxation without representation'. As we have seen in Chapter 3, Ministers are no longer responsible to the Monarch but are now responsible to Parliament. Today the House of Commons controls both the raising of money and the spending of it.

Discussion question

1 What is meant by the term 'grievance before supply'?

Since the Parliament Act of 1911 the House of Lords has no power to defeat or amend a Money Bill. A Money Bill is defined as 'A Public Bill which, in the opinion of the Speaker of the House of Commons, contains only provisions dealing with the imposition, repeal, remission, alteration or regulation of taxation'. If the House of Lords has not approved a Money Bill within one month after receiving it from the House of Commons then it automatically goes to receive the Royal Assent.

During the twentieth century the role of government has increased dramatically. Consequently the amount of money that it needs has also increased. In 1900 taxation accounted for only 10 per cent of the nation's income. Today it is around 40 per cent. Parliament has established three main principles in its attempt to control expenditure:

1 Any sum approved is a maximum and may not be exceeded without further approval.
2 Money authorised for one purpose may not be spent on something else.
3 Money granted for any purpose may be used only during the financial year (1 April to 31 March) for which it was voted. Surpluses cannot be carried forward.

Public expenditure procedure

Every government aims to keep public expenditure under control. Each November the Chancellor of the Exchequer presents his 'Autumn Statement' to Parliament. This is followed by a Public Expenditure White Paper, usually published in January. These give plans for future public expenditure.

Every year during October and November the government departments prepare their estimates of expenditure for the next financial year. These are sent to the Treasury who then prepare an overall picture to be presented to the Cabinet in January. The Treasury plays a key role in recommending what limits must be placed on public expenditure and hard bargaining will take place between them and the spending Ministers. The function of the Cabinet is to decide on priorities and where reductions in the estimates must be made. When the Cabinet finally approves the departmental estimates they are published (usually in February) and then debated in Parliament before the Chancellor of the Exchequer produces the Budget. By tradition there are two sets of estimates, the Defence estimates and the Civil estimates.

Budget procedure

Once the Cabinet has approved the level of public expenditure for the forthcoming year the Chancellor of the Exchequer in conjunction with the Treasury officials can begin the detailed work of deciding how to raise the money to meet this expenditure. The annual Budget is prepared and presented to the House of Commons in late March by the Chancellor. Strict secrecy is maintained right up to the announcement. Even the Cabinet are only informed a few days before the Budget statement. In 1947 Dr Hugh Dalton, the Chancellor of the Exchequer, spoke to a journalist on his way in to the House of Commons to make his Budget speech. As a result, he had to resign.

The Chancellor of the Exchequer usually starts his statement with a review of the previous year and the economic forecasts for the following year. He then announces his taxation proposals. A debate lasting several days in the House of Commons will follow on the Budget proposals and votes may be taken on some of them. The proposals are then put in the form of a Finance Bill. Part of this is debated by the whole House of Commons sitting as a committee while the more technical aspects are sent to a standing committee. The same procedure is adopted as for any other Public Bill (*see* Chapter 3). Normally the Finance Bill will receive the Royal Assent in July. However, under the provisions of the Provisional Collection of Taxes Act 1913 the Board of Inland Revenue is permitted to collect any proposed new taxes from the date of their announcement in the Budget.

Discussion question

2 Why is it so important that Budget proposals remain secret until the Chancellor of the Exchequer makes his speech in the House of Commons?

Consolidated Fund

All government receipts from taxes and other revenues are paid into one fund known as the Consolidated Fund. Payments on behalf of the government are paid out of this fund. Certain Officers of State are paid directly out of the Consolidated Fund, e.g. the Speaker, High Court Judges and the Ombudsman. The Fund also pays the Monarch's Civil List (*see* Chapter 3). The reason for these payments is to protect the political independence of the recipients. The payments are maintained continuously from year to year without the need for parliamentary debate and approval, except when alterations are necessary.

Supplementary estimates

These may be necessary:

- where an unexpected event occurs, e.g. the Falklands War or an outbreak of foot and mouth disease which necessitates a department spending more money than it had originally estimated
- where a department has underestimated the cost of a particular project.

Supplementary estimates are then presented by the Chancellor of the Exchequer to the House of Commons and are debated and approved in the normal way.

Parliamentary control over public expenditure

It has been generally recognised for many years that parliamentary control over government expenditure has been less effective than it should be. Until 1981 there were a number of Supply Days set aside each year where the opposition could choose the subject and scrutinise government expenditure in a particular area. In reality the opposition usually chose to have set-piece debates on particular subjects, e.g. the National Health Service and the detailed financial aspects were rarely discussed. This was recognised in 1981 when Supply Days were replaced by 20 Opposition Days. From 1971 to 1979 there was a Select Committee on Expenditure whose task it was to examine in detail government expenditure.

Departmental select committees

Departmental select committees were set up in 1980 to 'shadow' each government department. They are charged with 'examining the expenditure, administration and policy of their respective departments and associated public bodies'. They issue regular reports which are often debated in the House of Commons.

A select committee normally has about 11 members drawn from back-benchers in proportion to the party strengths in the House of Commons. Usually they put aside their party affiliations and aim to work as a united team. Occasionally there are majority and minority reports but this is unusual. The select committees can request Ministers and civil servants to give evidence and to be questioned but they cannot compel them to attend. However a refusal of such a request usually leads to a parliamentary row. The committees can also summon other bodies and individuals to come and give evidence. They can call for papers and records but on a few occasions the government has refused to release certain sensitive papers. The select committees have the power to employ research staff and advisers to help them in their work. Although these committees do not have the power of their counterparts in the United States they do provide a check on the activities of government departments. Their reports can cause embarrassment to the government (e.g. the Defence Committee Report in 1986 on the Westland Affair) and can lead directly to changes in legislation (e.g. abolition of 'sus' law in 1981).

Comptroller and Auditor-General

This post was first created in 1866, and is filled by an independent person whose salary is paid directly out of the Consolidated Fund. He or she now heads the National Audit Office created in 1983. His/her statutory function is to ensure that all expenditure is properly incurred; that Treasury sanction has been obtained where necessary and to audit all departmental accounts. In recent years the role has been extended to examining departmental expenditure with a view to discovering any waste or extravagance and also to making 'value for money' suggestions to government departments. He reports to the Public Accounts Committee.

Public Accounts Committee

This is a select committee of the House of Commons traditionally chaired by a senior opposition member. It has similar powers to the departmental select committees in that it can summon civil servants to give evidence and call for papers and documents. Its main role is to expose waste and inefficiency. Thus it operates 'after the event' and does not deal with current issues. In 1962 the Public Accounts Committee drew attention to the excessive profits made by Ferranti Ltd on a government contract for missiles. As a result, the company finally agreed to pay back over £4 million. On another occasion it drew attention to substantial savings that could be made by improved store purchasing methods in the National Health Service. The following year the new methods were put into effect.

Taxation

No-one likes paying taxes but it is now generally accepted that there are four criteria (originally suggested by Adam Smith, the eighteenth century economist) against which any tax should be judged:

1 **Equitable:** a good tax should be based on ability to pay. The criticisms of the community charge (poll tax) when it was introduced centred around whether or not it was equitable.
2 **Economical:** it should not be expensive to administer. The original dog licence fee was dropped when it was found that it cost more to collect than was obtained in revenue.
3 **Convenience:** the method of payment should be convenient to the taxpayer, e.g. PAYE which is collected at source from a person's income.

4 **Certainty:** the taxpayer must know how much he has to pay and when so that he can plan ahead. Thus the strong objection to retrospective taxation.

Taxes may be divided into certain categories:

1 **Indirect taxes:** these are usually taxes on expenditure. They can be sub-divided into **specific** taxes levied on each unit of the commodity purchased (e.g. excise duties) and *ad valorem* taxes levied on the price of the commodity (e.g. VAT). Indirect taxes are **regressive** in that they take up a larger proportion of the income of the lower paid.
2 **Direct taxes:** the taxes levied on the incomes of individuals and organisations. If the rate of tax increases with income then they are said to be **progressive**.

The following are examples of UK national taxes:

Direct	Indirect
Income tax	VAT
Corporation tax	Excise duties (petrol, drinks, tobacco)
Petroleum revenue tax	Motor vehicle duties
Inheritance tax	Customs duties
IBA levy	Betting and gaming
Capital gains tax	TV licences
	Stamp duty

Income tax, excise duties, VAT, corporation tax and petroleum revenue tax together account for about 65 per cent of total revenue from taxation. National insurance contributions, although not officially classified as a tax, have the same effect and account for a further 19 per cent of total revenue.

The main criticisms of indirect taxation are that it is regressive and also that it has a direct effect on the cost of living through the Index of Retail Prices. It thus tends to fuel inflation and may lead to higher wage demands which in turn accelerate the inflationary spiral.

The main criticism of a direct tax is that it is a dis-incentive to work and effort. In the case of individuals this will depend on their personal tastes. In some cases the individual faced by

higher taxation may work longer and harder in order to bring up their income to its original level. In other cases taxpayers may decide that it is not worth working so hard if a high proportion of their income is to be taken away in taxes. Alternatively, they may look for tax avoidance schemes to relieve the burden.

Discussion question

3 What are the main *economic* effects of reducing direct taxation and increasing indirect taxation?

Table 5.1 Sources of taxation on individuals and companies

	1978 (£m)	1982 (£m)	1988 (£m)
Taxes on income (e.g. income tax, corporation tax)	22 624	42 392	61 123
Taxes on expenditure (e.g. VAT, customs and excise duties)	22 756	46 467	75 029
Social security contributions	10 101	18 095	31 686

(Source: *HMSO Annual Digest of Statistics*)

As will be seen from Table 5.1 there was a shift from direct to indirect taxation during the 1980s. The standard rate of income tax was reduced to 25 per cent and the upper rate to 40 per cent. Similarly, the rate of corporation tax was reduced. One of the first actions of the Conservative Government in 1980 was to almost double the rate of VAT. The philosophy of the Conservative Government has been to allow people to keep a greater proportion of their income to spend as they please. On the other hand, the increase in indirect taxes hits hardest those living on low incomes.

The objectives of taxation are as follows:

1 Raise revenue to cover the government's expenditure. If the revenue raised is insufficient to meet the expenditure then there is a Budget deficit and the government will have

to resort to borrowing to make up the deficit. Alternatively, if the revenue exceeds the expenditure then there is a Budget surplus which can be used to pay off previous borrowing debts.

2 Redistribute income by putting higher taxes on the rich to pay for extra benefits for the poor.

3 Regulate the economy. When inflation threatens then taxes can be raised so that people have less money to spend. Alternatively, when a recession looms then taxes can be lowered to give people more money to spend and so revive consumption.

4 Attempt to discourage consumption of certain goods, e.g. a health tax on tobacco.

5 Encourage businesses to locate in development areas by offering them lower taxes if they do so.

6 Encourage businesses to invest their profits by having differential tax rates on distributed and undistributed profits.

Government management of the economy

All governments have four main aims in managing the economy:

- control inflation by maintaining a stable price level
- maintain full employment
- have a favourable balance of payments
- achieve economic growth.

It is rather like a juggler trying to keep four balls in the air at the same time. No government since 1945 has succeeded in doing this and each has had to formulate its own priorities. Britain's economic management since 1945 has not succeeded in producing steady economic growth, particularly when compared with our main competitors. No government has managed to develop a long-term strategy for industrial development. An attempt was made by the Wilson Government in the 1960s when it produced a national plan and set up a separate Department of Economic Affairs to implement it. However, the new department was unable to work harmoniously with the Treasury and the experiment was soon abandoned. One of the

problems has been that the Treasury has tended to think short term and devoted its efforts to controlling public spending. There has been insufficient long-term planning designed to produce economic growth. The 'stop-go' policies of the 1960s and 1970s were a hindrance to long-term industrial expansion.

Until 1979 all governments tended to adopt Keynsian policies to control the economy. Fiscal methods (i.e. changes in taxation) were used to influence consumption and production, while exchange controls were used to protect the balance of payments. In the 1950s and 1960s full employment (below three per cent) was maintained. There was, however, a low growth rate and in 1967 the pound was devalued. The aim of devaluation is to make Britain's exports more competitive in the world markets. In 1976 there was a crisis of confidence in the pound fuelled by high internal inflation rates. The Labour Government applied for a loan from the International Monetary Fund (IMF). One of the conditions of the loan was that Britain must reduce its public spending and take steps to curb the money supply. This was backed up by a statutory incomes policy. The pay restraint policy collapsed in the winter of 1978–9 and there was a series of very damaging strikes. The 'winter of discontent' was one of the main contributory factors to the Conservative victory in the 1979 general election.

Since 1979 fiscal policies have been largely replaced by monetarist policies. The main emphasis has been on reducing public spending and consequently the Public Sector Borrowing Requirement (PSBR) and also on setting strict money supply targets which were not always met. The immediate result was a rapid rise in unemployment which continued until 1987 and a decline in industrial output. After an initial rise inflation was reduced but in 1989 it started to rise again. High interest rates were used to try and control inflation.

Exchange controls were abandoned and the pound was allowed to float. In 1985 it reached a record low of US$1.1 to the pound but rose to around US$1.9 to the pound. By the end of the decade Britain had a record balance of payments deficit despite the benefits deriving from North Sea oil.

The decade ended as it began with an inflation rate above that of our major competitors and the consequent high interest rates proving a deterrent to firms to borrow money to expand their production. Nevertheless industrial efficiency improved considerably and this will prove valuable when the economic climate allows for increased investment.

People's real incomes rose — if only slowly — during most of the 1980s. Income tax rates were reduced, partly paid for by the privatisation of several major industries. Towards the end of the decade high interest rates hit those with mortgages whilst the introduction of the community charge to replace rates proved very unpopular. The strict restrictions on public expenditure had an effect on public services and there were demands for more expenditure particularly on education and the National Health Service.

The type of economic management we may expect in the 1990s may well depend on the result of the general election due in 1992. Whichever party wins will face an increasingly difficult task. North Sea oil revenues are expected to decline and after 1992 we shall have to face even stiffer competition from other European countries and possibly also from Eastern Europe and Asia.

Discussion question

4 Why have incomes policies not been successful in the past?

Written questions

5 Examine (a) income tax, (b) the community charge and (c) VAT and in each case see whether they meet the four criteria for a good tax as laid down by Adam Smith.

6 Referring to the figures given in Table 5.1:
(a) construct a pie chart showing the percentages of total revenue obtained from the various sources of taxation
(b) calculate the extra revenue which would be obtained by:
  (i) raising income tax by 1p in the pound
  (ii) increasing VAT by one per cent
  (iii) a 25 per cent increase in the car tax
(c) find out the equivalent figures for the latest year available and account for the increases in total revenue.

7 Write a brief account of the work of the Public Accounts Committee.

8 Produce a table showing:
(a) the percentage rate of inflation
(b) the percentage level of unemployment
(c) the percentage increase or decrease in industrial production in the UK for the most recent five years for which figures are available.

9 Produce a table comparing:
(a) the percentage rate of inflation
(b) the percentage level of unemployment
(c) the percentage increase or decrease in industrial production in the UK, Japan, West Germany, USA, France and Italy for the most recent year for which the figures are available.

10 Conduct a survey among about 20 of your friends and relations to find out which of the taxes they most object to and what changes in the taxation system they would like to see introduced. Design a suitable questionnaire for this purpose and present your findings in a report for discussion by your class.

6 Democracy at work

Introduction

True democracy implies that electors have a choice, not only between individuals, but also between different ideas and policies. Hence the recent transition in Eastern Europe from the one-party state to a multi-party system. A political party was defined by Edmund Burke as 'a body of men united for promoting, by their joint endeavours, the national interest upon some particular principle in which they are all agreed'. It is distinguished from a pressure group in that it seeks to become the government of the country and put its ideas into effect.

Political parties in Britain

For 200 years two parties have dominated politics in Britain. In the nineteenth century and until the 1920s it was the Conservatives (earlier known as Tories) and the Liberals (earlier known as Whigs) and since then the Conservatives and the Labour Party. In the 1987 General Election the Conservatives won 376 seats and Labour 229. Together they held 605 out of the 650 seats in the House of Commons. The other parties won only 44 seats and most of these were in Scotland, Wales and Northern Ireland. As we shall see later in this chapter the 'first past the post' voting system used in Britain favours the two-party system. No Independent MP has been elected since 1959. The party system is less rigid in local government elections and independent councillors have survived, particularly in rural areas, but even here their numbers have been very much reduced.

Conservative Party

The party originated in the late seventeenth century as the Tories who supported the Duke of York's claim to the throne. In the 1830s they changed their name to Conservatives and represented those who wished to maintain or conserve the traditional values in society. In the nineteenth century, particularly under the leadership of Benjamin Disraeli, they were identified on the one hand with imperialism and the expansion of the British Empire and on the other with social reform and the 'one nation' approach. Today, and particularly since 1979, they have taken over many of the nineteenth century Liberal ideas and are identified with free enterprise and the market economy.

Since 1945 the Conservatives have held office from 1951–64, 1970–4 and since 1979. Traditionally they have drawn their support mainly from the upper and middle classes but in recent elections have gained considerable support from the skilled working class and even from the semi-skilled and unskilled. There is a very clear regional bias. The South of England, with the exception of inner London, is almost exclusively Conservative whilst their support is much less in the industrial areas of the North of England, Wales and Scotland and in the inner city areas of London and the other large conurbations.

The leader

Since 1965 the leader of the Conservative Party has been elected annually by Conservative MPs. To win on the first ballot the candidate must obtain over 50 per cent of the votes of those eligible to vote and be ahead of the next

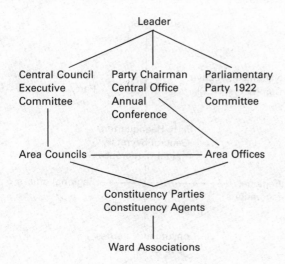

```
                        Leader

Central Council      Party Chairman    Parliamentary
Executive            Central Office    Party 1922
Committee            Annual            Committee
                     Conference

Area Councils ─────────────────── Area Offices

              Constituency Parties
              Constituency Agents

                 Ward Associations
```

Fig 6.1   Conservative Party organisation

candidate by at least 15 per cent of the electorate. If no candidate achieves this then a second ballot is held in which other candidates may join in. To win on this ballot the successful candidate must obtain more than 50 per cent of the electorate, i.e. Conservative MPs. If this is not achieved the top three candidates go into a third ballot and the alternative vote system is used.

Edward Heath was the first leader to be elected under this system but in 1977 he was defeated in the second ballot by Mrs Thatcher. She was re-elected unopposed until 1989 when Sir Anthony Mayer mounted an unsuccessful challenge.

In 1990 following the resignation from the Cabinet of Sir Geoffrey Howe, the Deputy Prime Minister, a challenge to Mrs Thatcher was made by Michael Heseltine, a former Cabinet Minister who had resigned over the Westland Affair in 1986. On the first ballot Mrs Thatcher obtained more than 50 per cent of the votes but did not fulfil the second qualification mentioned above. The voting figures were 204 to 152 with 16 abstentions. Surprisingly, she then withdrew from the election, and two other contenders, John Major and Douglas Hurd, then entered the contest with Michael Heseltine. On the second ballot John Major had a substantial lead but did not obtain 50 per cent of the votes. However, the other two candidates then withdrew in favour of John Major. On 28 November 1990 Mrs Thatcher resigned as Prime Minister and was succeeded by John Major. It is likely that, as

a result of this experience, the Conservative Party will seek to change its method of electing a leader.

Discussion question

1   Why do you think Mrs Thatcher withdrew from the Conservative Leadership Contest even though she obtained more than 50 per cent of the votes in the first ballot?

The leader of the Conservative Party has very extensive powers; and appoints the Party Chairman who, when the party is in office, is usually a member of the Cabinet. The leader is responsible for the organisation of the party, and also chooses the Cabinet and the Shadow Cabinet when the party is in opposition; makes party policies and approves the manifesto.

Annual conference

The Conservative Party holds an annual conference but it is not a policy-making body. Resolutions from constituencies may be discussed but rarely are votes taken. The main part of the conference is the leader's 'key-note' speech. Nevertheless it provides a medium for 'grass roots' opinions to be expressed.

Parliamentary Party

The Parliamentary Party consists of all Conservative MPs and meets weekly to discuss parliamentary business. It elects an executive committee known as the 1922 Committee. The Chairman of this committee is a senior back-bench MP and his main function is liaison between the leader and the Conservative MPs. He has considerable influence and can always obtain access to the leader.

Central Council

The Central Council consists of the leader, all Conservative MPs, adopted parliamentary candidates and four representatives from each constituency — a total membership of almost 4000. It serves as a two-way link between MPs and constituency associations. It appoints an Executive Committee to do the day-to-day work. One of its functions is to vet people who apply to be Conservative parliamentary candidates.

Constituency associations

Each constituency association has a full-time agent who is trained by Central Office. His/her main duties are to provide a link between the MP and the constituency association; to organise national and local election campaigns in his/her constituency; and to raise finance.

Central Office

Central Office co-ordinates general election campaigns; raises finance on a national basis; arranges speakers for local constituency parties; makes financial grants to constituencies where needed; and has an extensive research organisation providing information for MPs and local parties.

Finance

The Conservative Party is partly financed by membership contributions collected from ordinary party members but particularly at election times relies very heavily on donations from industry and commerce. Any public company making a contribution to a political party must declare it in their annual accounts.

Labour Party

The Labour Party was formed in 1900 by trade unions and socialists to provide 'a voice for the working class in Parliament'. Ramsay Macdonald led minority Labour Governments in 1924 and from 1929–31 but the first Labour Government with an overall majority came in 1945 under the leadership of Clement Attlee. Since then there have been Labour Governments from 1945–51, 1964–70 and 1974–9.

The Labour Party constitution states their objective as 'to secure for the workers . . . the full

Fig 6.2 Labour Party organisation

fruits of their industry . . . upon the basis of the common ownership of the means of production, distribution and exchange'. In practice this aim has never been carried out to its full extent. Public ownership or nationalisation, as it was more commonly known, was a major plank in the party programme until the mid 1980s but now it is seen as a means to an end rather than an end in itself. Under the leadership of Neil Kinnock it has accepted the market economy but believes there is a need for intervention to control the worst excesses of the market. It is concerned with achieving greater social equality through increased public expenditure on such services as health and education. Since its election defeats in 1983 and 1987 it has dropped many of its more unpopular policies, e.g. unilateral disarmament and withdrawal from the EC.

The leader

Until 1981 the leader of the Labour Party was elected by Labour MPs. Since that date the election is by an electoral college with 40 per cent of the votes cast by affiliated trade unions, 30 per cent by constituency parties and 30 per cent by MPs. Neil Kinnock in 1983 was the first leader to be elected in this way. The leader has considerably less power than his counterpart in the Conservative Party. When in office he will choose the Cabinet and have overall control of the day-to-day policy of the government but he does not have control over the party manifesto, although his influence will be great.

Annual conference

The annual conference is the supreme policy making body in the Labour Party. It debates resolutions forwarded by constituency parties and affiliated trade unions. If these are carried by a two-thirds majority they then become party policy. At the moment about 90 per cent of the votes at the annual conference are controlled by the block votes of the trade unions but there are proposals to reduce this percentage.

National Executive Committee

The National Executive Committee (NEC) is responsible for the day-to-day running of the party. Its membership consists of 29 members, 12 elected by the trade unions, 7 by the constituency parties, 1 from the socialist societies, 1 from the Young Socialists and 5 women members elected by all conference delegates. The Party Leader, Deputy Leader and Treasurer are also members. When the party is in opposition this body is very powerful as it may pronounce on day-to-day policy issues. In the past there have been frequent clashes with the Parliamentary Party. The NEC appoints the General Secretary and other full-time staff at party headquarters and is responsible for the organisation and financing of the party.

Parliamentary Party

The Parliamentary Party consists of all Labour MPs. It meets weekly to discuss the parliamentary programme. It holds annual elections for a parliamentary committee and the members elected form the basis of the Shadow Cabinet. The leader can allocate the members to particular front-bench posts but he must appoint all those elected.

Constituency parties

Details are given in Case Study 4 (p 63).

Finance

The Labour Party relies for its finances on membership contributions and trade union affiliation fees, but at general election times a large proportion of the finance is provided by the trade unions.

Other parties

The **Liberal Democrats** as they are now called, have 19 MPs. They are a combination of the traditional Liberal Party and a majority of the members of the Social Democratic Party (SDP) formed in 1981 by a group of MPs who broke away from the Labour Party, plus one Conservative MP. The SDP had considerable initial success winning some spectacular by-elections. They combined with the Liberals to fight the 1983 and 1987 general elections as the Alliance. However, in 1987 the SDP won only five seats and shortly afterwards a majority of the members voted to unite with the Liberals to form the Liberal Democrats. The Leader of the Liberal Democrats is elected by a secret ballot of all its members. The Liberal Democrats have had considerable success in local government elections, particularly in the South of England. The SDP remained in existence under the leadership of David Owen with two other MPs. It achieved little success and in 1990 dissolved itself. The three MPs now sit in the House of Commons as Independent Social Democrats.

The **Scottish National Party** (SNP) which advocates independence for Scotland won three seats in 1987 whilst its counterpart in Wales, **Plaid Cymru**, also won three seats.

In Northern Ireland elections tend to be decided on sectarian grounds. Attempts to introduce traditional party politics there have not succeeded and in a recent by-election a candidate standing as a Conservative received little support. The two Protestant Parties are the Official Unionists with ten seats and the Democratic Unionist Party with three seats. The two Catholic Parties are the Social and Democratic Labour

Party with three MPs and Sinn Fein with one MP. The latter has never taken his seat as he refuses to take the oath of loyalty to the Crown. The two Protestant Parties want Northern Ireland to remain part of the UK while the aim of the two Catholic Parties is a united Ireland.

The party system

The party system has long been established in British politics. Indeed the leader of the opposition receives a salary paid out of taxation and each of the political parties represented in Parliament receives a sum of money, based on the number of seats held, to help defray their parliamentary expenses.

In some countries, e.g. Germany, the party organisations receive state finance. This is to enable them to be independent of particular vested interests. As we have seen earlier, in this country the Conservative Party relies heavily on donations from industry and the Labour Party is largely financed by the trade unions. The expense of conducting elections is very considerable and those political parties not receiving money from outside sources are at a disadvantage.

Whilst it is generally accepted that party politics are an essential part of national elections there is some doubt as to whether it should play such a prominent part in local government elections.

The electoral system

Who can vote?

In order to qualify for a vote a person must be at least 18, a UK, Commonwealth or Irish citizen and have their name on the electoral register which is compiled annually. Certain people are disqualified from voting. These include:

- members of the House of Lords (although they can vote in local government and European elections)
- persons serving a prison sentence of one year or more
- persons of unsound mind
- persons convicted of corrupt or illegal election practices.

Since 1989 persons living abroad for less than 20 years may also be entitled to vote. Most people vote in person by going to the polling station but some may have a postal vote if they are sick or have moved to another constituency. Certain groups of servicemen may appoint a proxy to vote on their behalf.

Who can be a parliamentary candidate?

Any person who is over the age of 21 with certain exceptions (which are mentioned on p. 28 in Chapter 3) can be a parliamentary candidate.

Discussion questions

2 Do you think the voting age should be reduced to 16?
3 Should British subjects who permanently live abroad be able to vote in British elections?

The British system

The British system is based on 650 single member constituencies where the candidate with the highest number of votes in each constituency is automatically elected.

The advantages of this system are:

- it is simple to understand and easy to operate
- constituencies are kept to a reasonable size (average 65 000 electors) and this enables the MP to look after his constituents
- it normally produces a clear result in party terms which leads to strong and effective government.

The disadvantages are:

- it favours larger parties at the expense of the smaller, and minority interests may not be represented in Parliament
- in some constituencies where one party has a very large majority a vote for another party is in effect a wasted vote
- the seats won bear little relationship to the percentage of votes obtained by each party. For example, in 1987 the Conservatives won only 42 per cent of the votes but gained 58 per cent of the seats, while the Alliance won 22½

per cent of the votes but only 3 per cent of the seats.

In recent years there has been a growing demand for a fairer voting system based on some form of proportional representation (PR). It was one of the major planks in the Alliance election manifesto in 1983 and 1987. A growing number of Labour and Conservative MPs now support PR. It is already used in Northern Ireland for elections to the European Parliament and in some local elections. This was done to ensure adequate representation for the minority Catholic population. Every other country in the EC has some form of PR and it is possible that Britain may fall in line for the next European elections due in 1994. We will now look in more detail at some of the PR systems in use in other countries.

The alternative vote

There are single member constituencies and each elector places the candidates in order of preference by placing 1,2,3 etc. against their names. The first preference votes are counted and if one candidate has more than 50 per cent of all the votes cast then he is automatically elected. If no candidate has more than 50 per cent then the candidate with the least number of first preference votes is eliminated and his second preference votes are distributed among the other candidates. This process continues until one candidate has more than 50 per cent of the votes. This system is used in Australia.

The second ballot

Again this involves single member constituencies. If no candidate has 50 per cent of the total vote then the top two candidates contest another election a week later. This is used in France.

The party list

Each political party produces a national list of candidates in order of preference. The elector votes for a party rather than an individual. If a party wins 40 per cent of the vote then it would be entitled to 40 per cent of the seats and enough

names would be taken from the party lists to fill these seats. To avoid having a multiplicity of small parties some countries have a cut-off point. A party will only be entitled to seats in Parliament if it achieves a certain percentage of the national vote.

The disadvantages of the list system are:

- the elected MPs do not have constituencies and may be remote from the voters
- the elector has no choice between individuals
- the party apparatus has too much control in that it can determine who should be elected by the order of the list.

The additional member system

The elector casts two votes: one for the party and one for the individual. A proportion (one half in Germany) of MPs are elected in constituencies and the remainder through a list. The party lists are used to correct the unfairness caused by the 'first past the post' system.

Single Transferable Vote (STV)

This system uses multi-member constituencies and is the type of PR supported by the Liberal Democrats. It is used for parliamentary elections in the Irish Republic and several other countries. Voters have to put the candidates in order of preference. The counting procedure is complicated.

The advantages of STV are:

1 It produces a Parliament where the seats gained by each party are proportional to the votes cast.
2 It enables voters in each constituency to choose between candidates, e.g. in a four-member constituency he may like three of the candidates of a particular party but not the fourth. He can then put that candidate low down his list of preferences. Under the 'first past the post' system if he does not like his party's candidate his only alternative is to vote for another party.
3 As in most multi-member constituencies it is likely that MPs of more than one party will

be elected, thus reducing the concept of the wasted vote;

4 As one party may not have an overall majority in Parliament it cannot do exactly what it wants ('the elective dictatorship' described by Lord Hailsham) but will have to listen to the views of the other parties. This should lead to more moderate government.

The disadvantages of STV are:

1 The size of the constituencies will be very large and this will make it difficult for an MP to keep in touch with his constituents.
2 It could destroy the concept that an MP once elected represents all his constituents whether or not they voted for him.
3 It could lead to hung Parliaments where no party has an overall majority and this could result in weak government.
4 The counting procedure is complicated and difficult for the ordinary person to understand.

Electoral reform will undoubtedly be on the political agenda during the 1990s. It will only come about if one or both of the larger parties are convinced that it is necessary. Much will depend on the result of the 1991-2 General Election.

Discussion question

4 Do you think the present voting system in the UK is fair? Does it lead to good government? If not, which alternative system would you recommend?

The MP

In a speech to his constituents Winston Churchill said '. . . the first duty of an MP is to do what, in his faithful and disinterested judgement, he believes is right and necessary for the honour and safety of the country. His second duty is towards his constituents, of whom he is the representative and not the delegate. Only in the third place does his duty lie with the party organisation or programme'. Not all MPs would agree with this order of priorities but all would agree that an MP

does have several loyalties which sometimes conflict.

Members of Parliament have a loyalty to their own consciences to do what they believe to be right. They have a loyalty to the constituents who elected them. They are the only people who can speak on their behalf in Parliament. They have a loyalty to their constituency party who selected them as candidates in the first place. If they continually disregard their views they may find themselves de-selected when the next general election comes along.

The MPs are expected to support their party's policies in Parliament particularly when they are in government. Each Parliamentary Party appoints a number of their members as Whips. Their duties are to arrange the business of the House of Commons and its timetable; to advise MPs how to vote on the issues coming before Parliament; and to ensure that if an MP is absent for a vote he/she is properly 'paired' with an opposition MP similarly absent. If an MP intends to vote against the party line or abstain he/she is expected to inform the Whips beforehand and they will try and persuade him/her to change his mind.

Most MPs attend Parliament from Monday to Thursday and on Fridays if there is particular business in which they are interested. They will be expected to take their fair share of standing committees. Opportunities for speaking in major debates may be limited but they will normally table questions (written and oral) to Ministers and seek the occasional adjournment debate. These are usually reported in the local press and allow constituents to keep in touch with their activities. In addition, they will probably have to answer at least 100 letters (more if there is a particular campaign in progress) each week, spend time meeting constituents as well as reading a mass of parliamentary and other publications (*see* examples of letters received by MPs in Case Study 2). If an MP is wise he/she will tend to specialise in one subject and make him/herself an expert in it.

Most MPs spend the weekends in their constituencies. They will hold a 'surgery' to which constituents bring their problems, make visits to factories, etc., speak to local organisations and often open fetes, bazaars, etc. They must also keep in close touch with their constituency party and very often will be expected to speak at public and party meetings in other constituencies.

Payment and allowances

MPs receive a salary of about £25 000 a year — much lower than most of their European counterparts. They receive an allowance of about £23 000 to enable them to employ secretarial and research assistance. This must be paid to designated people. Very few MPs are lucky enough to have an office of their own and usually have to share with one or more others. Other allowances include cost of accommodation in London (except for MPs with London constituencies), free postage and free travel between their constituency and London. There is also a contributory pension scheme. If MPs have any other source of income, including gifts and free trips, they must declare it in the Register of Members' Interests.

Candidates

When an MP dies or resigns, a by-election is held in his constituency. On average there are about six by-elections every year. Any candidate in a general election or by-election must be nominated by at least ten electors. A deposit of £500 has to be made which is returnable if he receives more than five per cent of the votes cast in the subsequent election.

Pressure groups

Pressure groups are groups of people who seek to influence the policy of a government by persuasion. They are distinguished from political parties in that they do not seek election to Parliament. They often have spokesmen in Parliament and direct contacts with the Civil Service. Pressure groups are usually classified as either 'interest' groups or 'cause' groups but many cannot be clearly defined as either.

Interest groups

These are set up to further the interests of a particular group of people. Examples:

- Confederation of British Industry
- Trade unions
- British Medical Association
- National Farmers Union.

They are very often consulted by government when it is proposing legislation in their particular field.

Cause groups

Some of these like RSPCA, the RSPCC, the Howard League for Penal Reform, Age Concern and the Child Poverty Action Group are set up to further the cause of a particular group in society whilst others such as CND, the Lord's Day Observance Society and Greenpeace are concerned with specific political issues.

Arguments for pressure groups

1 In a complex society it is rarely possible for an individual acting on his own to influence government policy so there is a need for like-minded people to join together for concerted action.
2 They play an important part in educating the public about the issues in our society, e.g. Shelter's campaign on behalf of homeless people (*see* Case Study 5).
3 They can provide information to Ministers and MPs which is valuable when coming to decisions on current issues.
4 They enable minority views to be expressed and to receive publicity in the media.

Arguments against pressure groups

1 Many of the interest groups are strong and may have too much influence on governments, e.g. the CBI on a Conservative Government and the trade unions on a Labour Government.
2 As many of the interest groups represent producers the interests of the ordinary consumers may not be protected.
3 Some of the stronger pressure groups can exert undue pressure on a government, e.g. a threat by doctors to withdraw from the NHS or by the TUC to call a general strike.
4 Some pressure groups use dubious tactics to

try and intimidate MPs. This occurred during the abortion debate when some MPs received threatening telephone calls.

5 Some pressure groups may encourage people to break the law to further their cause, as in the animal rights campaign.

It is certain that pressure groups are here to stay and it is probable that their numbers will increase. They will play an important part in influencing public opinion and putting pressure on governments. On the other hand, governments have to be concerned with the long-term interests of the country and will not always be willing to bow to that pressure. In the last resort in a democratic system of government it must be the elected Parliament that decides.

Discussion question

5 Do you think you are ever justified in breaking the law, even if you believe strongly that your cause is just?

Government and the media

One of the hallmarks of a democratic state is that the media — TV, radio and the press — should not, except in wartime, be under government control.

Both the BBC set up in 1927 (*see* Case Study 10) and the IBA established in 1954 were independent bodies not subject to governmental control. Recent changes in the structure of commercial TV, as evidenced in the Broadcasting Act 1990, has not altered this basic fact. Both organisations have to maintain political impartiality and, particularly during election periods, have to maintain a political balance in both news bulletins and current affairs programmes. The Broadcasting Act 1990 set up the Broadcasting Standards Council covering both BBC and ITV, to which complaints about the content of programmes can be made.

Attempts at various times by governments to influence the contents of programmes have been strongly resisted. The one example of direct government interference is the law forbidding TV and radio to interview directly representatives of Sinn Fein, although they can report what they say.

The government in Britain has little control over the press. From time to time the government may issue a 'D' notice urging editors not to print certain matters in connection with defence and national security. It is, however, a voluntary self-censorship agreed by the newspaper industry. The Monopolies and Mergers Commission has powers to investigate media take-overs to prevent too great a concentration of ownership.

Statutory bodies have been set up to deal with complaints from members of the public into such matters as unbalanced reporting, intrusion of privacy and sex and violence in programmes, but these mainly concern matters of taste and are not an attempt to censor the political content. Of course, both broadcasting and the press are subject to the laws of defamation and obscenity. Everyone accepts that a free press is essential to a democracy but there is growing concern about some of the methods used by the press and the sensationalism used to increase their circulation figures. It is likely that if the press is unable to put its own house in order legislation may follow based on the 1990 Calcutt Report on Privacy.

Written questions

6 Explain in detail the method used for counting the votes in an election held under the single transferable vote (STV) system.

7 In each of the following cases explain, giving your reasons, how you think your MP should vote:

(a) The majority of electors in his constituency through a local referendum have voted in favour of the return of capital punishment. The MP is strongly opposed to this on conscientious grounds.

(b) The government has decided to place new naval shipbuilding orders in a shipyard in the north of England where there is high unemployment. The MP representing a low unemployment area with a shipyard is convinced that this is in the national interest but knows that the outcome will cause more unemployment in his own constituency.

(c) The MP's party is in office and his government is proposing to take some action which is strongly opposed by his local constituency party.

8 Explain the duties of the Press Council and state whether you think it has been an effective body.

9 You live in a beautiful village and are the Chairman of the local residents' association. The government has chosen an area just outside your village for the storage of nuclear waste. Write a report to present to the association indicating what action can be taken to try and persuade the government to change its mind.

10 List the main recommendations of the report of the Calcutt Committee on Privacy.

CASE STUDY 4 Southampton Labour Party

Case study situation

Richard Bates began his working life as a 'Bevin Boy' in the Derbyshire mines at Ilkeston where he first became a member of the Labour Party. ('Bevin Boys' were named after Ernest Bevin, Minister of Labour during the Second World War when they were called up to serve in the mines instead of the armed forces.) His interest in the party led to his involvement in party administration at an early age and now he is one of the longest serving and most experienced party organisers in the country. He has been employed by the Labour Party for 40 years at their local offices in Bedfordshire, Huntingdonshire and the Isle of Ely, Ipswich and Southampton (his present appointment). During this time he has provided administrative support at numerous elections for parliamentary and local government candidates. Richard Bates has himself now been elected to serve as a councillor on the Southampton City Council (*see* Case Study 6). His position with Southampton Labour Party is in the process of being re-organised to widen the scope of his operations in order to encompass the work of some of the adjoining labour party offices in the Solent Area.

Labour Party organisation

Figure 6.4 shows the administrative and committee structure of the Labour Party and Richard Bates' position in it. Further details of the organisation of the Labour Party, including the composition of the National Executive Committee are given in Chapter 6.

The Constituency General Management Committee consists of delegates from branch meetings and affiliated trade unions and it elects members to serve on the Constituency Executive Committee. The General Management Committee considers local and central government policy matters; compiles the panel of local government candidates; arranges the selection of parliamen-

Fig 6.3 Richard Bates, Labour Party organiser

Administration

Committee structure

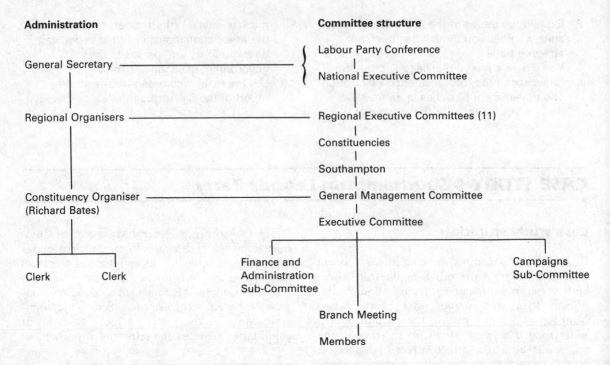

Fig 6.4 Organisation chart for Labour Party administration and committees

tary candidates by individual party members; elects delegates to attend party conferences; submits resolutions to the party annual conference and mandates their delegates on how to vote on matters before the party conference; oversees local party administration; organises campaigns on local and national issues; and arranges membership campaigns.

Constituency administration

The committee procedures and rules for administration are laid down in the Labour Party Constitution and Standing Orders and the rules for expenditure of candidates at elections are prescribed in the Representation of the Peoples Act.

The major tasks involved in Richard Bates' office include:

1 **Local party annual meeting**: issuing agenda and reports; writing minutes; communicating information to branches and affiliated organisations; administering the election of officers and committee members; arranging for local MPs or prospective parliamentary candidates to address the meeting.

2 **Committee meetings**: servicing the monthly executive meetings, general management committees and their sub-committees.

3 **Parliamentary elections**: supporting candidates for general elections and by-elections.

4 **Local government elections**: preparing candidates for local government elections; inviting branches to nominate candidates; setting up campaign committees; compiling panels of candidates; preparing and printing election addresses and other election leaflets — Richard Bates prepares these with desktop publishing and offset litho printing methods as in his own election address illustrated on p. 65, acting as agent for the candidates.

5 **Membership campaigns**: organising membership recruitment campaigns including mailing literature to new electors and mailing regular progress reports to all electors on the electoral registers.

6 **Financial control**: controlling expenditure with the assistance of a voluntary treasurer.

Labour
Leading ⌡ the way

All elections are important - the one to be held on May 3rd is even more so. It is an opportunity to show your support for Southampton's Labour Council; to express your concern and disgust with Tory policies - such as the poll tax and high mortgage rates, to mention just two, and is your opportunity to elect a Labour Councillor to work for the benefit of Coxford and its people.

Whilst Council resources are limited, Coxford should have a fair share of them to enable improvements to be made within the ward. Regarding any proposed development in the ward, or on its boundaries, the interests of Coxford people must be taken into account and the development only allowed if those interests are not harmed.

Living nearby in Shirley I shall be available to meet any of you who have problems and need the assistance of a local councillor. Your support on Thursday 3rd May will enable me to do that and will show your support for our Labour Council.

Richard A Bates

General election campaign

The agent is involved in the following ways:

- meeting with the candidates to plan the campaign
- drawing up a timetable for public meetings

and press conferences and making the necessary arrangements for them
- making the necessary arrangements for visiting dignitaries
- arranging for the candidates to visit factories, shopping precincts, etc.
- drafting and printing election addresses and introductory pamphlets for delivery to voters — each candidate is allowed one postage-free delivery to voters
- co-ordinating the work of canvassing officers who are responsible for organising teams of volunteers to visit people in their homes
- polling-day organisation, i.e. co-ordinating arrangements for checking in voters and knocking up those who have not been to the polling booths.

Finance

Eighty per cent of the local constituency party organisation's income is raised by lotteries and the remaining 20 per cent from membership subscriptions; £5.80 of the member's £10 subscription is spent on head office administration and the balance remains with the local party and the member's branch. The local constituency party requires income to pay for rent, rates, insurance, wages, campaign expenses, etc. Richard Bates estimates that the cost of preparing and distributing an A4 leaflet to 80 000 houses in the city is about £400. One of the organiser's major problems in administration is that it is difficult to undertake forward planning with any certainty because financial resources fluctuate according to the number of paid-up members and the income from lotteries received in any one year.

Computerisation

The Southampton Office uses computers for word processing, financial records, membership records (a database) and desktop publishing. A computerised election program containing the local electoral register data is used and adapted to provide the political affiliation of voters and reference to those with postal votes. This program is used not only for communicating with the electorate at election times, but for writing to new electors in membership campaigns and for communicating with voters on local issues.

1 (a) Design a leaflet for a local political party to be sent to electors on a current issue of local importance. If possible use desktop publishing to prepare your leaflet.
   (b) You are asked to prepare a checklist for a new clerk who has recently joined your office setting out the procedure to be used for producing and distributing leaflets to electors.
2 (a) Draft a three-week general election campaign programme for your local parliamentary candidate.
   (b) Justify the need for each item included in the programme.
3 Draft a resolution for your party's annual conference raising a matter about which you feel strongly.
4 Compare the organisation and financing of the Labour Party with one of the other political parties.

1 (a) Role play, with video recording, a meeting of the Constituency General Management Committee in which each member of the group argues the case for submitting their resolution to the party's annual conference (as prepared for Task 3 above).
   (b) Discuss and evaluate the relevance of each of the resolutions and identify the skills which contributed to a successful and persuasive presentation.
2 Discuss:
   (a) the advantages and disadvantages of forming larger political party administrative groups comprising several constituencies
   (b) to what extent the party 'machine' wins votes for the candidate
   (c) in what ways a local government campaign would differ from a parliamentary election campaign
   (d) Richard Bates' dilemma in attempting forward planning on resources which rely predominantly on income from lotteries.

CASE STUDY 5 Shelter — National campaign for the homeless

Introduction

In this case study we take a look at the administration and activities of a well-known pressure group. Shelter is a national campaigning organisation which:

• advises people on their rights
• campaigns for decent homes everyone can afford
• ensures that governments, local authorities and the public are always informed about the homeless and those who are badly housed
• works nationally and locally against housing injustices
• supports housing projects run by homeless people.

Through its members, groups, housing aid centres and network of supporters Shelter campaigns for new policies, new initiatives and renewed commitment to help homeless and badly housed people.

Statistics

Shelter's estimates of homelessness in England:

1 126 240 households were accepted as homeless in 1989 representing 362 300 individuals. This figure is more than double the figure recorded 10 years ago and an increase of 7.4 per cent on the 1988 figure.
2 There are no national statistics for single

homelessness, but CHAR, who campaign for single homeless people, estimate a figure of two million.

3 156 000 young people are estimated to be homeless in Britain. Centrepoint have estimated that there are at least 50 000 young homeless people in Central London between the ages of 16 and 19.

4 The London Research Centre estimates that in London black people represent 40 per cent of those accepted as homeless by London Authorities.

5 42 per cent of homeless households in 1989 were outside the big cities.

6 11 633 households were placed in bed and breakfast accommodation during 1989. Recent figures comparing the cost over the first year of bed and breakfast accommodation with building new homes to rent are:

	London	Elsewhere
Paying a B & B hotel bill	£14 600	£5 475
Building a home to rent	£ 8 200	£5 000

7 30 000 people were helped by Shelter Housing Aid Centres in 1989.

Shelter's achievements

Through its housing aid centres and independent housing aid projects, Shelter provides practical help to people who are homeless or have other urgent housing needs. As well as housing aid work, centres organise local campaigns, e.g. the West Midlands Housing Aid Centre is encouraging and helping people to get urgent repairs to their homes, whilst a new project in Merseyside is focusing specifically on homeless young people. Many housing aid workers also give talks on housing issues to tenants associations, churches, schools and youth and community groups. In order to monitor their cases and help identify national trends in housing needs, each centre has a computerised system for recording case details.

Cases supported by Shelter

1 The Whites, who have five children, were living in a bed and breakfast hotel after being evicted by their building society because of £700 mortgage arrears. Now, the local authority was going to force them to leave the hotel because it had decided they were 'intentionally' homeless and not entitled to a council home. One of Shelter's housing aid centres referred them to a solicitor and, with the family's permission, arranged for media coverage of the case. The family were eventually given a loan by another building society and bought back their original home on a new mortgage.

2 Mr Carter, who lives in a privately rented bedsit, is mentally ill and had been on his local authority housing list for eight years. His landlord was trying to evict him, and he was badly injured in an attack which he believed his landlord had arranged. By the time Mr Carter came to Shelter's housing aid centre, he was eager to move out, but he could not find a place that he could afford. Shelter's housing aid workers wrote immediately to 15 housing associations, asking them to put Mr Carter on their lists, and wrote to the local environment health department asking for a management order to be served on Mr Carter's landlord. Mr Carter is now living in a home provided by a housing association, and his health and well being are much better.

3 Mr and Mrs Jones lived in a flat in need of repair and had a protected shorthold tenancy. The landlord had given them their notice to quit and had also issued a summons for alleged rent arrears. At that time, Mrs Jones was pregnant. While making enquiries, Shelter housing aid workers found that their flat was in a very bad state of repair and helped to arrange for a counterclaim to be made against the landlord for failure to carry out his legal duties to keep the flat in good repair. Shelter advised Mr and Mrs Jones' solicitor about the repair problem. As they were likely to be made homeless in the very near future, Shelter also arranged for them to apply as homeless to the council. At the end of the two months, the landlord had dropped the rent arrears claim because of the clients' counterclaim and Mr and Mrs Jones were re-housed by the council.

National housing aid and advice network

With financial support from the Department of the Environment, plans are now under way for a national housing aid and advice network which will be run jointly by Shelter and the Citizens Advice Bureaux (CAB). It is based on a model pioneered by Shelter for several years in Dagenham and Crawley. The CAB will give information and advice on the more straightforward issues, such as benefits, while Shelter will concentrate on the more complicated cases.

The Housing Act 1988

This Act came into force in early 1989 and, according to Shelter, is already threatening the security of all those living in rented homes. Under the Act, local authorities now have to compete for the ownership and management of council homes; housing associations have to look for private money instead of depending on government grants; and privately rented property is no longer subject to rent controls.

The government maintains that the Act will improve the efficiency of local authorities, widen tenants' choices and increase the number of properties available for private rent. Shelter consider that it will have the reverse effects and that it is more likely to send rents soaring, reduce security of tenure and increase homelessness.

Shelter campaigned strongly against the introduction of this Act. Since its introduction, Shelter has been working — and continues to work — to prevent the most damaging implications of the Act from becoming a reality. Shelter's research section is monitoring the effects of the new Housing Act, particularly its impact on the private rented sector.

Campaigning

Shelter's six ways of achieving campaign objectives are as follows:

1 Break each objective down into specific tasks and allocate these to members of the group.
2 Draw up a campaign timetable with deadlines for completion of each task.
3 Arrange regular meetings with the group members to ensure that everyone knows what everyone else is doing and how the whole campaign is progressing — you may want to make one person responsible for coordinating the overall campaign operations.
4 Ensure that the campaign allows everyone to get involved and is not restricted to those who know about housing.
5 Make regular checks to ensure that all your objectives are still working towards your campaign aim.
6 Remember to exploit all the publicity possibilities with press releases, photo opportunities, etc.

Shelter's income and expenditure

The 1989 figures are given in Table 6.1.

Table 6.1 Figures extracted from the report and accounts for 1989

Income	1989 (£)	1988 (£)
Donations:		
Fundraising	1 216 145	1 051 062
Covenants	845 658	626 569
Legacies	399 417	336 960
Grants	576 815	528 510
Income from fixed assets (investments) and interest receivable	157 235	143 694
Publications, training and conferences	241 631	175 226

Expenditure	1989 (£)	1988 (£)
Project expenditure	1 211 793	1 095 401
Grants allocated	399 671	344 586
Publications, information, campaigning and conferences	672 588	655 972
National and regional fundraising	539 970	446 034
Central administration and financial services	336 032	321 086

Communications

Shelter employs 140 staff (including 70 at head office) and they are assisted by a large number of voluntary workers. The following methods are used to communicate information to staff and the general public.

1 **Magazines:**
   - *Roof* — Shelter's housing magazine published every two months
   - *The Adviser* — published jointly by NACAB and Shelter bi-monthly for housing advisers
   - *Parliamentary News* — a weekly compilation of extracts from *Hansard* concerning housing
   - Shelter Progress Reports.

2 **Guides:** on such topics as:
   - buying your home with other people
   - housing finance
   - leaving home
   - rent arrears and the courts
   - rights for homeless
   - poll tax — don't pay twice.

3 **Reports:** on such topics as:
   - doing time — experience of homeless people in bed and breakfast
   - voidwatch — taking action on empty properties
   - the allocation of council housing
   - a decent home makes all the difference — the work of housing associations in inner cities.

4 **Circulars:** *Campaign News* (internal).

5 **Meetings:** Minutes of management meetings are distributed to section heads for the information of staff in their sections; monthly staff briefing meetings are held for discussion of current developments, e.g. the Charities White Paper, European Housing Forum, Health and Safety at Work Act, etc.

6 **Computers:** The computer network with 28 terminals provides electronic mail and access to a database consisting of a mailing list and parliamentary casework.

Case study situation

Our contacts at the London headquarters of Shelter were Vaughan Lindsay, the Assistant Director for Staffing and Resources, and his Personal Assistant, Dorota Mosowicz. Their positions in the Shelter organisation and the staff in their division are given in the organisation chart in Fig 6.5.

Each member of staff including the Director and Assistant Directors have individual work programmes and targets. Vaughan Lindsay's current year's key objectives were:

- to ensure all basic administrative systems are appropriate and effective
- to improve the quality of the office environment at the London Offices
- to achieve a saving of £15 000 on last year's level of expenditure
- to provide appropriate management accounts on a monthly basis
- to implement the recommendations of the auditors
- to meet the Department of the Environment requirements for funding
- to prepare financial systems for the next financial year
- to produce draft accounts for audit by June
- to set up personnel systems and procedures to consolidate work already started in order to make the new line management structure effective and supportive and to improve communications, information sharing and co-operative working between sections
- to reduce staff turnover by five per cent by introducing and developing good employment practices
- to recruit Department of the Environment-funded staff for the national housing aid network.

The Assistant Director of the Staffing and Resources Division is responsible for implementing Shelter's equal opportunities policy; acting as Company Secretary; liaising and negotiating with the unions; organising staff development programmes; organising core administrative functions for the Shelter organisation; implementing Shelter's personnel and health and safety policies; and managing the development of computer systems throughout the organisation.

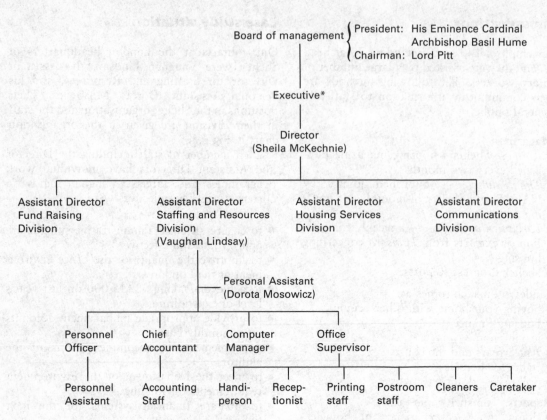

*The Executive comprises six members of the Board, the Director and the Assistant Directors

Fig 6.5 Shelter Headquarters organisation chart with detailed structure of the Staffing and Resources Division

Personal Assistant's job description

Dorota Mosowicz is responsible for providing administrative and secretarial support to the Assistant Director, for running Shelter's routine administrative functions and providing a key contact point for the division. Her duties and responsibilities include:

1 **Administrative**
   - typing and word processing
   - maintaining an up-to-date filing system
   - servicing meetings: arranging dates, times and venues, circulating papers, taking minutes and making any travel arrangements
   - holding and organising the Assistant Director's diary
   - acting as first line of contact for telephone and face-to-face enquiries and correspondence
   - being responsible for drafting the Assistant Director's correspondence, where appropriate
   - standing in for the Assistant Director at meetings and briefings, where appropriate
   - photocopying and distribution of documents.

2 **Supervision**
   - working unsupervised
   - supervising any temporary staff within the section.

3 **Development**
   - assisting the Assistant Director to ensure that projects are followed through and implemented

- drafting and compiling monthly newsletters in conjunction with the Personnel Department
- assisting with background research for projects initiated by the Assistant Director
- supporting the Assistant Director in meeting the Division's aims and objectives.

4 **Communication**
- assisting the Assistant Director to ensure good communication between the Division's staff and the rest of the organisation
- acting as a link for the Division/ information holder

5 **Financial**
- controlling the flow of invoices coming in for the Assistant Director to code and authorise
- authorising and coding invoices amounting to less than £250
- also authorising invoices which have had purchase orders signed by the Assistant Director.

Administrative systems

Dorota was involved in setting up and maintaining efficient and reliable administrative systems involving staff at regional offices and at the housing aid centres and one of the problems she encountered was in gaining the support of staff to accept prescribed office systems, especially those who lacked administrative skills and who were not convinced of the necessity to comply with laid down procedures.

STUDENT ACTIVITIES FOR INDIVIDUALS

1 Prepare Shelter's estimates of homelessness in England in visual or graphic form to support a case for action.
2 Contact your local office of Shelter and the CAB to find out the estimated number of homeless people in your area and what action is being taken to draw attention to it. Incorporate your findings in an article for a local newspaper.

3 As a result of the group meeting in Task 2, draw up a checklist of the action to be taken in the campaign.
4 Write notes to accompany the extracts of income and expenditure in Shelter's annual report comparing the figures for the two years and explaining their significance.
5 Write a memo to the Assistant Director for Staffing and Resources suggesting the methods you would advise him to use to reduce staff turnover by five per cent.

STUDENT ACTIVITIES FOR GROUP WORK

1 (a) Identify the different Acts of Parliament which Vaughan Lindsay will need to comply with in exercising his responsibilities.
   (b) In small groups find out how this legislation affects Shelter's organisation (each group allocated different Acts of Parliament).
   (c) Each group to present its findings to the class.
2 Roleplay a meeting called for the purpose of organising a campaign to try to influence the government or your local authority on a matter about which your class feels strongly.
3 Discuss:
   (a) The significance of the estimates prepared in Task 1 for individuals. What are the main reasons for homelessness and what action could be taken to reduce it?
   (b) The place of pressure groups in public administration. Why should they be necessary in a democracy?
   (c) Will the Housing Act 1988 have the effect of increasing homelessness (as predicted by Shelter) or will the removal of rent controls reduce it by providing more homes?
   (d) How should Dorota set about convincing staff of the necessity to comply with laid down procedures?
   (e) What is meant by 'making the new line management structure effective and supportive'?

Part C

Local government

7 The structure of local government

As mentioned previously Britain is a unitary state and sovereignty rests with the Westminster Parliament. Local authorities were established by Acts of Parliament and the structure and powers of local government can be, and frequently are, changed by central government. This is in direct contrast to the State Governments in the USA whose powers are enshrined in their constitution. A future British Parliament could, if it wished, pass an act abolishing local government.

What distinguishes local authorities from other de-centralised administrative bodies is that they are elected bodies with powers to levy taxes and to a limited extent make local laws.

Why have local government?

It is generally recognised that some areas of public adminstration need to be responsive to local circumstances. The problems of the inner cities are, for example, very different from those of the rural areas. Some services, such as refuse collection, are essentially local in character. However, some services previously administered by local government, have been taken away and passed over to non-elected bodies, e.g. health authorities. In 1967 the Maud Committee on Management in Local Government pointed out that local administration of public services was essential but such government need not be administered by local democratically elected bodies.

Development of local government

The Industrial Revolution transformed Britain from an agricultural to an industrial society. Large urban areas developed as people left the land to work in industry. These changes brought with them new problems of poverty, disease, inadequate housing and sanitation and the need for education. The existing local services could not cope and a variety of *ad hoc* bodies were set up to deal with particular problems. Town councils had been created in 1835 but they did not apply to all urban areas. It was eventually realised that a uniform system of local government was needed to bring together the functions of the *ad hoc* bodies.

The Local Government Act of 1888 divided the country into county councils, county boroughs for the larger towns and cities and the London County Council. These councils were elected bodies. The Local Government Act 1894 sub-divided the county councils into urban and rural district councils and delineated the powers and responsibilities of each tier of local government. In rural areas a third tier — parish councils — was created for all parishes with a population of over 200. The county boroughs remained as all-purpose authorities. In 1899 metropolitan councils were created for the boroughs within the County of London.

After 1945 there was considerable pressure for further local government reform. Population movements and in particular the growth of the larger urban conurbations meant that the 1894 division between urban and rural areas was no longer applicable.

The Herbert Royal Commission, which was set up to enquire into London government, reported in 1960 and the Redcliffe-Maud Royal Commission to deal with local government in England (except London) reported in 1969. The main proposals of Redcliffe-Maud were:

1 There should be 61 new local government areas replacing the existing counties and districts.
2 Fifty-eight of these areas should be governed by single tier authorities.
3 In the three conurbations surrounding Liverpool, Manchester and Birmingham there should be a two-tier system.
4 The country (including London) should be divided into eight provinces each with a provincial council — not directly elected — to deal with provincial strategy, economic planning and social and economic development in co-operation with the central government.

This scheme was strongly opposed by the existing county and district councils and the Conservative Government elected in 1970 brought forward its own alternative proposals in the Local Government Act of 1972. This instituted a two-tier system throughout the country and was strongly opposed by the existing county boroughs who lost their powers over such major functions as education and the social services. Meanwhile most of the recommendations of the Herbert Commission had been put into effect by the London Local Government Act of 1963.

Discussion question

1 What are the advantages and disadvantages of a two-tier system of local government?

The metropolitan counties comprised the six largest urban conurbations — West Midlands, West Yorkshire, Tyne and Wear, Merseyside, South Yorkshire and Greater Manchester — while the 36 metropolitan district councils varied

in size with the largest being Birmingham with over one million population.

Since 1 April 1986 the metropolitan county councils have ceased to exist and their powers have been transferred to the metropolitan district councils. Most of the metropolitan county councils were controlled by the Labour Party and were regarded by the Conservative Government as high spending councils opposed to the government's policy of reducing public expenditure. At the same time, the Greater London Council was also abolished and most of its powers transferred to the London boroughs. This produced other problems and *ad hoc* bodies had to be set up to deal with those services, e.g. the fire service, which were not suitable to be dealt with by the London boroughs.

The Inner London Education Authority (ILEA) which had been a committee of the Greater London Council (GLC) was then given independent status and elections for it were held in 1986. However, two years later in the Education Act 1988 it was finally abolished and ceased to exist on 1 April 1989. Powers over education have been transferred to the London boroughs.

The London Residual Body (LRB) was appointed by the government to tie up all the loose ends resulting from the abolition of the GLC. One of its main tasks is to sell off all the former GLC buildings. It was originally appointed for five years but may now last longer as it has picked up some other residual duties subsequent to the abolition of the ILEA.

Local government structure in Scotland

Local government structure in Scotland was reorganised in 1975 with a two-tier structure. How

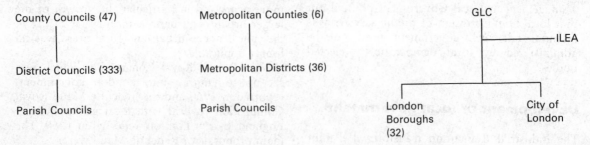

Fig 7.1 New local government structure for England and Wales (after 1974)

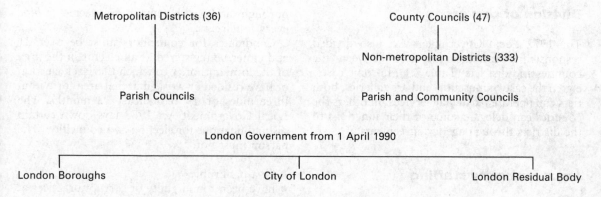

Fig 7.2 Local government structure for England and Wales since 1 April 1986

long this will last may depend on future developments with regard to devolution. There is still a strong demand in Scotland for a separate Scottish Parliament.

The community councils in Scotland are not strictly a tier of local government as they have no statutory powers (Fig 7.3). Their main function is to assess and express local opinion.

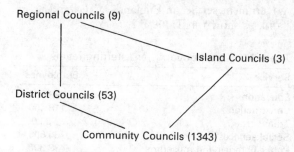

Fig 7.3 Local government structure in Scotland (since 1975)

Table 7.1 Distribution of local government services in England and Wales

Service	Metropolitan Districts	County Councils	District Councils	London Boroughs
Education	*	*		*
Social services	*	*		*
Housing	*		*	*
Fire service	*	*		Ad hoc authority
Police	*	*		Home Office
Strategic planning	*	*		*
Transport — roads	*	*		*
Road maintenance (urban unclassified)	*		*	*
Local planning and building regulations	*		*	*
Trading standards	*	*		*
Refuse disposal	*	*		*
Refuse collection	*		*	*
Leisure	*	*	*	*
Museums	*	*	*	*
Environmental health	*		*	*
Tourism	*	*	*	*
Cemeteries and crematoria	*		*	*
Smallholdings and allotments	*		*	*
Libraries	*	*		*

Division of powers

The 1972 Local Government Act also divided responsibility for local services between the counties and districts (Table 7.1). In some cases, e.g. in the case of museums and art galleries, both tiers can operate particular services. In others the counties can delegate some of their functions to the districts through agency agreements.

Local authority staffing

Local government is one of the major employers of labour in the country. In 1989 over two million people were employed in the local government service in England, Wales and Scotland, as shown in Table 7.2.

Table 7.2 Local government staffing levels

Service	Employees
Education	993 700
Construction	118 400
Transport	3 200
Social services	284 500
Public libraries and museums	39 300
Leisure and tourism, recreation, parks and baths	92 000
Environmental health	22 800
Refuse collection and disposal	41 300
Housing	73 000
Town and country planning	25 900
Fire service	47 400
Other services	306 500
Total of above	2 048 000
Police service	193 400
Court administration, probation, etc.	25 900
TOTAL	2 267 300

(Source: *HMSO Monthly Digest of Statistics*)

Local government elections

County councillors are elected on the basis of single member electoral divisions and there are elections every four years. District councils are divided into wards which normally have three councillors, one-third of whom retire at a time. District council elections are held in three out of every four years, i.e. in those years when there are no county council elections. London

boroughs and parish councils are elected *en bloc* every four years.

Candidates for councillors must be over 21 and either be registered as an elector in the area of the local authority to which they seek election or have resided or worked in that area (or within three miles of it) for at least 12 months. The Local Government Act 1972 lays down certain disqualifications for election as a councillor. The person must not:

- be a bankrupt
- have been found guilty of corrupt practices at a previous election
- have been convicted of an offence punishable by three months or more imprisonment without the option of a fine, during the previous five years
- be an employee of the council to which they are seeking election.

New rules are proposed arising from the Widdicombe Report 1986 which would prevent some employees of one local authority from standing for election to another local authority.

Everyone over 18 who is on the electoral register (compiled annually) may vote in local elections. In fact the average vote is around 40 per cent and at one recent parish council by-election only one per cent of the electorate voted.

Discussion question

2 How do you think a larger percentage of the electorate could be persuaded to vote in local elections?

Councillors are unpaid but may receive an allowance for attending council and committee meetings. Particularly in the larger urban areas being a councillor involves a great deal of time. It is not unusual for a councillor who is the Chairman of an important committee to spend two or three days a week on council business. This makes it very difficult for many people to serve as councillors and their average age is above that of the population as a whole. Political parties are finding it increasingly difficult to find suitable candidates. It should be noted that under the provisions of the Employment Protection (Consolidation) Act 1978 (as amended by the

Employment Acts 1980, 1982 and 1988) employers are required, under certain circumstances, to permit employees who hold public positions, such as members of a local authority, to have reasonable time off to perform their duties.

In many European countries a proportion of the councillors are full time and paid a salary. This has not found favour so far in Britain but the argument is probably not yet finalised.

Discussion question

3 Do you think there is a case for having all or some paid councillors?

The committee system

As you will have noticed from Table 7.1, a local authority administers a wide range of services. It would be impossible for the full council to deal with everything so all councils, with the exception of some parish councils, operate a committee system. Since 1974 the number of committees has been reduced in the interests of efficiency.

Some committees (e.g. education, social services and police) have a statutory basis. Most councils now have a Policy and Resources Committee which operates as a management committee. Examples of committee structures are given in Case Study 6 (p. 83) for a District Council and in Case Study 7 (p. 91) for a county council.

Most committees consist solely of elected councillors but some have co-opted members with specialist knowledge, e.g. representatives of teachers serving on the Education Committee. By statute one-third of the members of the Police Committee are magistrates.

Most councils also set up a wide range of sub-committees which report to the main committee, e.g. the Education Committee may have sub-committees to deal with schools, further education, etc.

The press and the public have a statutory right to attend all council and committee meetings, but not sub-committees. They may be excluded for particular items if an appropriate resolution is passed by the council or committee.

Party politics in local government

Since 1918 there has been a gradual extension of party politics into local government. The process started in the urban areas but since 1945 has been extended to most parts of the country. Today nearly all county and district elections — and even some parish elections — are fought on party lines. In 1985 only 15 per cent of all councillors described themselves as independent (Widdicombe Report 1986) and the proportion has been reduced since then. For example, Hampshire County Council had a considerable number of independent councillors in the 1950s and 1960s but now has only one out of a total council membership of 102. However, many of the previous independent councillors were members of a political party, usually Conservative, but chose to fight local elections under the 'independent' label.

The introduction of party politics brought about a change in the way many councils were organised. Today most important policy decisions are made in the party group meetings which are held prior to the full council meeting. Members are then expected to vote at the council meeting in the way decided by the group and may be subjected to disciplinary procedures if they do not conform. There may also be similar group meetings held before the meetings of the individual committees.

There are arguments for and against party politics in local government.

Arguments for party politics in local government

1 Parties have declared policies and this ensures that the council has a continuous and coherent policy which the council officers can follow.
2 Decision making in the full council is quicker and the decisions are more predictable.
3 Party politics has increased interest in local elections and encouraged more people to vote.
4 The electorate is accustomed to voting on party lines in general elections and prefer to vote for policies rather than individuals.

Arguments against party politics in local government

1 Many local issues are not party political in character and councillors should use their own judgement and not be subjected to a party 'whip'.
2 Overall policy matters may be decided by non-elected local party activists.
3 Some able people who are not party activists have little chance of being elected.
4 The positions of committee Chairmen are usually allocated on party lines instead of choosing the best person.
5 Where one political party controls a particular council for a long time there is the danger of complacency and even corruption.
6 Many local elections are fought on national issues and the results reflect the popularity or unpopularity of the government at Westminster at that particular time.

A development in the 1980s has been that a third party — the Liberal Democrats (formerly the Alliance) — has made spectacular gains in local elections, particularly in the South of England. This means that many councils are 'hung' with no one party having an overall majority.

Discussion question

4 Do you think party politics in local government is a good or bad thing?

The management of local government

Local government expenditure accounts for over 25 per cent of total public expenditure in Britain and it is one of the largest employers in the country. It is 'big business' and, therefore, needs efficient management.

Local authorities, like central government, operate through departments. Each department will have a Chief Officer who is responsible to the appropriate committee. In central government most Permanent Secretaries of government departments are generalist administrators, whereas most chief officers of local authorities are specialists. In some cases, for example in education and the police, the Chief Officer has

to be approved by the appropriate Minister to ensure that they are properly qualified and suitable.

Organisational structures for local authorities are illustrated in Case Study 6 (p. 82) for a district council (note the use of directorates by the Southampton City Council) and in Case Study 7 (p. 89) for a county council.

Before 1972 many local authority departments tended to work in isolation and were controlled only by financial restraints. The council's chief officer (usually called the County Clerk or Town Clerk) was invariably a lawyer who gave legal advice to the various departments but was not necessarily a manager. As the work of local authorities increased this system proved to be unsatisfactory.

The 1972 Bains Committee Report on 'The New Local Authorities: Management and Structure' coincided with the re-organisation of local government which took place in that year. The main recommendations were:

1 There should be a corporate approach to management which looked at the local authority's work as a whole. Departmentalisation should be discouraged.
2 A Chief Executive Officer should be appointed, who should be the leader of a management team responsible for implementing the council's overall policy and ensuring that resources are efficiently used. The Chief Executive Officer should also constantly review the organisation and administration of the authority.
3 Each council should appoint a Policy and Resources Committee whose function should be to recommend objectives and priorities, co-ordinate the implementation of policy decisions made by the council and efficiently manage resources.
4 The number of committees should be reduced and should be based on programme areas, e.g. housing, leisure, etc.
5 There should be greater co-operation between counties and districts in the same area and also with local voluntary agencies. In other words, a community approach should be adopted.

Most councils have adopted many of these recommendations. Chief Executives have been appointed, some from outside local government but others who were previously specialists. The Chief Officers now regard themselves as part of a management team. In some areas, including Southampton — the subject of Case Study 6 — the Chief Officers have been re-named Directors and their departments are directorates. However, it would be too optimistic to say that departmentalism has been eliminated. It varies from one local authority to another.

Discussion question

5 How do you think departmentalism in local authorities can be reduced further?

Democratic control

Members of a board of directors of a private company are responsible to their shareholders, but the shareholders will not normally be involved in the day-to-day management of the company. They will only become involved if the company is not succeeding in producing adequate returns.

The management team of a local authority is responsible all the time to the elected councillors. It is the councillors who make the policy and the management team who carries it out. The full-time officers have an important influence on policy but their advice may not always be accepted. Councillors take ultimate responsibility and their success or failure will be judged by the electorate.

Although, as stated earlier, local government is 'big business' it cannot be run on purely commercial lines. Basically local government provides a service to the public and in most cases there is no immediate measurable return. However, in recent years local democracy has been increasingly threatened by central government control. This is discussed further in the next chapter.

Written questions

6 Your next-door neighbours are proposing to build an extension to their house. In your opinion, this extension, if built, would reduce the light in your living room.

Explain the procedure that your neighbours must follow before they build their extension and the rights that you have to object.

7 The plot of land next to your house is vacant and is being used as a rubbish dump. Not only is it unsightly but you have seen rats there and there is an unpleasant smell. You do not know who owns the land. Explain clearly what steps you could take to have the nuisance remedied.

8 A small child in your neighbourhood is constantly appearing with bruises on his face, arms and legs. You suspect that he is being abused and you report the matter to the local social services department.

Explain what powers they have to investigate the complaint and what action they could take. What rights do the parents of the child have?

9 You live in a small village and your seven-year old child attends the local village primary school which has 60 pupils. The Education Committee of the County Council is proposing to close this school and transfer the pupils to another school which is three-and-a-half miles away. You are very pleased with the education that your child is receiving at the village school and you would like her to continue her education there.

Explain what steps you could take to persuade the Education Committee not to close the local school and the procedure the committee must adopt in order to close it.

10 Referring to Table 7.2 produce a similar table with the same services for your local county council and district council. Draw attention to any major differences compared with the national figures.

CASE STUDY 6 Southampton City Council

Case study situation

Wendy Gardiner is a Training Officer in the Directorate of Personnel and Management Services at Southampton City Council specialising in women's development. She was recently appointed to this position after working for two years as a Personnel Training Assistant with the City Council. Wendy left school at the age of 16 to attend the Eastleigh College of Further Education for a BTEC National Diploma Sandwich Course which provided a broad business background and the necessary work skills for her career. The course gave her the opportunity to 'sample' personnel work during the six months sandwich employment which she spent in various departments (including personnel) at the offices of the Independent Broadcasting Authority. On completion of the course Wendy worked for a short period as a Customer Sales Assistant with an engineering company and then joined Winchester City Council as a Personnel Clerk. In this position she gained useful experience in the personnel field and was responsible for organising a youth training scheme and serving as a leader in Outward Bound Schemes.

After a period of three years with the Winchester City Council she moved to her present employer to specialise in training. Wendy continued her studies on a day release basis gaining the Certificate in Personnel Practice and later qualifying as a Graduate of the Institute of Personnel Management with a distinction in Employee Relations.

Case study organisation

Southampton, a district council within the County of Hampshire, has a population of more than 200 000. Its world-famous port is of great importance to the city but with the decline in port activities in recent years, there has been a diversification of commercial activities. Many national and international companies now have their headquarters in Southampton and it is one of the largest office centres in the South East outside London. Southampton is widely considered to be the south coast's leading shopping centre and has many major departmental stores as well as a wide range of specialist shops. The city council employs approximately 2200 people, of whom 1620 are engaged in administrative, professional, technical and clerical posts.

Council committees

The council, composed of all elected members, is the supreme policy making body, but the volume of business necessitates delegation of decision making through a framework of committees and sub-committees, each responsible for particular

Fig 7.4 Wendy Gardiner, Training Officer at Southampton City Council

areas of services. Each full committee has 15 members, with political groupings broadly represented in a similar proportion to their membership of the full council. Much of the council's power is delegated to these committees and for day-to-day working purposes they are autonomous in many matters, but issues of major importance or those involving expenditure of substantial sums of money must be referred by the committees to the full council for approval.

The Policy and Resources Committee is responsible for determining the authority's overall priorities and policies; co-ordinating the activities of the service committees; the overall financial policy; approving the revenue budget and capital programme; and recommending the rate of local taxation to the full council.

Organisational structure of the council

The organisational structure of the council (*see* Fig 7.6) is based on directorates, each headed by a Director who is required to advise the council on policies within their area of responsibility.

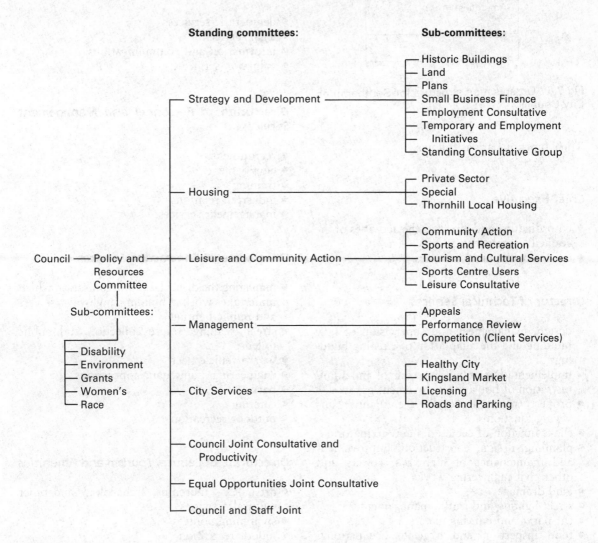

Fig 7.5 Committee structure for Southampton City Council

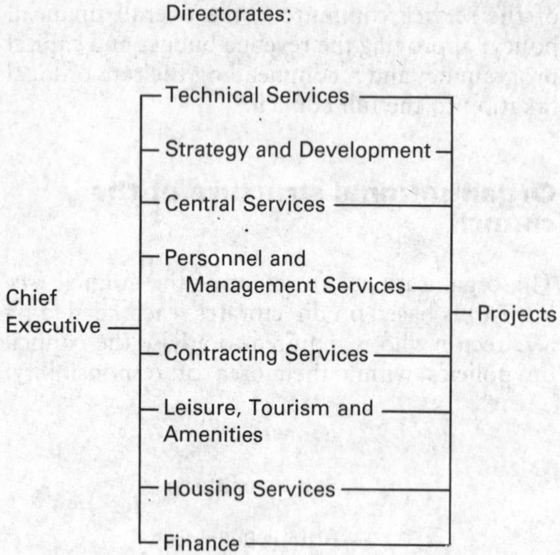

Directorates:

Chief
Executive

- Technical Services
- Strategy and Development
- Central Services
- Personnel and
  Management Services
- Projects
- Contracting Services
- Leisure, Tourism and
  Amenities
- Housing Services
- Finance

Fig 7.6 Organisation structure for Southampton City Council

Their functions are as follows.

Chief Executive

- co-ordinating and directing the activities of the council's employees
- equal opportunities schemes.

Director of Technical Services

- design, management and supervision of new building and the adaptation of existing buildings
- implementation of building control and administration of housing improvement grants
- property maintenance and the quantity surveying function
- client function of cemeteries and crematoria
- planning, design, construction, improvement and maintenance of highways, sewers and other civil engineering works
- land drainage
- street lighting and traffic management
- car parks and parking meters
- food inspection and hygiene, occupational health enforcement, pollution control, housing

inspection, control of pests, nuisances, disinfection, health education and port health duties.

Directorate of Strategy and Development

- strategy and information
- development policy and promotion
- environmental planning and control
- major projects and co-ordination.

Directorate of Central Services

- democratic services
- legal services
- information and communications
- valuation services.

Directorate of Personnel and Management Services

- recruitment
- employment
- training
- industrial relations
- management services.

Directorate of Contracting Services

- managing the direct labour organisation which undertakes work in building, highways, sewers and public lighting
- street cleaning, refuse collection and public toilets
- works vehicle fleet
- engineering maintenance operations
- parks
- catering
- outdoor recreation.

Directorate of Leisure, Tourism and Amenities

- art gallery, museums, archaeology and other cultural activities
- swimming pools
- indoor recreation
- entertainment centres and public halls

- promoting and developing tourism
- allotments
- community development services
- promoting conferences
- special events, including the annual South-ampton Show, Balloon Festival, etc.

Directorate of Housing Services

- council houses
- housing assistance to the private sector
- housing advice centres

Directorate of Finance

- supervising and controlling the income and expenditure of the city, advising on financial policy
- financial accounting
- internal auditing
- collecting rates and community charge
- paying salaries, wages and pensions
- central purchasing and supplies service

Personnel and management services

Traditionally, the personnel and management services role has been based on centralised control and prescriptive national agreements. The emerging need, with the development of the commercial approach (competitive tendering for services, etc.) and greater local flexibility in matters such as conditions of service, is for the personnel function to be more concerned with strategic management and the achievement of corporate goals involving the personnel manage-ment process; human resource management; supporting directorates with specialist and tech-nical advice; advising the directors' management team and council; and safeguarding the well-being of employees.

The range of work undertaken by the Person-nel and Management Directorate includes:

1 Management services
    - organisation and method reviews
    - work study reviews
    - management development: structures, 'styles, attitudes, etc.
    - performance reviews

2 **Employee relations**
    - industrial relations
    - employment law
    - conditions of service
    - contracts of employment
    - salary reviews
    - employee communication and consultation

3 **Recruitment and training:** assisting direc-torates with:
    - recruitment and selection of staff including job analysis, advertising, testing, short-listing, interviewing and induction training
    - staff development practices
    - career counselling and advice
    - providing equal opportunities
    - re-deployment of staff

4 **Information and resources**
    - voluntary severance and early retirement
    - labour market trends
    - long service awards
    - computerised personnel database
    - monitoring manpower budgets
    - employee information and statistics
    - the suggestion scheme

5 **Training and employment initiatives:** em-ployment, training and re-training to meet the needs of employers and the unemployed including:
    - Youth Training Scheme
    - Information Technology Centre
    - Community Programme Agency

6 **Health and safety**
    - advice on health and safety
    - safety inspections, surveys and audits of workplaces
    - accident procedures
    - joint consultation with safety representa-tives
    - safety training
    - liaising with Health and Safety Executive, Fire Brigade and insurance companies

7 **Occupational health:** an advisory service to management, employees and trade unions on all aspects of occupational health care.

The training function

The training officers organise and run training and development courses for all members of staff

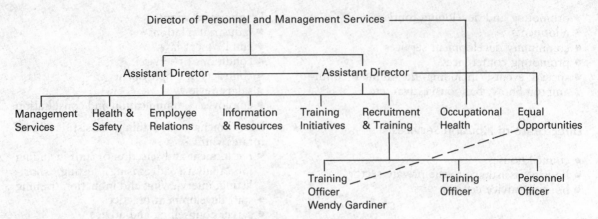

Fig 7.7 Organisation chart for Personnel and Management Services

employed by Southampton City Council. A comprehensive range of in-house courses are arranged in all aspects of personnel and management services and those of particular relevance to administrative staff include:

- dealing with the public
- effective presentation — for staff who have to give talks or speak to groups
- induction awareness — for staff responsible for arranging induction training
- introduction to management
- letter writing
- making meetings work
- managing change
- making effective use of time
- supervisory development
- understanding competition in local government
- handling disciplinary problems at work
- problem solving and decision making
- personal safety awareness

Wendy Gardiner is responsible to the Recruitment and Training Manager, as indicated in Fig 7.7.

Equal opportunities programme

Southampton City Council is an equal opportunities employer. It operates a job-share scheme and with the exception of a limited number of jobs, all of them are open to be shared. Job sharing is a form of employment where two people divide the duties and responsibilities of one full-time job. Job sharing may be attractive to those with family responsibilities; with a disability; who wish to combine work with part-time education; and who wish to ease into retirement. Under the scheme each employee holds an individual contract of employment as a permanent employee. The salary and conditions of service of the post are divided between the job holders according to the hours that they work. Each sharer must work at least 16 hours per week and cannot hold more than one job-share post. The Council also supports the objectives of the Data Protection Act 1984.

Wendy Gardiner is currently seconded from 'main stream' training to a post which is responsible for equal opportunities training, primarily to develop, market and organise skills training for women in all occupations as part of the authority's equal opportunities programme. The courses include:

1 'A Personal Development Programme' — a course for women on one afternoon per week for 10 weeks.
2 'Staying Safe: Personal Safety for women' — a programme of eight one-hour weekly sessions.
3 Skills blocks (one- and two-day courses for women) consisting of:
   - introduction to management
   - stress management
   - presentation skills
   - interviewing skills
   - personal effectiveness at work.

The following is the procedure Wendy uses for promoting and administering training courses:

1 Training needs are identified by managers as a result of meetings and 'career progression reviews' with staff, then through meetings of training co-ordinators and personnel administrative officers (each directorate appoints an administrative officer responsible for co-ordinating and carrying out training needs analysis).

2 The Training Officer writes objectives to meet the identified needs and develops course programmes, including course aims and content, duration, venue, dates and times.

3 The training room or conference centre is booked.

4 The course is advertised by memos or leaflets which are sent to the administrative officers of each directorate for circulation to Managers.

5 The course details are also circulated to training co-ordinators who ensure that all staff within their departments receive copies.

6 The staff who express an interest in attending the course apply through their manager to the departmental Personnel Administrative Officer who sends a nomination form with the names of applicants to the Training Section.

7 A delegate list is drawn up and sent to applicants together with course details and any pre-course work which may be required.

8 The course is costed as a charge on the Equal Opportunities Section budget containing:
 • tutors' fees
 • use of training room/conference centre
 • refreshments
 • course administration and development
 • course materials.

9 At the conclusion of the course evaluation forms are completed by the participants in a 'wash-up' session to provide feed-back for the Training Officer and Managers on the effectiveness of the training and to modify future courses, if necessary, in the light of the conclusions reached.

10 The content of the evaluation forms is discussed at a trainees' meeting with their manager and together they decide how skills and knowledge gained on the course can be transferred to the workplace.

11 If requested, a meeting with the Training Officer, Manager and course participant(s) is arranged to discuss the outcome of the course and the role the Training Officer can play to further develop the skills gained on the course by the participants. Sometimes a further day's training is arranged, say three months later, where all course participants return to evaluate how the course has helped them in the workplace and if any further training is needed.

12 The course evaluation forms and all other records are kept on a working file in the Training Section for each course held.

Wendy is conscious of the problems involved in encouraging her trainees to be more assertive, to cope with criticism, to balance multiple commitments and to improve their self-image and self-presentation. The trainees are often reluctant to raise any of their personal inadequacies in a meeting with others and may also resent the presence of a younger, less experienced person as their tutor. Wendy endeavours to overcome these 'barriers' by providing a relaxed environment and by coaxing the participants to gain confidence in their personal skills and abilities.

In addition to the training courses which Wendy organises, the authority seeks to establish equal opportunities for women by offering schemes for job sharing, child care and career re-entry opportunities.

Financial constraints on training

With the heavier workload arising from increased demands made upon local government services, there is a tendency for funds and accommodation for training to be cut to the minimum, thus creating problems for the Personnel and Management Directorate to offer adequate training provision.

Computer services

Most of the computing and word processing facilities at the Civic Centre currently operate from a mainframe computer with distributed terminals but stand-alone micro-computers are also used.

A 'PROFS' electronic mail system is currently used by 166 members of staff providing them with computerised transmission of notes and messages, diary entries, automatic reminders and a bulletin board. The introduction of this system has resulted in a considerable reduction of paper passing through the internal mail and a much quicker method of transmitting internal memos. It is planned to extend these facilities to more staff in the near future.

A computerised system for the storage and retrieval of information, known as STAIRS, is also in use throughout the Civic Centre. This is a mainframe data base which is accessed via personal computers or terminals through which searches can be carried out in a few seconds. The retrieval function has a powerful 'search' command which enables the user to find a word or string of words held within the data base. The system is used primarily for storing council minutes and reports and providing an easy and reliable means of extracting data from these records. In the Directorate of Personnel and Management Services computer systems are used for recruitment records, training budgets, response analysis statistics for staff advertisements and for maintaining records of an employment agency for temporary staff.

Staff career progression scheme

A staff career progression scheme operates at Southampton City Council to provide scope for the advancement of employees consistent with their acquired experience and enhanced skills. Periodic review interviews are carried out by the employee's immediate superior with the aim of establishing what the employee is expected to do in his/her post, how well they do it and what they are capable of doing. The review may cover the following.

- **qualifications:** those already held, those the employee is studying for and the anticipated results
- **experience:** experience of work in the current post and experience of other related jobs
- **professional knowledge:** establish whether the

employee is up to date
- **innovation:** establish the extent to which the employee is capable of developing new methods and approaches
- **communication:** the ability of the employee to communicate orally and in writing to supervisors, colleagues and the public
- **relevance of work:** to determine the effectiveness of the work produced by the employee
- **output:** the employee's capability of meeting target dates
- **initiative:** the extent to which the employee can take action without being prompted
- **persistence:** the employee's ability to persevere in the face of difficult situations
- **adaptability:** the ability of the employee to adjust to changing circumstances
- **persuasiveness:** the ability to convince others of a point of view
- **self-confidence:** the employee's belief in his/her ability
- **reliability:** the extent to which the employee is dependable, trustworthy and consistent
- **responsibilities:** for example, attendance at meetings, supervision of others, reporting hierarchy, i.e. immediate superior, more senior officers, chief officers or directorate management team
- **areas for development:** e.g. any weaknesses, suggestions for further development, assessment of the employee's potential.

A form is completed by the reviewer and the employee adds his/her comments. The completed form is seen by the reviewer's superior to ensure that an objective assessment has been made. A representative of the Personnel and Management Services Directorate may also be involved in review interviews as a 'neutral' observer.

Communication

Weekly team briefing meetings at different levels of staff are conducted to facilitate communication and the development of ideas within directorates. Each briefing meeting is limited to 8–10 members of staff.

Public relations

Public relations are handled by a Public Relations (PR) unit in the Directorate of Strategy and Development but all staff involved in meeting the public are expected to maintain a high standard of efficiency and co-operation. Statements of policy have to be cleared at the directorates' meeting before being disseminated to the press.

5 Pressure on accommodation for increased services has resulted in a suggestion that the training room should be used for other purposes. Write a memo to the Director of Personnel and Management Services justifying the retention of the room for training purposes.

STUDENT ACTIVITIES FOR INDIVIDUALS

1 Prepare (a) a departmental organisation chart and (b) a committee organisation chart for your local district council and compare them with the charts supplied for Southampton City Council.
2 Newly appointed staff are required to attend a two-day induction course. Devise (a) an induction course programme for administrative staff joining Southampton City Council and (b) a checklist of the arrangements you would make for the course.
3 A school party visiting the Civic Centre asks you the following questions: What is 'an equal opportunities employer'? Why are some jobs excluded from Southampton's job-share scheme? In what ways does the authority support the objectives of the Data Protection Act 1984?
   Prepare notes or a record on a tape recorder of your answers to these questions.
4 Devise a form which may be used for conducting career progression/staff appraisal interviews in order to assess an employee's strengths, weaknesses, effectiveness, potential for further responsibilities, need for further training, etc.

STUDENT ACTIVITIES FOR GROUP WORK

1 Discuss:
   (a) Why you think it was necessary for Southampton City Council to organise women's training courses within their equal opportunities programme.
      Identify the legislation which applies to equal opportunities in employment.
   (b) What you consider to be the purposes of a local authority PR unit. Is there any danger of it being construed as 'party politics on the community charge' and, if so, what safeguards are needed to ensure that the PR unit acts in a non-party political way?
   (c) How you would solve the problem of complaints by staff that 'no one tells us anything'. What are the advantages and disadvantages of team briefing meetings? What other forms of communication might be used?
2 Prepare the course material for one of Wendy Gardiner's courses for developing assertiveness and confidence in her trainees and role play a training session using the material.
3 Draw up a checklist of points to be covered in the short course 'Understanding Competition in Local Government'.

CASE STUDY 7 Hampshire County Council

Case study situation

Lorna Leverett is employed as a Senior Salaries and Wages Assistant in the County Treasurer's Department of Hampshire County Council situated in Winchester. Her position in the department is indicated in Fig 7.8. Lorna began her career with the Hampshire Authority at the age

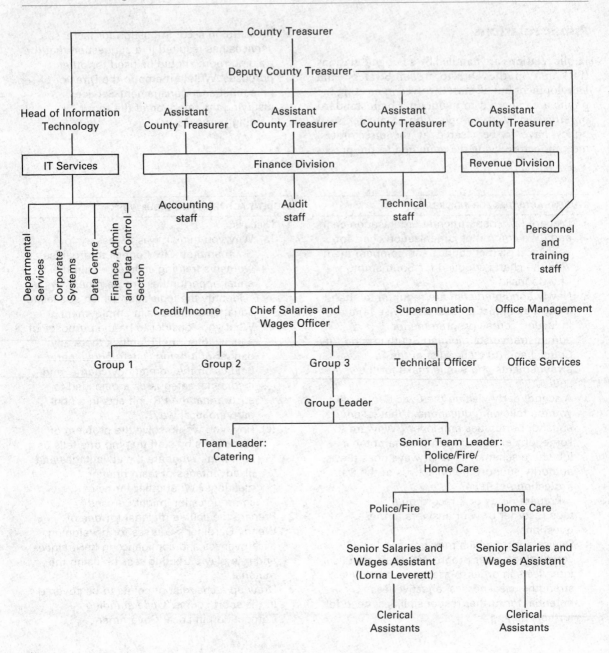

Fig 7.8 Organisation chart for County Treasurer's Department

of 17 after spending a year at a sixth form college to study for additional GCE subjects. Apart from six months' work in the Treasurer's Office Services Section at the commencement of her career and a year spent at B&Q as a Payroll Clerk, Lorna has specialised in local government salaries and wages work, firstly as a Clerical Assistant and for the last three years as a Senior Assistant. She has taken advantage of the facilities provided for further education by attending day-release courses at local colleges, gaining the BTEC National Certificate and, at the time of writing this case study, she was in the second year of a BTEC Higher National Certificate Course.

The county council

Hampshire, one of the three largest counties in England, provides a wide range of local govern- ment services for over one and half million people in 13 district councils, including the city of Southampton, the subject of Case Study 6. The principal committees of the county council, their functions and departments responsible for admi- nistering the services are shown in Figs 7.9 and 7.10.

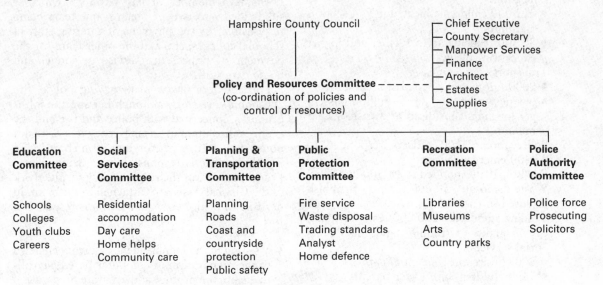

Fig 7.9 Hampshire County Council committee structure

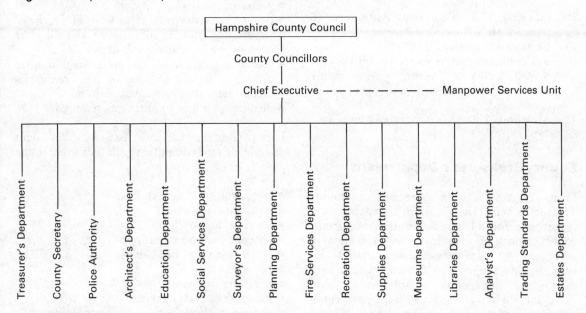

Fig 7.10 Hampshire County Council departmental structure

The following key service indicators reveal the nature and size of the tasks undertaken by the county council:

1 **Revenue expenditure:** in excess of £800 million.
2 **Capital programme:** in excess of £70 million.
3 **Education:**
   - 212 000 children educated in 734 schools and units
   - 86 300 students at 15 further and higher education colleges.
4 **Transport:**
   - 9000 kilometres of roads to maintain
   - bus networks provide 77 million passenger journeys subsidised at a cost of £3.5 million.
5 **Police force:** 3100 officers responded to 99 400 emergency calls.
6 **Fire brigade:** responded to 18 500 incidents.
7 **Waste disposal:** 750 000 tonnes of rubbish disposed of each year.
8 **Trading standards:** 290 000 tests for quantity or quality by trading standards officers
9 **Social services:**
   - 600 children in residential care
   - 1100 children with foster parents
   - 2800 elderly accommodated in 60 residential homes.
10 **Libraries:** 17.5 million book issues from 76 libraries and 24 mobile libraries.
11 **Countryside services:**
   - 4.2 million visitors to recreation sites
   - 7000 acres of country parks, nature reserves, historic sites and open spaces managed.
12 **Museums:** 200 000 visitors to 81 museums.

County Treasurer's Department

Lorna Leverett is a member of the County Treasurer's staff. The Treasurer's Department is responsible for all aspects of finance for the county council and employs some 450 staff, of whom over 40 are professional accountants. This responsibility ranges from the calculation, estimating and allocation of the authority's budget (£785 million in a recent year) to the payment of salaries, wages and pensions to 83 000 employees and pensioners and the payment of the vast number of bills incurred by the council's wide range of activities. The department also runs the county council's large computer installation with its IBM 3090/200E computer system.

Payroll group

Lorna is a member of Pay Group 3 which is subdivided into two pay teams; one team being responsible for the payment of catering staff in schools, colleges, etc. and the other team for the payment of police, fire service personnel and home care staff.

Lorna works in the team paying police, fire and home care staff, although her specific job is primarily concerned with police and fire and she is only called upon in an emergency to assist with home care staff. As the organisation chart in Fig 7.8 shows, she is responsible to a Senior Team Leader and shares the responsibility for the work of the Clerical Assistants attached to the team. In her role of Senior Assistant Lorna is responsible for:

- assisting in the management of a team engaged in the preparation of computer-based payrolls to ensure the prompt and accurate preparation of pay in accordance with agreed deadlines;
- preparing payroll input data
- dealing with payroll output from IT Services
- supervising and training junior clerical staff engaged on similar payroll duties
- consulting with staff of a similar level in other departments and sections of the Treasurer's Department on pay related matters
- dealing with pay enquiries, as required.

Lorna and the Clerical Assistants key data directly into the computer to effect changes to the payroll resulting from:

- employment of new staff
- termination of staff
- absence due to illness
- absence due to maternity
- promotions and upgradings
- pay awards
- overtime payments
- income tax code changes
- absence without pay, e.g. industrial disputes
- all other variations to pay records which may

occur from time to time, e.g. changes in trade union deductions, attachment of earnings orders, changes in bank account details, etc.

All data input is checked by Lorna or her Senior Team Leader using a computer printout. They are also responsible for checking the completed payroll prior to its despatch and payment on the 15th of each month.

Paying people is, however, only part of Lorna's duties as she also assists with:

- training new members of staff
- answering pay enquiries, either verbally or in writing, from employees and the staff of the employing department or central government departments (Inland Revenue and Department of Social Security)
- annual jobs which include archiving records and preparing statistical returns.

To fulfil her role, Lorna is expected to have a good knowledge of statutory regulations regarding income tax, national insurance, statutory sickness pay and statutory maternity pay, as well as being conversant with several sets of conditions of service. In addition, she has to have the ability to communicate well with anyone from other members of the team to irate employees. During the course of her day she may, for example, be asked:

- 'Why am I paying more tax this month without an increase in pay?'
- 'I am getting married next month. What do I need to do to claim the higher personal allowance?'
- 'I am leaving the authority next week. How will my new employer know how much tax to deduct?'
- 'I am off work with tonsilitis and my doctor says that I will not be fit to return to work for two weeks. What am I expected to do about my pay?'
- 'I have heard that I might be able to receive statutory maternity pay while I am away from work having my baby. Can you please advise me if this is so?'
- 'Why was my National Insurance contribution increased last month as a result of the reimbursement of course fees and travelling expenses which I had paid for my day-release course?'

Lorna normally deals with pay enquiries by telephone but occasionally she writes letters or memos, especially if the employee requires information for the Inspector of Taxes. She writes these in longhand and delivers them to the Secretarial Services Unit for typing.

All data relating to wages and salaries of staff is highly confidential. Printouts are always locked in filing cabinets and access to computer files controlled by a system of 'sign on passwords'. Paperwork relating to pay is shredded when it is no longer required in the office and all visitors to the office are escorted by a member of the staff to ensure confidentiality of information on desks.

Additional reference sources for the activities:

Employer's Guide to Pay As You Earn (Board of Inland Revenue)

Employer's Manuals on:
- *National Insurance Contributions*
- *Statutory Sick Pay*
- *Statutory Maternity Pay*
(Department of Social Security)

STUDENT ACTIVITIES FOR INDIVIDUALS

1 Lorna's Team Leader has suggested that, in view of the large number of pay enquiries received, it would be a good idea to issue all new entrants to the authority with an explanatory leaflet about pay. Draft a leaflet which could be used for this purpose answering the questions raised in the case study and any other matters which you consider relevant.

2 Obtain the annual report from your local county council and write a report comparing its key service indicators with those given in the case study, using appropriate diagrammatic illustrations.

3 Draft a letter for Lorna to send to the employee who raised the final question relating to NI contributions.

4 Suggest which local authority department you would contact to deal with each of the following situations:

(a) an application for a grant for higher education

(b) a query concerning your community charge

(c) to report a meat pie bought from your local supermarket with a matchstick in the middle of the pie

(d) to request a pedestrian crossing outside your college where the road is very busy and difficult to cross

(e) to request additional policemen in your area because of the frequent break-ins which have occurred in recent weeks

(f) you are a member of your local football team and have been asked by the players to complain about the unsatisfactory standard of council pitches

(g) to make a complaint concerning a big hole in the pavement outside your house.

STUDENT ACTIVITIES FOR GROUP WORK

1 Study the Chancellor of the Exchequer's last budget proposals and discuss how they affect:
(a) the work of the payroll team;
(b) other aspects of the county council's work.

2 Prepare a presentation with visual aids to be given to a visiting party of overseas students on the administration of your college; its relationship with the county council, the training and enterprise councils and the business community and how recent changes in managing the college budget have affected college administration.

3 Discuss the ways in which central government control over local government has increased during the last decade.

4 Discuss what benefits are received (a) by individuals and (b) by employers from the payment of:
• income/corporation tax
• community charge/rates
• national insurance
• superannuation.

5 Suggest examples from your own area of:
(a) any conflicts that may arise between the county and district councils and the reasons for such conflicts and
(b) co-operation between county councils and district councils, such as agency agreements.

8 Local government finance

Local government expenditure accounts for about a quarter of total public expenditure. Since 1979, one of the main planks of the Conservative Government's economic strategy has been the reduction of public expenditure. It has inevitably come into conflict with some local authorities, particularly the urban Labour controlled authorities, who wish to spend more to improve their services. The story of the 1980s was the attempt by central government to exercise greater financial control over local government. We shall examine this in more detail later in this chapter but before doing so we must look at how local government spends its money and from where it obtains its income.

Expenditure

The local government financial year runs from April 1st to March 31st. Every autumn the spending committees of the councils start preparing their estimates of expenditure for the following year. These will be carefully scrutinised by the Treasurer's Department and then by the Policy and Resources Committee. Very often they will instruct the spending committees to make cuts in their estimates. In December or January the national government will tell individual councils how much government grant they are to receive. In March the full council will decide on the level of the community charge to be levied for the following year. There is usually a political debate between those who want to improve services and are prepared to raise the level of local taxation to meet the increased costs and those who see it as their main priority to keep the level of taxation as low as possible.

County councils are by far the biggest

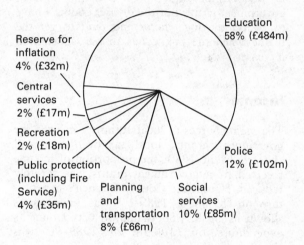

Fig 8.1 Hampshire County Council spending 1989–90

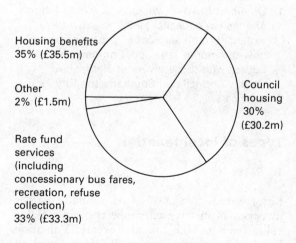

Fig 8.2 Southampton City Council spending 1989–90

spenders. Education is the most expensive service followed by the police and social services. Hampshire County Council (*see* Case Study 7) spent £839m in 1989–90, as shown in Fig 8.1. Southampton City Council (*see* Case Study 6) spent £100.5m in 1989–90, as shown in Fig 8.2.

There are district council elections in three years out of every four and the level of local taxation can have a significant effect on the election results. This often creates problems as the district councillors have little or no control over the expenditure of the county councils (by far the largest amount) or over the level of government grant. But the district councils have to collect the local taxes and tend to get the blame when the public has to pay substantial increases.

Income

The main sources of local authority income are government grants, local taxation, fees and charges. In the 1980s the proportion of income received from government grants was severely reduced. Hampshire County Council's expenditure of £897m in 1989–90 was financed as shown in Fig 8.3. Southampton City Council's expenditure of £100.5m in 1989–90 was financed as shown in Fig 8.4.

Discussion question

1 Obtain from your own local authority (county and district councils) tables to show the expenditure on services in your area and how the money is raised. Compare the figures with those given for Hampshire County Council and Southampton City Council.

Types of local taxation

1 Rates

Rates were a local tax levied annually on the owners of property. Each property had a rateable value fixed by the Inland Revenue Valuation Department. Rateable value (RV) was based on the rental value of the property in the open

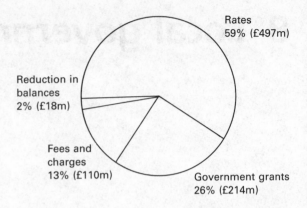

Fig 8.3 Hampshire County Council's sources of income 1989–90

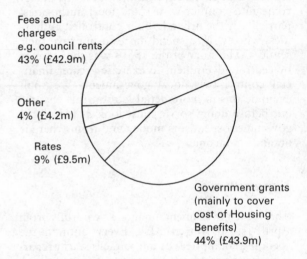

Fig 8.4 Southampton City Council's sources of income 1989–90

market. There were periodic re-valuations of all property. Charities usually paid half the full rate whilst agricultural land and buildings were exempted. Domestic ratepayers paid a lower rate of poundage than commercial and industrial properties. A rate rebate scheme was available for those householders with small incomes and this meant that a significant proportion of householders paid little or no rates. Rates could be paid in ten monthly instalments.

Calculating the rate poundage

Each local authority calculated the amount that it needed to raise from the rates. This was its total expenditure less income from other sources, e.g. government grants. It also calculated the total rateable value of all the properties in its area, for example:

total needed ÷ total RV = rate per £

In 1989–90 the rate levied by Hampshire County Council was calculated as follows:

total needed £497m ÷ total RV £238m = Rate per £ of rateable value 210.2p

Similarly, the Southampton District rate was calculated as follows:

£9.5m ÷ £31.9m = 29.8p for every £ of RV

Thus the total rate in the £ for a Southampton property was:

210.2p + 29.8p = 240p

For domestic properties there was a reduction of 18.5p making a total rate poundage payable of 221.5p.

A householder living in a property with a rateable value of £240 would pay 240 × 221.5p = £531.66 in rates during the year.

The advantages of the rate system were:

- cheap and easy to collect
- difficult for householders to evade
- long established and understood by the public.

The disadvantages of the rate system were:

- as it was a tax levied on property only those who owned or rented property paid and so contributed towards the cost of local services. Less than 50 per cent of the adult population paid rates.
- It was a regressive tax which bore little relation to the ability to pay. One house could be occupied by a single person on a modest fixed income whilst the identical house next door could contain three wage-earners, yet the amount paid on both properties was the same.

2 Community charge (poll tax)

In both the 1983 and 1987 general elections the Conservative Party promised to abolish the rating system. In 1989 the government introduced the community charge in Scotland and in 1990 in England and Wales. It replaced domestic rates. Most people over the age of 18 now pay at least part of the personal community charge. There are some exemptions, e.g. those under 19 who are still in full-time education; those serving prison sentences; those whose main home is in a NHS hospital, nursing home or residential care home; the severely mentally disabled; and members of some religious orders who have no income.

Students over the age of 19 taking a full-time course of education pay 20 per cent of the personal charge payable at their term-time address. There is a community charge benefit scheme for those on low incomes, similar to the previous rate rebate scheme, except that everyone pays at least 20 per cent. Every individual receives a bill but husbands and wives are jointly responsible for payment of their charges.

Those who own second homes or empty properties pay a standard community charge in addition to the personal charge.

A collective community charge is paid by landlords of hostels and houses in multiple occupation. They either collect it from their tenants or add it to their rent.

Commercial and industrial properties continue to pay business rates. The level is set by the government and annual increases are limited to no more than rises in the Retail Price Index. Local councils collect this rate but only keep a proportion of the money raised depending on how many adults live in the area. All properties were re-valued and the new valuations applied from 1 April 1990. In some parts of the country, particularly the south of England, re-valuation has meant substantial increases in rates for commercial and industrial properties.

The advantages of the community charge are:

- Many more people now pay towards the cost of local services. Almost everyone pays at least 20 per cent.
- Local authorities have to be more responsible in their expenditure plans. Previously high

spending authorities could raise rates in the knowledge that very few of their electors paid the full rate.

- Businesses are now protected against large annual increases in their rates.

The disadvantages of the community charge are:

- The community charge bears no relation to the ability to pay. The millionaire pays the same as the person earning £70 a week.
- Many people on relatively low incomes pay more than they did under the rating system.
- The charge is expensive to collect. Compilation of the community charge register and regularly updating it is a major operation involving more staff than rate collection.
- It is much easier to evade payment thereby causing a higher charge on those who do pay.

During its first year of operation the community charge proved very unpopular. The amount levied in most areas was much greater than that anticipated by the government and the level of non-payment was much higher than under the rating system. When John Major became Prime Minister in November 1990 the first pledge of his new government was to make a fundamental review of the community charge. He appointed Michael Heseltine, a long-term opponent of the community charge, as Secretary of State for the Environment to make this review.

Discussion question

2   Compare the advantages and disadvantages of the rating system and the community charge.

3 Other possible types of local tax

(a) *Local income tax*
This would undoubtedly be the fairest scheme as it is directly related to the ability to pay. All earners would contribute to the cost of local services. The big disadvantage is the cost of collection. The present Inland Revenue income tax system is based on where people work and not where they live.

(b) *Capital value tax*
A tax on the capital value of all properties. The main disadvantages are that only property owners would pay the tax and a major valuation process would have to be undertaken.

(c) *Sales tax*
A tax on all goods sold in the area. This would duplicate the existing value added tax for many goods and services. It is a system which is widely used in the USA.

Government grants

The amount of government grant to a particular local authority depends on a combination of needs and resources and includes amounts for housing benefits. Such key service indicators as the number of children of school age; the number of miles of road to be maintained; total adult population, etc. are taken into account. Central government fixes the amount that it believes the particular local authority needs to spend. This is known as the Grant Related Expenditure Assessment (GREA).

If the local authority proposes to spend more than this then its grant aid from government may be reduced and it will have to make up the difference from local taxation. In 1984 the Rates Act gave the government power to place an upper limit on the amount that the local authority could levy in rates (rate-capping). In January 1990 the government announced that similar provisions would apply to the community charge. In December 1989 the government published a list of what it thought the community charge should be in each local authority. These figures were strongly disputed by many local authorities who claimed that the government had seriously under-estimated the amount that they needed to spend to maintain local services.

Capital expenditure

Local authorities borrow money for major capital projects, such as new schools, houses, etc. For example, in 1989–90 Hampshire County Council had new capital projects totalling £77 million.

In recent years high interest rates have made borrowing very expensive and interest repayments are a significant factor in revenue expenditure resulting in an increased level of taxation. Prior to 1980 local authorities had to apply to central government for loan sanction to borrow money for major capital projects. Since 1980 they have had to apply for capital expenditure approvals which means that there are now controls over what they may spend rather than what they borrow.

Controls have also been imposed on spending from the realisation of capital assets. For example, local authorities may only spend a proportion of the money they receive from the sale of council houses and flats.

Control by central government

Most people accept that there must be some central government control over local government. It is the method and extent of that control which produces the political arguments. On the one hand, local authorities wish to retain a degree of independence to run affairs in their areas according to their assessment of local needs. They do not wish to become merely an administrative agent for central government. On the other hand, central government wishes to ensure that its policies are carried out and not thwarted by the action of recalcitrant local authorities.

Reasons for control

1 Finance

Local services are expensive to operate. They form a significant part of total public expenditure. Part of their revenue comes from central taxation. The government naturally wishes to keep control over total public expenditure and the overall level of taxation.

2 Standards

Some essential services, e.g. police and education, must maintain a national minimum standard and

it is the function of central government to ensure that this happens.

3 Prevention of corruption and illegal practices

Central government has a duty to prevent corruption either by officials or councillors and also to ensure that local authorities act within the law. For this reason accounts must be audited by government appointed auditors.

Methods of control

1 Control by legislation

All local authorities are created by statute and can be abolished by statute, e.g. the Greater London Council. All actions of local authorities must be carried out under the provisions of a statute, otherwise they are *ultra vires* (beyond their legal power). Some statutes impose duties on local authorities while others give them permissive powers. Local authorities often complain that duties are imposed upon them under successive statutes but that the government does not provide the necessary cash to carry out these duties.

Occasionally local authorities may seek extra powers through a Private Local Bill but there are strict conditions attached including permission from the Minister for the Environment. Local authorities may also make local by-laws but these have to be approved by the Home Office.

2 Administrative control

(a) Standards control
As we have seen, central government has the duty to maintain minimum standards in many of the services administered by local authorities. Traditionally this has been done by the responsible Minister issuing circulars of advice to local authorities. The concept was that there should be a genuine partnership between national and local government. There has been a tendency in recent years for statutes to give Ministers enabling powers to issue detailed directions to local authorities on how they should run their services.

An example of this is the national curriculum in schools.

(b) Financial control

We have already discussed the financial controls imposed on local authorities. These have been very much tightened during the 1980s. Capital expenditure control, grant related assessmental control and rate-capping have all reduced the financial independence of local authorities.

The Local Government Finance Act 1982 established the Audit Commission (*see* Case Study 14). As well as taking over the duties of the District Auditors in checking the accounts to see that no expenditure not authorised by statute has been made, it also has the role of seeking greater efficiency and value for money. Some see this as another example of central government interfering with local autonomy but others welcome its reports as a way of preventing wasteful expenditure.

Councillors who authorise expenditure not permitted by statute may be brought before the courts. If they are found to have acted unreasonably they may be surcharged and have to pay back the unauthorised expenditure out of their own pockets. This happened to many Liverpool councillors in the mid-1980s.

(c) Inspection

The education and police services have an inspectorate appointed by central government. HM Inspectors of Education visit schools and colleges and issue reports on the individual institutions. Similarly, Home Office Inspectors visit each local police force and report on their efficiency.

(d) Inquiries

The Minister may hold a public inquiry when a local authority is planning to take some action which may impinge upon the private rights of individuals. Similarly, an individual may, in certain circumstances, appeal to the Minister against a planning decision made by a local authority.

(e) Default

Some statutes empower a Minister to take over the functions of a local authority which is not carrying out its statutory duty. This power is rarely used, although threats to use it were made in the 1980s. Also, certain local authority chief officers, e.g. education, police and social services, have to have their appointment ratified by the appropriate Minister.

3 Judicial control

Local authorities are corporate bodies subject to the rule of law. They can sue and be sued. The three main forms of judicial control are:

- **Mandamus:** an application may be made to the courts for a writ of mandamus where it is alleged that a local authority is not doing what it is obliged to by statute.
- **Prohibition:** this prohibits a local authority from taking action which it has no legal power to do and where it proposes to do a lawful act in an unlawful manner.
- **Injunction:** to restrain the local authority from proceeding on a course of action which is *ultra vires*.

Summary

Historically there has always been a partnership between central and local government. However, during the 1980s this partnership has undoubtedly been strained. The Conservative Government had as one of its main economic objectives the need to reduce public expenditure. This brought it into direct conflict with some local authorities. As a result of this conflict several Acts of Parliament have been passed giving central government more control over local government expenditure.

The government also had a firm belief that private enterprise was more efficient than public enterprise. Some functions of local authorities have been transferred to the private sector whilst others, e.g. refuse collection and school meals have had to be put out to competitive tender in which both the local authority and private firms compete for contracts. Most local authorities have set up separate organisations run on commercial lines to compete with private enterprise organisations but the local authority is still responsible for any losses incurred by these organisations.

There has also been some increase in direct control from Whitehall over matters which had previously been in the hands of the local authorities. The 1986 Education Act removed the right of local authorities to negotiate over teachers' pay. This revived a long-standing argument that, to relieve the burden of local taxation, certain essential costs, such as teachers' pay, should be transferred from the local authority budget to the national exchequer. Previously local authorities had strongly opposed this on the grounds that they would lose their independence, but the loss of negotiating rights plus the establishment of a national curriculum has meant that much of this independence has been lost in any case.

In contrast, the Education Reform Act 1988 has devolved power away from local authorities in the other direction. School and college governors are now responsible for managing their own budgets, as illustrated in Case Study 8 relating to Cantell School.

There is little doubt that the role of local authorities has declined during the 1980s. Many councillors fear that they are losing much of their independence and are in danger of becoming mere agents for national government. This controversy will certainly continue in the 1990s.

Discussion questions

3 What are the main reasons for the control exercised by central government over local government?

4 Find out from your school or college authorities how they are affected by the 1988 Education Reform Act.

5 To what extent is it true that local government has 'become mere agents for national government' and, if so, why has this development occurred?

Written questions

6 (a) Why did the rating system last for so many years?

(b) What were the main reasons which caused the government to replace domestic rates by the community charge?

(c) Why has the introduction of the community charge caused so much public controversy?

(d) What are the main advantages and disadvantage of a local income tax?

(e) What are the main advantages and disadvantages of a local sales tax?

(f) Should certain items of local government expenditure, e.g. teachers' salaries and police salaries be transferred to the National Exchequer?

(g) Should some local authority services be transferred to the private sector? If so, which ones and why?

(h) What, if any, should be the extent of national government control over local government expenditure and the level of local taxation?

When answering this question you should refer to the Layfield Committee Report on Local Government Finance published in 1976.

7 Your local district council has recently passed a resolution, against the advice of its officers, to:

(a) make a cash grant to the Campaign for Nuclear Disarmament and

(b) allow CND to hold a conference in the Town Hall free of charge.

As a local community charge payer you object to this expenditure. What steps can you take to find out whether the council has acted within its legal powers? If it subsequently transpires that the council have acted *ultra vires* what action can be taken and by whom?

8 Construct pie charts, similar to those in Figs 8.1–8.4 for your local county council and district council.

CASE STUDY 8 Cantell School

Introduction

Most of the case studies in this book relate to the structure and administration of head offices of large public undertakings but in this case we turn our attention to the point at which a public service is implemented, i.e. a place of learning. Cantell School is a mixed comprehensive secondary school catering for the needs of 883 12 to 16-year-old pupils in the City of Southampton. The school assumed its present name in 1986 when two schools — Glen Eyre and Hampton Park — were amalgamated to counter the effects of falling rolls. Cantell School aims to provide a community which allows its pupils to develop to the full their academic potential and their wider interests. Besides providing pupils with essential academic qualifications, the school seeks to help them to become personally and socially aware and better able to contribute as developing adults to the local and national community.

Case study situation

Tony Ford, the Administrative Officer, was our contact when we visited the school. He has held this post for two years, following a career in the armed forces where he served as a Chief Clerk with the Royal Corps of Transport. His final posting was involved with the administration of transport at the headquarters of NATO. Tony Ford's position at Cantell School and the responsibilities of his staff are shown in the organisation chart in Fig 8.5.

Job description

The Administrative Officer at the school is responsible to the Head Teacher for the following:

- budgetary control
- management of non-academic staff, including their supervision, employment, salaries and training. Contracts of employment are issued by the county council
- ordering and control of administrative equipment and supplies
- office administration throughout the school
- administration of repairs to buildings and equipment
- Schools Information Management System (SIMS) — a computer program with a data base for creating staff and pupil records, timetables and examination entries and results
- administration of school meals — this service, together with cleaning, is undertaken by private contractors.

Communications

Communications within an organisation of this size with approximately 900 pupils and 90 staff are crucial for maximising human resources in order to achieve the school's objectives. The Head Teacher, Mr D Burge, uses the following methods to communicate with his staff and students:

- regular weekly meetings every Monday for 15 minutes to inform staff of the week's activities, visitors to the school, new admissions, matters of pastoral care, etc.
- daily bulletins with information for staff and pupils concerning new admissions, leavers, house changes, etc.
- weekly bulletins for staff dealing with changes in personnel, absences, etc.
- assemblies
- house meetings } for communicating with
- tutorials   } pupils
- noticeboard notices — general information for all personnel

Local Management of Schools (LMS)

The Education Reform Act 1988 transferred a major part of the financial management of schools from the local authority to the governing bodies of individual schools. At the time of our visit Cantell School was taking part in a pilot

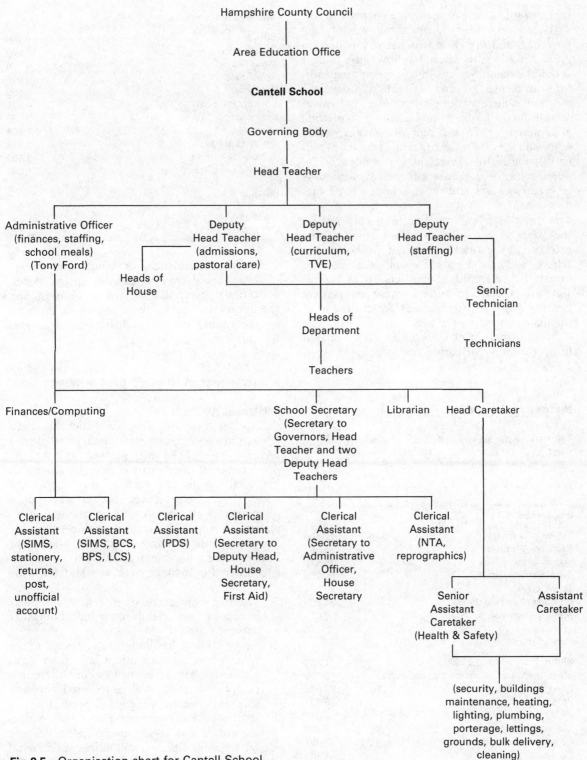

Fig 8.5 Organisation chart for Cantell School

scheme for LMS organised by the county council.

LMS is intended to give the school, the governors and the Head Teacher in partnership greater freedom to determine how their budget should be spent. Savings in one type of expenditure can be used to fund desirable new developments. Resources will be allocated to individual schools on the basis of pupil numbers to provide a minimum of 75 per cent of the aggregated school budget. Up to 25 per cent of the funds will be distributed to take account of small schools, pupils with special educational needs, variations in premises costs and other school-related factors.

Staffing costs will be allocated to schools on the basis of the average salary costs of the teachers in the Local Education Authority but schools will be charged the actual salary costs of the staff they employ. Some schools in Hampshire are expected to suffer a severe cost penalty because many of their teachers are at the top of the main professional grade.

Local management schemes are to be phased in over a four-year period commencing in April 1990.

Budgeting for LMS

The following items make up a school's budget for LMS:

	£
Employees	
Full-time teachers	1 012 466
Part-time teachers	35 961
Supply staff	18 652
Administrative staff	59 266
Technicians	22 234
Caretakers and cleaners	61 862
Midday supervisors	7 073
Premises	
Minor repairs (up to £250)	11 155
Maintenance of buildings and grounds	19 250
Energy	33 635
Rates	66 731
Water	2 845
Sewerage	4 254
Fixtures and fittings	2 451
Furniture	1 260

Supplies and services	
Books	16 284
Stationery	11 960
Materials	4 474
Apparatus	9 616
Equipment	6 459
Educational visits	4 225
Examination fees	27 320
Postage	1 400
Office expenses	7 323
Telephone rentals	2 100
Telephone call charges	1 840
Income	
Lettings	21 850
Other charges	620

Central services such as education welfare officers, school crossing patrols, special needs, educational psychologists, music support, and the library service will continue to be financed by the county council and are excluded from formula funding.

Management of the LMS pilot scheme

A Clerical Assistant has been engaged to operate the special computer program which has been devised to create the necessary budgetary control records. Tony Ford was pleased to have the opportunity of taking part in the pilot scheme as it is enabling his staff to learn more about the scheme and be prepared for it when it is obligatory in all schools. The up-to-date budget statements which the system produces monthly are essential for management in controlling their budgets. The following problems were, however, encountered in managing the new system:

1 Training was given on the new computer system but not in implementing a budgetary control system.
2 Access to data has had to be restricted to the office where the computer is held. In order to give more staff access to this data additional computer terminals will be required involving substantial items of capital expenditure.
3 Difficulties have been experienced when placing orders and paying invoices electronically on a system which is still in its experimental stage and does not always function properly.

4 In LMS the senior staff have greater involvement in all aspects of the school in determining financial priorities, e.g. the Administrative Officer is involved in matters which were previously the responsibility of the academic staff and academic staff find themselves involved in staffing and financial matters.

A member of the governing body is appointed as Financial Governor with responsibility for overseeing financial matters.

STUDENT ACTIVITIES FOR INDIVIDUALS

1 Write a memo from Tony Ford to his clerical staff explaining the significance of the new computerised budgetary control statements and the changes in administration which are necessary to manage the school's budget for LMS.
2 Run a software program with the figures given on pp 104–5 in order to prepare a school's budget. What benefits are gained from computerising this procedure?
3 Prepare a report of the School Management meeting held in Task 2 for group work.
4 School meals and cleaning services are already privatised at Cantell School. Identify another service which could be privatised and, as a member of the governing body, write a letter to the Head Teacher putting forward your case for the privatisation of this service.
5 Discuss the organisation of one of your local schools with the Head Teacher or a member of his/her staff and draw up an organisation chart. Identify the similarities and differences of your chart with the Cantell School's chart. Suggest the reasons for any differences identified.

STUDENT ACTIVITIES FOR GROUP WORK

1 Discuss:
   (a) the advantages and disadvantages of

delegating financial management to individual schools
   (b) the strengths and weaknesses of the different methods of communication used at Cantell School and consider other methods which might be used in this situation
   (c) the implications and possible solutions to the problems encountered by Tony Ford in managing the LMS pilot scheme
   (d) the role, if any, of each of the following in the financial control of Cantell School:
   1 Head Teacher
   2 Financial Governor
   3 Administrative Officer
   4 County council
   5 Department of Education and Science
   6 Audit Commission
   7 Local Ombudsman
   (e) why the school meals and cleaning services were privatised and what effect this development would have on the school
   (f) the ways in which a school can raise additional finance to supplement its allocated budget.
2 (a) Role play a school management meeting in which members of the group prepare and present coherent arguments for the following increases in their budgets:
   (1) additional teacher in Mathematics to reduce class sizes in this subject
   (2) computer terminals to enable senior staff to manage their budgets;
   (3) new textbooks to meet the requirements of the national curriculum;
   (4) an additional Clerical Assistant to handle LMS financial records;
   (5) repairs to buildings;
   (6) educational visits abroad to support increased language tuition for the national curriculum;
   (7) new classroom furniture.
   (b) Prepare a joint report prioritising these items for the Head Teacher to submit to the governor's meeting.

Part D

Other public sector organisations

9 The quasi-government sector

In Chapter 1 the public sector was defined as 'all those organisations and activities which need to be financed from public funds'. In earlier chapters we examined central and local government. In this chapter we shall examine those organisations which are financed, but not directly controlled, by government.

Public corporations

These are commonly known as the nationalised industries. The object is to combine commercial freedom and public accountability. The Minister appoints the Chairman and Board Members who then have responsibility for the day-to-day management of the corporation.

A few public corporations existed before 1945. They included the Port of London Authority, the Central Electricity Board (CEB), the London Passenger Transport Board, the British Broadcasting Corporation (BBC) (the subject of Case Study 10) and the British Overseas Airways Corporation (BOAC).

A big surge in nationalisation came during the Labour Government of 1945–51. The Bank of England, coal, gas, electricity, transport and steel were among the industries taken into public ownership. The following Conservative Government de-nationalised steel and parts of road transport but also created the Atomic Energy Authority and the Independent Broadcasting Authority (IBA).

The Labour Governments of 1964–70 and 1974–9 extended public ownership with the inclusion of airways, airports, shipbuilding and ship repairing, ports, the aircraft industry, steel (again!) and parts of the motorcar industry. The Post Office, formerly a government department, became a public corporation and was later divided into the Post Office and British Telecom. In some cases, notably British Petroleum (BP), the government bought shares in the industry to obtain a controlling interest. In other cases individual companies were taken into public ownership. Even the Conservative Government of 1970–4 had to purchase Rolls Royce to avoid it going into bankruptcy. The National Enterprise Board (NEB), set up in 1975, had powers to extend public ownership into manufacturing industry by purchasing shares in individual companies. Many companies in the computer and electronics industries became mixed enterprises, i.e. part public and part private. The NEB was disbanded by the Conservative Government in the early 1980s.

Characteristics of public corporations

1 They are created by statute and can sue and be sued in their corporate names.
2 They are publicly owned and even though they may raise some capital from private sources there are no shareholders.
3 Their employees are not civil servants.
4 The Chairman and Board Members are appointed by the Minister, usually for a fixed term.
5 They are subject to parliamentary scrutiny of their long-term objectives and the examination of their annual report and accounts but not in respect of the day-to-day management of their affairs.
6 Their revenue is obtained from the goods and services they provide. They may borrow from the Treasury for long-term capital develop-

ment and also from private sources. They may receive grants and subsidies.

7 They are not solely profit-making. The original intention was that they should break even taking one year with another but today they are expected to make an annual return on capital.

Arguments for public ownership

1 Many of the nationalised industries were monopolies and it is important that they are operated in the national interest and not just for private profit.
2 Only the government is able to provide the major capital investment needed in many of these industries. This was probably true in 1945 but is less valid today. Even the Channel Tunnel is being built with private money.
3 The public ownership of major industries enables the government to control investment, prices and employment in the economy.
4 A nationalised industry is not bound entirely by the profit motive and so may at times provide services below cost if there are social reasons for so doing. An example is the keeping open of unprofitable railway lines.
5 It is important for strategic reasons to keep certain industries under public control (e.g. atomic energy) or to keep some industries in existence (e.g. shipbuilding).

Arguments against public ownership

1 The lack of a real profit motive removes the spur to efficiency and many nationalised industries become large bureaucratic organisations.
2 Some abuse their monopoly power and there is very little chance for consumers to influence policy. Many of the consumer councils set up by the nationalised industries were ineffective.
3 Some nationalised industries were prevented by statute from diversifying into other areas when their own market declined.
4 They are often prevented by political interference from taking sound commercial decisions, e.g. raising prices.

5 There is the political argument that extensive public ownership makes for a too powerful state and diminishes the freedom of the individual.

In recent years these arguments have lost much of their force. As we shall see later in this chapter the Conservative Government since 1979 has privatised a large part of British industry and the Labour Party no longer regards public ownership as a major plank in its programme. The controversy in the 1990s is likely to centre on the extent of government control over industry rather than on the question of ownership.

Discussion question

1 Do you think the public corporation is the best organisation for a publicly owned industry? What are the possible alternatives?

Quangos (Quasi Autonomous Non-Governmental Organisations)

These are mainly publicly funded organisations outside the industrial sector. There are many hundreds of them. Most are established by Act of Parliament or by orders made under an act but some have been created by the administrative act of a Minister. Their day-to-day activities are not subject to parliamentary control. Some have been established to implement government policy directly, e.g. the Monopolies and Mergers Commission, whilst others are concerned with matters in which government departments do not wish to be directly involved, e.g. the Arts Council.

In January 1980 a Government White Paper listed 489 quangos with decision making powers and a further 1561 with advisory responsibilities. Since then several have been abolished but others created. Most quangos serve a useful purpose. They can get things done without too much political interference. Some exercise a regulatory role (e.g. the Health and Safety Commission and Executive and the Office of Fair Trading) whilst others like the Advisory, Conciliation and Arbitration Service (ACAS) are concerned with settling disputes.

The main criticism directed against quangos is that there are too many of them; there is inadequate parliamentary control over their expenditure; and they confer too great a power of patronage on Ministers who appoint their members.

In addition to those mentioned above some of the more important quangos are the British Council, British Tourist Authority, Countryside Commission, Criminal Injuries Compensation Board, Equal Opportunities Commission, Forestry Commission, Medical Research Council, Milk Marketing Board, National Consumer Council, Race Relations Board, Sports Council, Training Commission and, of special importance to students, the Business and Technician Education Council. The BBC and IBA are classified by many as quangos. They both have the public corporation structure but are not industrial producers.

Discussion question

2 Choose any quango and examine how it operates. Do you think it is effective?

National Health Service

The National Health Service (NHS) was established in 1946 (Fig 9.1). Its aim was to provide a comprehensive health service to all citizens which was to be free at source. The first charges introduced in 1950 caused a major political row and led to the resignation of several Ministers, including Aneurin Bevan who had been Minister of Health when the NHS was created. Since then charges have been introduced for a range of provisions, e.g. prescriptions, dental treatment, eye tests, etc. Nevertheless, charges only account for three per cent of the total expenditure on the health service; 81 per cent is met out of general taxation and 15 per cent comes from National Insurance contributions. The total cost of the NHS for 1989–90 is estimated at over £25 billion.

The regional health authorities (as in Case Study 9) whose members are appointed by the Secretary of State are responsible for the long-term planning of the health service within their region.

The district health authorities have their Chairman appointed by the Secretary of State. At the present time some of the other members are appointed by the regional health authorities and

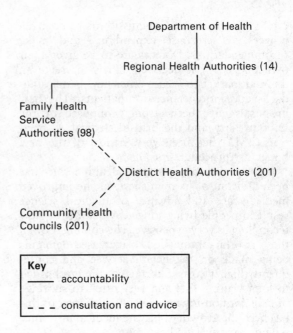

others by local authorities. Present government legislation proposes to abolish the local authority representation. District health authorities are responsible for the provision of hospital services, maternity, mentally handicapped and the whole range of health services in their area. They are expected to work closely with the local authority social services and joint-funded services can be established.

The community health councils are there to represent the consumers, i.e. the patients, and often draw attention to the lack of facilities in a particular area.

The family health service authorities, formerly the family practitioner committees, are responsible for the work of general practitioners, dentists, chemists and opticians. They are accountable to the regional health authorities.

Recent government legislation has the objective of making the health service more efficient. Health authorities and individual hospitals are to be given more financial control over their own affairs. Some hospitals may opt out and become self-governing trusts. Health service managers have been appointed, some from outside the

Fig 9.1 Structure of the NHS in England and Wales

NHS, and the Audit Commission is to be given powers to scrutinise expenditure and make recommendations. Doctors are to be given their own budgets. The declared aim is to create an internal market to secure efficiency, better standards and more choice for patients. The new proposals have been strongly opposed by the Labour Party and the British Medical Association (BMA) has been very critical of the new budgetary procedure for GPs.

In many ways the National Health Service has been a victim of its own success. The improved medical care and advance of medical science result in people living longer. Much of the new technology is very expensive. The combination of these two factors has led to increased demands being made on the health service and consequently higher costs. Shortage of finance has led to long waiting lists and very often to shortage of beds for non-urgent cases. A side effect of this has been the growth of private medical insurance schemes and private hospitals.

The decade of privatisation 1980–90

Between 1945 and 1979 there was a general acceptance that Britain should have a mixed economy. As we have seen the Labour Government of 1945–51 undertook a major programme of nationalisation. At the time each act was opposed in Parliament by the Conservatives, but during their 13 years of government from 1951–64 only steel and part of road transport were transferred back into the private sector. There was a continual argument about Labour proposals to extend nationalisation still further but little discussion about returning the basic public utilities to the private sector.

There was a general acceptance of a *fait accompli*. It was argued that the continual threats of nationalisation and de-nationalisation created a climate of uncertainty which was harmful to industry. In any case many of the nationalised industries were making a loss and would not be attractive to private enterprise. Instead the Conservative Government contented itself with trying to run the publicly owned industries more efficiently.

The extensions of public ownership by the Labour Governments of 1964–70 and 1974–9 were more strongly opposed and Conservative spokesmen often gave an undertaking to return these industries to private ownership. But the Heath Government from 1970–4 was too pre-occupied with the EEC and industrial relations to undertake any major privatisation programme. Indeed it actually took Rolls Royce into public ownership when that company was threatened with bankruptcy.

It was not until after 1979 when a Conservative Government led by Mrs Thatcher came to power that the climate changed radically. As we saw in Chapter 1, one of Mrs Thatcher's main aims was 'to roll back the frontiers of the state'. After 1979 her government embarked upon an extensive and continuing programme of privatisation:

Year	Undertaking privatised
1979	International Computers (ICL)
1980	Ferranti Electronic
	Fairey Aviation
1981	British Aerospace
	British Sugar Corporation
	Cable and Wireless
1982	Amersham International
	National Freight Corporation
1983	Associated British Ports
1984	British Telecom
	Enterprise Oil
	Jaguar Cars
	Naval Shipbuilding Yards
	Sealink Ferries
1985	Britoil
1986	British Gas (Case Study 1)
1987	British Airways
	British Airports Authority
	Rolls Royce
	British Petroleum
1988	British Steel
	Bus Services
1989	Water Authorities
1990	Electricity (except Nuclear Power Stations)

Many of the above were privatised by a share flotation on the Stock Exchange with the general public encouraged to purchase shares. In some cases shares could be purchased over a period of time and incentives were given (e.g. reduced gas bills) to encourage people to invest. There has been a public demand for shares. Most of the issues were over-subscribed. In some cases shares have been purchased with the object of a quick re-sale at a profit.

Some of the companies privatised were sold privately and in many cases employees were given an allocation of shares and allowed to purchase others at an advantageous rate. In one case, the National Freight Corporation, the organisation was sold completely to its managers and employees.

The only remaining publicly owned industries are British Coal, British Rail, the Post Office, Atomic Energy, Nuclear Power Stations and the Bank of England. Parts of British Rail, e.g. hotels and ferries have been privatised whilst the Post Office has been divided into sections with the probable intention of privatising parts of its operations. The original intention was to privatise all the electricity industry but difficulties have arisen over nuclear power stations which are not attractive to the private sector.

Arguments for privatisation

1 A main objective in the government's economic policy is to reduce public expenditure and the Public Sector Borrowing Requirement (PSBR). The borrowing of nationalised industries played a significant part in the PSBR. If industries are freed from government borrowing restrictions they can raise capital in the market to expand and modernise. This was one of the main arguments put forward in the case of water privatisation.
2 Proceeds from the sales can be used to finance tax cuts. It has been a contributory factor in the reduction of income tax to 25 per cent.
3 Private enterprise is more efficient than public enterprise and greater efficiency leads to lower prices. There has been little evidence of this as yet.
4 People should be encouraged to become shareholders and therefore take an active part in the capitalist system. This follows logically from a very successful Conservative campaign to create a property-owning democracy through the sale of council houses. Widespread share ownership would also discourage a future Labour Government from embarking on a programme of re-

nationalisation. The Conservatives used this argument very effectively in the 1987 general election campaign.
5 Employee share ownership would encourage workers to take a greater interest in their companies and so reduce industrial disputes and improve management/worker relationships. This has proved a great success in the case of the National Freight Corporation where the whole organisation was purchased by employees but has been less successful in other companies where employee share ownership is only a small fraction of total share ownership.

Arguments against privatisation

1 Important national assets should be kept under national control. Some industries, e.g. shipbuilding and shiprepairing should be kept alive for strategic reasons. They are needed during national emergencies, e.g. during the Falklands' crisis.
2 Long-term interests are being sacrificed for short-term gain. It is argued that many of the industries have been sold too cheaply to encourage individuals and institutions to purchase the shares.
3 If monopoly industries are in private hands there is a danger that the public could be exploited in the interest of private profit.
4 If the major utilities are run solely for profit the service element that many provide will disappear, e.g. unprofitable bus or rail services to remote areas will be curtailed causing considerable hardship to the residents.
5 Most of the shares sold to the public will end up in the hands of the large financial institutions. The idea of wider share ownership may well be a myth rather than a reality.

Whether privatisation continues into the 1990s depends on the result of the next general election. Should the Labour Party win that election some of the privatised industries could be taken back into public ownership, although it is not clear what form that public ownership would take and whether private shareholders would have any part to play.

Competitive tendering

An alternative to privatisation is to compel the public sector to compete with the private sector. Competitive tendering has been enforced in parts of the operation of local government and the health service. Examples are catering, refuse collection and council house maintenance. In other cases the publicly owned industries have lost their monopoly rights. The intention is to make the public sector more efficient by compelling it to compete with the private sector and so reduce prices to the consumer. There is some evidence that competitive tendering has forced public bodies, e.g. local authorities, to become more cost conscious but only time will prove whether this will be translated into lower price

Discussion questions

3 Distinguish between the public and private sector.

4 Do you think employee share ownership has improved industrial relations?

5 Conduct a survey among your friends and relations to find out how many of them purchased shares in the privatised industries? How many have since sold their shares? What was their main reason for either deciding to purchase or not to purchase?

Written questions

6 Examine in detail either British Coal, British Rail or the Post Office. The following questions are designed to provide a guideline for your study.

(a) Who appoints the Chairman and Board Members?
(b) What is the management structure of the organisation?
(c) What parliamentary control and/or scrutiny is there over the activities of the organisation?
(d) What judicial control exists over the activities of the organisation?
(e) What financial control does government exercise? Does the organisation have to make a profit?
(f) What powers does the organisation have to borrow money for expansion or modernisation?
(g) How does the organisation fix its pricing policy? Is there any government interference?
(h) Examine industrial relations in the industry. What mechanisms have been established for negotiation with the relevant trade unions?
(i) What arrangements have been made for dealing with complaints from consumers? Are they effective?
(j) Does the organisation expect to be privatised and if so how? Have any alterations to the structure of the organisation been made with a view to eventual privatisation?

7 Find out how many hospitals in the area of your district health authority have decided to or are thinking of becoming a self-governing trust. Explain the procedures involved in obtaining self-governing status and the advantages and disadvantages to the hospitals concerned in becoming self-governing.

CASE STUDY 9 Wessex Regional Health Authority

Our visit to the Wessex Regional Health Authority's headquarters was at a time when major changes were in the process of being made in the roles, responsibilities and funding of hospitals and health authorities following the White Paper on the Future of the National Health Service and the subsequent National Health Service and Community Care Act 1990.

Management structure

Figure 9.2 shows that the Wessex Regional Health Authority (RHA) is accountable to the Secretary of State for Health for the provision of health services in Dorset, Hampshire, Wiltshire, the Isle of Wight and parts of Avon and Somerset. Hospital and community health servi-

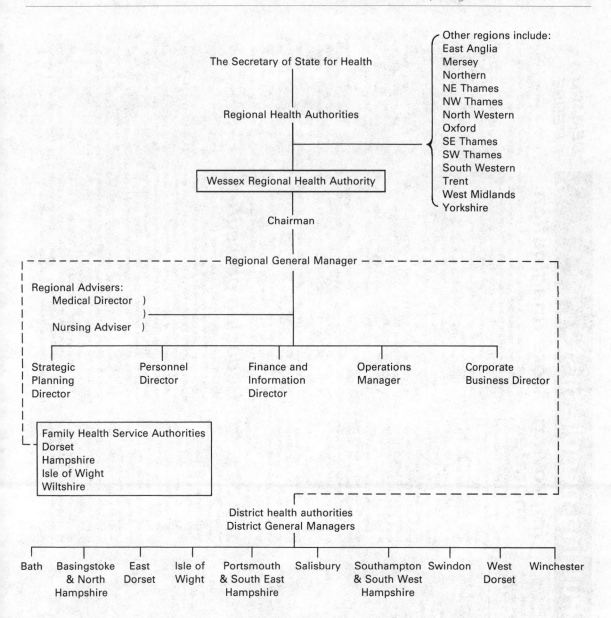

The Secretary of State for Health

Other regions include:
East Anglia
Mersey
Northern
NE Thames
NW Thames
North Western
Oxford
SE Thames
SW Thames
South Western
Trent
West Midlands
Yorkshire

Regional Health Authorities

Wessex Regional Health Authority

Chairman

Regional General Manager

Regional Advisers:
Medical Director)
)
Nursing Adviser)

Strategic Planning Director | Personnel Director | Finance and Information Director | Operations Manager | Corporate Business Director

Family Health Service Authorities
Dorset
Hampshire
Isle of Wight
Wiltshire

District health authorities
District General Managers

Bath | Basingstoke & North Hampshire | East Dorset | Isle of Wight | Portsmouth & South East Hampshire | Salisbury | Southampton & South West Hampshire | Swindon | West Dorset | Winchester

Fig 9.2 Organisation chart for Wessex RHA management structure

ces are managed by ten district health authorities. The RHA plans, monitors and finances these services and also manages a number of others on a regional basis. Local family doctor, dental, optician and pharmacy services are managed by four family health service authorities on a county basis. The RHA became managerially accountable for these committees in April 1991.

Statistics

The Wessex RHA covers an area of 1 075 119 hectares, has a population of 2 916 000, employs 42 943 staff and provides 208 hospitals with 16 379 beds. In 1989–90 revenue expenditure for the day-to-day running of services in the Wessex RHA was £707m and capital expendi-

Putting people first

UNLESS action is taken now, the NHS in Wessex could, in a few years' time, find itself short of one of its most vital resources – staff. The labour market is shrinking yet the demand for health care is continuing to expand. How can the NHS avert a crisis in care?

NEEDS of staff who work for the NHS deserve to be given as much attention as those of patients, according to a major new strategy document produced by the Regional Health Authority.

"Putting People First: A Human Resource Strategy for Health Services in Wessex" argues that more could and should be done to support the workforce and to help them do their job more effectively.

It states that there is a "need for managers, at all levels, to give time to their staff, to care for them, to recognise their achievements and to guide and influence their development as well as their current activities."

As an organisation concerned with the care of people in the community, the NHS must ensure that the well-being and motivation of the people who work for Service receives a higher priority.

However, health authorities, it warns, are facing a demographic timebomb which could threaten the NHS's ability to meet demand and improve services.

Armed

The Service must be "ARMED" to meet the problems caused by a marked decline in the number of school leavers seeking work, and a substantial increase in the demand for care – mainly from increased numbers of elderly people.

The NHS in Wessex must improve the way it "Attracts, Recruits, Motivates, Educates and Develops staff," and the Strategy calls for action on three fronts: to reduce the demand for staff, to improve the way staff are utilised and to compete more effectively in the labour market.

More effective manpower information systems will need to be developed, and training and development need to be given an even higher priority to help staff reach their full potential and to achieve a satisfying career in the NHS.

Mr. Alex Selkirk, Regional Personnel Director, said that "Putting People First" reflects a belief that the Service should demonstrate that its concern for patients is matched by a concern for staff.

"It is no use asking staff to provide better care for the patient if management is not prepared, at the same time, to offer better care for staff – this approach is indivisible," he said.

"The staff of the NHS are its greatest asset and its most valuable resource. Without them – their skills, talents and sense of vocation – we can achieve nothing."

Improving morale

THE NHS benefits from one of the most highly committed work forces in the country, but, says the Strategy, staff should be given more help to improve their morale and motivation.

They should be given regular feedback on their efforts, communications between all levels of the Service needs to be improved and individual contributions, be it long service or extra work, need proper recognition.

Improvements should be made to the way training and development needs are identified. Staff should be helped to meet their own work objections and career aspirations.

Shift patterns and working routines should be devised which make the most effective and flexible use of staff and which reflect peaks and troughs in demand.

Unnecessary absenteeism and poor employee relations will need to be tackled, says "Putting People First," and the contribution of occupational health initiatives should be given increased priority.

More training in management techniques will need to be given to front-line health staff as they become more involved in decisions about the use of resources, and effort should continue to reduce the hours worked by junior medical staff.

Increased emphasis will also be placed on the use of facilities which help staff make more effective use of their time, such as centralised surgical units or more modern and better equipped buildings.

More imagination

BETTER benefits and working conditions, improved training and more imaginative recruitment campaigns will be needed if the NHS is to maintain an adequate supply of staff.

"Putting People First" recommends a comprehensive package of measures to help the NHS compete more effectively in the labour market against stiff competition from rival organisations.

● There should be more flexible shift and working routines; health authorities should consider allowing some people to work from home. The NHS will also have to be more attractive to mature recruits and those wishing to work part-time.

● Working conditions will need to be improved, including the extension of occupational health, child-care and career-break schemes.

● Staff benefits, such as sports facilities and clubs, should be of sufficient quality to compete with those offered by other employers.

● The NHS should build closer links with schools, colleges and the community, upgrade its recruitment material and improve its recruitment and selection procedures.

● Better training and development programmes will help to offer greater career satisfaction.

The strategy wants health authorities to adopt more progressive personnel policies to help staff make an even greater contribution to the work of the NHS.

It also urges the improvement of schemes to allow staff to benefit from the NHS's massive purchasing power, offering reduced rates for everything from holidays to cars.

Reducing pressures

HEALTH authorities need to do more to reduce the work pressures of increasingly scarce staff.

Expansion plans will need to be carefully scrutinised, argues "Putting People First", to ensure that they are not only needed, but also staffed and funded properly. Staff should be given clearly defined duties and proper training. This should help eliminate gaps in services and the duplication of effort. Full advantage should be taken of new rules which allow local pay flexibility, and staff should receive an appropriate rate for the job.

New information systems, now being developed across hospitals in the region, should also help reduce the demand for staff by freeing front-line personnel from time-consuming paperwork.

The Strategy says that more needs to be done to direct resources towards pressure points in the Service – be it specialities with long waiting times or wards and departments coping with heavy workloads.

DEMAND INTENSE

THE NHS can no longer rely simply on the labour market to provide all the recruits it needs, says the Strategy.

The number of school leavers is falling: by the turn of the century, the number seeking work will have dropped by 25 per cent. Those with between five GCSEs and two 'A' levels, the group from which the NHS has recruited traditionally, will fall by 30 per cent.

Demand for this shrinking pool of labour will also be more intense. It is estimated that by the year 2000 some 2.2 million jobs will have been created nationally.

Competition for new recruits will be much fiercer than it is today, particularly for trainees and those with skills which can be used by a variety of employers.

Even those trained in specific health care jobs could be tempted by high wages and better conditions to leave the Service; and, as the NHS battles to meet its staff needs, the demand for care will be increasing substantially.

New treatments, therapies and technologies are being developed, offering the chance of improved care for increasing number of people. The population of the region is also getting older – the very group of people who need most health care.

Between now and the year 2001, the number of people living in Wessex will increase to nearly 3.2 million – a rise of more than ten per cent, and more than twice the national average.

It is expected that the demand for acute services will increase by 30 per cent. over the next ten years.

Fig 9.3 'Putting People First', an article in *Link*

ture for new buildings and major items of equipment was £51m. In 1987–8 Wessex expenditure on health care per head of its population was £238 compared with the national average of £271 (1988–9 prices). The NHS is a labour intensive organisation with about 75 per cent of all expenditure used on paying staff.

Health services are now treating record numbers of patients — in fewer beds — due to increases in funding, better techniques, greater use of day surgeries and improvements in community services, as indicated in Table 9.1. It is aimed to continue making better use of expensive hospital resources and develop methods of providing care that permit people to return home more quickly. Local services are aiming to treat 33 per cent more hospital patients, within an increase in revenue of just 10 per cent (in real terms) by the end of the next ten years.

Communications

A joint consultative committee with representatives from management and staff meet regularly to discuss proposals for policy changes, e.g. the smoking policy for public areas.

A monthly newspaper *Link* is circulated to all health staff throughout the region to provide them with information about future plans and policies, new developments and initiatives in health care, news affecting the NHS and its personnel, as well as sporting and recreational activities.

An information sheet *Update* is also circulated to all staff at the RHA's headquarters to provide a channel of communication on such matters as staff and organisational matters, new office systems and procedures, etc.

Personnel policy

The article 'Putting People First' (*see* Fig 9.3), which was published in the *Link* newspaper, discusses a human resource strategy for health services in Wessex and recommends measures which should be taken to help the NHS compete more effectively in the labour market against competition from rival organisations.

Table 9.1 Changes in hospital activity

	1980/1	1988/9	Change (%)
Day cases	42 310	64 666	+53
Inpatient cases	318 509	396 898	+25
Outpatient cases	1 661 864	1 790 659	+ 8
Available beds	18 837	15 841	−16
Average length of stay	17.4 days	13.9 days	−20

Case study situation

Ellie Man joined the Wessex RHA headquarters staff 18 months ago after completing her full-time education at a sixth form college. She is employed as a Payroll Officer in the Salaries Section of the Finance and Information Department, as shown in Fig 9.5.

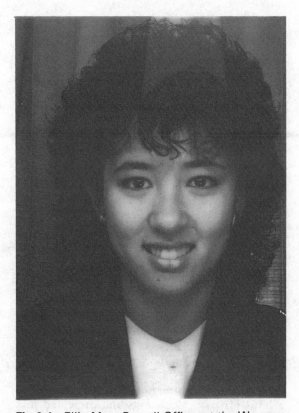

Fig 9.4 Ellie Man, Payroll Officer at the Wessex RHA

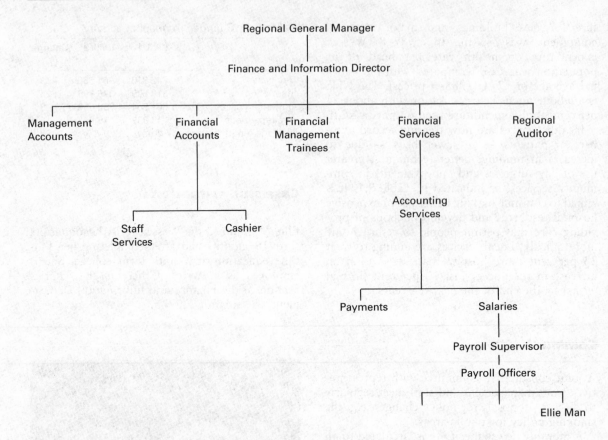

Fig 9.5 Organisation chart for the Wessex RHA Finance and Information Department

Ellie's job entails recording the source data for the computer for doctors, consultants and senior registrars. The information is supplied to the Salaries Section by the Personnel Department and involves changes in salaries, allowances, superannuation and income tax codes. The standard payroll system which is used is one of a number of financial applications which are part of an integrated data processing accounting and information management system. It is based on the application of standard payments and deductions in which the computer permanently holds information in relation to each employee; each district within the authority; the region; and the Whitley Council NHS pay and conditions of service. All the information is stored and used as a basis for pay calculations and presented in a variety of output documents, including pay slips and income tax P60 forms (summaries of tax deducations issued to employees at the end of the tax year).

In addition to providing data for the computer Ellie handles telephone queries from staff concerning their pay and deductions. It was obvious that she gains satisfaction out of doing a job well by making sure that staff receive their correct pay on time. There are strict rules concerning confidentiality of information relating to pay — the staff in the Salaries Section are not allowed to divulge any information to others and the office has to be manned at all times.

Training

The work of a Payroll Officer is of a specialised nature and job training is done by sitting next to an experienced Administrative Officer for the first month. New employees are allocated a 'sponsor' to assist them in settling in and familiarisation of the organisation. A checklist is issued to sponsors to ensure that they give new entrants all essential information such as rules concerning attendance (flexitime procedures), absence, smoking, private telephone calls, holidays, etc.

When Ellie began work at the RHA headquarters she also took part in a day's induction course, organised and conducted by Sallie Woodford, the Personnel Development Officer. This is an in-house course for all levels of staff covering:

- the role and organisation of the RHA including a film *Wessex — the caring team*
- personnel and employment issues including training, consultation, health and safety, grievance procedures and conditions of service
- salaries, superannuation, etc.
- legal requirements such as the Data Protection Act, Health and Safety at Work Act (including first aid), trade union membership, etc.
- fire safety and evacuation procedures.

Staff can apply to attend external training and further education courses if they are relevant to their work. It is essential that the training is beneficial to the employee's department as well as to the individual. The authority pays 75 per cent of the cost of the course (including books, travelling expenses and examination fees) on the understanding that it is repaid if the employee should not complete the course or leave the employment of the NHS within two years of completion or during the course.

Staff appraisal

Annual staff appraisal forms are completed for all staff based on discussion of their work performance, achievement of targets for the previous year and the setting of objectives for the next year. During the course of this discussion any training needs are identified in order to support the employee in achieving their objectives. Whilst this exercise provides a stimulus for career development for the majority of staff it is not always viewed in the same light by staff who may be in their mid or late careers or those who lack the incentive to retrain for new roles or

develop their careers any further.

The staff appraisal forms are agreed and signed by three parties:

- appraisee (the employee)
- appraisor (the employee's immediate line manager)
- grandparent (the appraisor's immediate line manager)

STUDENT ACTIVITIES FOR INDIVIDUALS

1. Using the statistics given in the case study for the Wessex RHA:
   (a) calculate the estimated number of hospital patients in 1998–9
   (b) prepare charts:
   (1) illustrating the numbers of day cases, inpatient cases and outpatient cases dealt with by Wessex RHA in 1988–9;
   (2) contrasting Wessex RHA expenditure on health care per head of its population (1987–8) with the national average for that year.
   (3) contrasting the expenditure on health care per head of population by your local RHA with the national average for the most recent available year.
   (4) contrasting waiting lists in your local RHA with the national average.

2. (a) Prepare a summary of the article reproduced from the Wessex *Link* newspaper, 'Putting People First'.
   (b) In a memo to the Personnel Director comment on the Human Resources Strategy produced by the RHA and put forward your own ideas to 'avert a crisis in care'.

3. You are required to assist in an induction course at Wessex RHA by conducting a seminar on 'legal requirements'. Prepare the handout which you would give to new employees.

4. (a) Compare a computerised payroll procedure with a manual payroll procedure.
   (b) Explain how income tax code numbers are calculated and the employee's involvement in this procedure.

1 Discuss:

 (a) why the staff appraisal exercise 'may not always be viewed in the same light by staff who may be in their mid or late careers or those who lack the incentive to retrain for new roles or develop their careers any further'. How would you deal with such cases?

 (b) why a 'grandparent' is involved in staff appraisal schemes.

 (c) why it should be essential for training to be beneficial to the employee's department as well as to the individual.

 (d) the changes affecting the local family doctor following the White Paper on the Future of the NHS and the subsequent National Health Service and Community Care Act 1990. What are the reasons for these changes, how will patients benefit from them and what are the disadvantages?

2 Draw up a checklist for 'sponsors' of newly recruited staff and role play a session in which each member of the group discusses two or three items from the checklist with the employee.

3 Investigate the ways in which your organisation uses, or could use, integrated data processing accounting and information management systems and discuss your findings with the other members of your group.

CASE STUDY 10 The BBC

In this case study we take a glimpse at the operation and organisation of the BBC — one of the public corporations and described in the White Paper on Broadcasting as 'the cornerstone of British broadcasting . . . to provide high-quality programming across the full range of public tastes and interests, including both programmes of popular appeal and programmes of minority interest, and to offer education, information and cultural material as well as entertainment.'

Michael Checkland, Director-General, in his statement for the annual report, states that the BBC is facing up to the new era of increased competition in broadcasting — made visible by the arrival of the Sky satellite service — with a three-fold strategy of maintaining programmes of range and quality, co-operating with new broadcasters and new technologies, and continuing to be cost-effective in programme operations.

The White Paper's suggestion that 'the BBC should progressively replace the licence fee as its source of funding by subscription' has been considered. The BBC's research indicated that subscription would be unlikely to prove a realistic substitute for the licence fee, though it could be a source of additional income. The BBC is exploring the scope for specialist services downloaded to users during the night hours. An experimental service of information for doctors, operated by a specialist company, has been introduced and it is hoped to offer additional services on subscription. The revenue from these services could help to keep down the level of the licence fee, although it is thought unrealistic to expect such income to make a significant contribution in the near future.

The BBC's constitution and role

The BBC is governed by a Royal Charter which defines its objects, powers and obligations, its constitution and the sources and uses of its revenues. A Licence and Agreement, granted by the Home Secretary, prescribes the terms and conditions of the Corporation's operations.

The powers, responsibilities and obligations laid upon the BBC are vested in the Board of Governors, who exercise them through a permanent staff headed by the Director-General, as Chief Executive Officer, and the Board of Management (Fig 9.6). Governors are appointed by the Queen in Council on the nomination of the government of the day. Through its directorates,

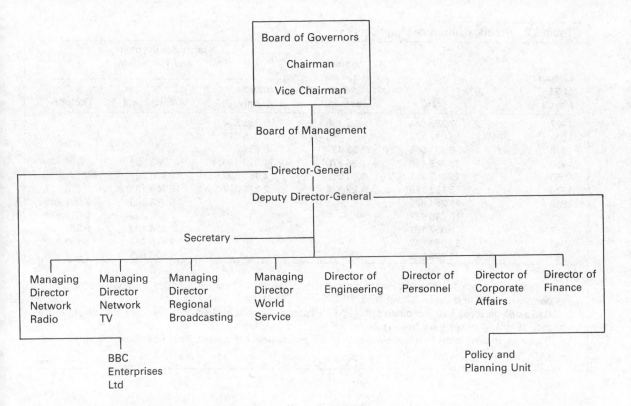

Fig 9.6   BBC's Board of Management

divisions and departments, the BBC is responsible for the whole broadcasting process, from the planning, commissioning and making of radio and TV programmes and their technical and engineering infrastructure, through to transmission over the air, by means of its own network of transmitters.

The work of the BBC is controlled and administered by the following directorates:

- Network Television
- World Service
- Regional Broadcasting
- Network Radio
- Personnel
- Finance
- Engineering
- Corporate Affairs.

The present Charter came into force on 1 August 1981 and is for a period of 15 years. It lays down the powers and responsibilities of the BBC in meeting its objectives. It requires the BBC to appoint national broadcasting councils for Scotland, Wales and Northern Ireland, a general advisory council and regional and local radio advisory councils. The BBC is required to make arrangements for obtaining from the public views and opinions of its programmes and for considering any criticism and suggestions made.

Finance

The BBC's domestic radio and TV services are financed by the TV licence fee (Table 9.2). The BBC earns extra income through its own commercial company, BBC Enterprises Ltd. Their commercial activities include the sale of programmes overseas and books, videos, records, tapes and other products linked to BBC pro-

Table 9.2 Broadcasting receiving licences

Licences at 31 March	Total	Issued free for blind persons	Issued for payment radio and TV combined		
			Radio only	Monochrome	Colour
1927	2 269 644	5 750	2 263 894		
1930	3 092 324	16 496	3 075 828		
1940	8 951 045	53 427	8 897 618		
1950	12 219 448	56 376	11 819 190	343 882	
1960	15 005 011	54 958	4 480 300	10 469 753	
1970	18 183 719	22 174	2 279 017	15 609 131	273 397
1980	18 284 865	–	–	5 383 125	12 901 740
1985	18 715 937	–	–	2 896 263	15 819 674
1987	18 953 161	–	–	2 414 496	16 538 665
1988	19 354 442	–	–	2 220 482	17 133 960
1989	19 395 963	–	–	1 926 805	17 469 158

Notes:

i   In 1947 there were 14 560 combined radio and monochrome TV licences; in 1968 there were 20 428 combined radio and colour TV licences.

ii Radio-only licences and combined radio and TV licences were abolished on 1 February 1971; from that date TV-only licences have been issued.

iii Dealer's demonstration fees and accommodation and residential care licences have been excluded from the figures.

grammes. BBC Enterprises Ltd also produces *Radio Times*.

The BBC's World Services, which broadcast in English and 36 other languages, are not financed by the licence fee, but receive instead parliamentary grants-in-aid.

The level of the licence fee is currently determined by the Retail Price Index (RPI), a formula which has the advantage of making long-term planning easier. Its drawback is that the BBC's income cannot keep pace with broadcasting costs which, largely because broadcasting is a labour-intensive industry, rise faster than general inflation. This, in turn, inhibits the BBC in their efforts to reduce the gap between the pay levels of many of their staff and that of their counterparts outside the BBC. Among the difficulties this creates for the BBC is in competing in the broadcasting labour market with ITV, the growing independent production sector and, increasingly, satellite channels, which are not limited by the RPI.

The corporation is required to submit audited accounts, as part of its annual report, for presentation to Parliament.

Government controls

The licence contains a clause which confers on the government the power to determine what the BBC may or may not broadcast and this could enable the government to ban programmes. This clause has never been invoked to ban a programme, but it was used in October 1988 to restrict broadcast coverage of statements supporting terrorism in Northern Ireland. The corporation has always vigorously defended its freedom, which is rooted in its Charter obligations and its duty to the public, to exercise independent judgement in its programmes.

Other important licence clauses which place obligations on the BBC include the following:

- to broadcast an impartial account day by day of the proceedings of both Houses of Parliament.
- to broadcast official announcements whenever asked to do so by one of the government's Ministers.
- to refrain from expressing its own opinion on current affairs or on matters of public policy, other than broadcasting.

- to forbid the broadcasting of subliminal messages, i.e. transmission of TV images of very brief duration which might convey a message or influence the minds of the audience without their being aware of what has been done.
- to refrain from carrying advertising — the BBC's policy is to avoid giving publicity to any individual, product, firm or organised interest except when this is necessary in providing informative programmes.

The Home Secretary regulates broadcasting generally, and is answerable to Parliament on broad policy matters, but otherwise the BBC is independent in the day-to-day conduct of its business.

BBC services

These include:

- TV — two national TV networks BBC1 and BBC2
- Radio — five national radio networks Radios 1–5
- World Service — worldwide broadcasting through radio
- Educational Broadcasting
- Teletext — the BBC's service CEEFAX offers 600 pages of news and information on BBC1 and BBC2: home and foreign news, sports news and results, city and financial news, weather and road, rail and air information are updated throughout the day and broadcast at all times when BBC TV transmitters are on the air. Note: CEEFAX is an additional broadcast service only available to those with a TV set fitted with a teletext decoder.

Regions

There are the following four English regions each with a Head of Broadcasting responsible for regional TV and local radio in their areas:

Midlands	— Birmingham
North	— Manchester
South and East	— Elstree, Herts
South and West	— Bristol

BBC Scotland (Glasgow), BBC Wales (Cardiff) and BBC Northern Ireland (Belfast) make TV and radio programmes for the networks and for their own regional audiences.

Case study situation

During our visit to the BBC we looked particularly at the work of the Secretarial and Clerical Services Department where we met Dipti Bhayani who is the Secretary to Mrs Yvonne Pierce-Goulding, Manager of Secretarial and Clerical Services. Dipti joined the BBC in December 1988 and was appointed to her present position in August 1989. She studied secretarial subjects at school, followed by 'A' Levels at the Harrow College of Higher Education and is currently studying for professional qualifications of the Institute of Personnel Management. Before working for the BBC Dipti gained clerical experience with British Gas.

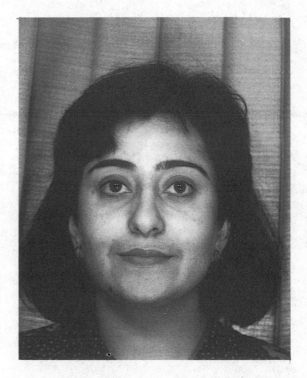

Fig 9.7 Dipti Bhayani, Secretary in the Secretarial and Clerical Services Department of the BBC

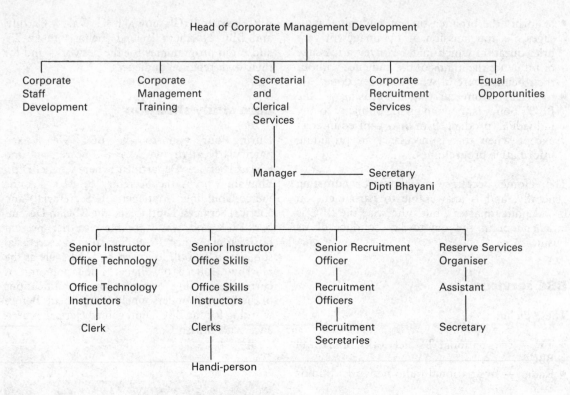

Fig 9.8 Organisation chart for BBC's Corporate Management Development Division

Secretarial and Clerical Services Department

This is a department of the Corporate Management Development Division as shown in Fig 9.8. It is responsible for providing:

- 'in-house' secretarial and clerical training courses
- recruitment of clerical and secretarial staff for the BBC in London
- reserve services, i.e. employment of temporary staff to provide office attachments for short-term relief.

The department provides a wide range of courses and seminars for approximately 2500 trainees per year covering:

- shorthand and typewriting
- word processing
- minuting meetings
- telephone technique
- organising day and diary
- communication skills
- manager-secretary team work
- the electronic office
- spreadsheets
- databases
- customised systems

The training of supervisors and junior, middle and senior managers to corporate level is catered for separately in the Corporate Management Training Department.

Staff are recruited for a wide range of secretarial and clerical jobs including:

- secretarial posts in support departments such as programme publicity, artists' contracts, copyright, design and scenic services, personnel, engineering, BBC enterprises, etc.
- finance: programme accounts, costing, salaries, etc.

- news information clerical duties
- library and registry services
- film and tape despatch
- administrative and accommodation services
- telephonists and receptionists
- newsrooms — VDU or auto script operators and dictation typists
- data preparation operators
- personnel administration clerks.

The BBC employs around 30 000 staff country-wide, including over 4000 secretaries or clerks.

Secretarial support services

Dipti's job as Secretary to the Manager of Secretarial and Clerical Services consists of the following duties:

- typing correspondence from manuscript drafts using a word processor
- composing and typing routine letters and memos
- keeping the Manager's office diary and making appointments
- arranging meetings and business lunches
- recording and passing on telephone messages
- receiving visitors and informing reception of their expected arrival
- maintaining an efficient filing and bring-forward system
- supervising trainees who work in the office for practice sessions
- deputising, when necessary, for the clerk to courses
- serving as a liaison point for queries about reserve services
- providing a point of contact for messages for people attending courses, including the administration of notifications of sick leave.

Dipti sometimes experiences difficulty in communicating with staff operating from different buildings throughout the city, but this should prove easier when many of the corporate administrative departments move shortly to a purpose-built headquarters in White City, located close to Television Centre. At the same time, it is planned to computerise the recruitment procedures operated by the department.

Recruitment

Linda Ronaldson, a Recruitment Officer at the BBC, told us that when recruiting office staff she looked for the following skills and qualities:

- a good general education to GCSE level (English Grade C)
- an application form which is well written and accurate
- accurate proof reading — tested at interview
- competent shorthand/typewriting — tested at interview — for secretarial staff
- competent spelling, numeracy and filing skills — tested at interview — for clerical staff
- realistic understanding of the occupational role
- good organisational and planning skills
- knowledge of new technology or interest in being trained
- effective oral communication
- social integration
- active listening
- ability to solve problems
- adaptability
- stress tolerance.

STUDENT ACTIVITIES FOR INDIVIDUALS

1 Using the statistics on broadcasting receiving licences (p. 122):
   (a) prepare a chart to illustrate the figures and
   (b) comment on the trends to date and the likely trends in the future.
2 Write a letter to the BBC suggesting an alternative method of financing the BBC to replace or supplement the licence fee.
3 Prepare a job description, job specification and advertisement for the post of Clerk in the Office Technology Section of the Secretarial and Clerical Services Department.
4 In a memo to the Departmental Manager suggest what steps should be taken to computerise the recruitment procedure.
5 You are required to assist in supervising the trainees who work in the office for practice sessions. Draw up a checklist of 'do's' and 'don'ts' on handling telephone calls.

STUDENT ACTIVITIES FOR GROUP WORK

1 Discuss:
   (a) the forms of control exercised over the BBC. Why are they imposed? Are they necessary, and if so, are they adequate?
   (b) the White Paper's suggestions for the future funding of the BBC.
   (c) the implications of using the RPI to determine licence fees.
   (d) competition in broadcasting. Is it in the interests of the public? Can and should the BBC compete with the independent companies with their advertising incomes?

2 Make a presentation (using visual aids) to a group of overseas visitors explaining the government's role in the operation of the BBC and how the BBC differs from ITV.

3 Demonstrate to your group the uses which may be made of the CEEFAX service within your own organisation.

Part E

The international scene

10 The international scene

The British Commonwealth

At the end of the war in 1945 about one quarter of the world's population belonged to the British Empire. Australia, Canada, New Zealand and South Africa had been given their independence earlier though they still owed allegiance to the British Crown. Since 1945 most of the other states have been granted independence. A few like Pakistan, Burma and South Africa left the British Commonwealth but most remained. It now consists of 49 independent sovereign states — 18 accept the Queen as Head of State, 26 are republics whilst five have their own monarchs. Some still accept the Privy Council as the final Court of Appeal in their legal system whilst others have their own Supreme Court.

For many years the Commonwealth played an important role as an economic unit. Preference was given to goods from Commonwealth countries but this has largely disappeared since Britain joined the European Community.

The Queen is accepted as the Head of the Commonwealth but it is in her personal capacity and not as the British Crown. Britain's links with the Commonwealth are historical and emotional rather than legally binding, as in the case of the EC. In recent years the Commonwealth has been under considerable strain, particularly over the question of apartheid in South Africa, when the British government under Mrs Thatcher took a different view from most of the Commonwealth nations. The Queen has played an important role in keeping the Commonwealth together (*see also* Chapter 3).

A Commonwealth Secretariat was set up in 1965 to act as an administrative agency, making sure that there is proper communication between member states and on occasions putting forward the collective view of the Commonwealth on matters of international concern.

The United Nations (UN)

The United Nations Organisation now has over 150 members covering all parts of the globe. It has two constituent parts: the General Assembly and the Security Council. The General Assembly holds regular meetings of all its members and each nation has one vote irrespective of its size or population. It has few executive powers. More important is the Security Council consisting of 15 members. Five of these (China, France, UK, USA and the USSR) are permanent members whilst the other ten members are elected every two years. Decisions must have the support of nine of the 15 members but this must include all five permanent members. This means that each permanent member has a veto and in the early days this was used particularly by the USSR on many occasions.

The Security Council's main task is to maintain international peace and it has peacekeeping forces (comprised of soldiers from member countries) in several countries, including the Lebanon and Cyprus. However, the UN has not been able to deliver as much as its founders had hoped. This is largely because the super powers have followed their own diplomacy with scant reference to the UN and because the veto in the Security Council has stultified many peacekeeping efforts. In the 1990 dispute over the Iraqi occupation of Kuwait there was an encouraging measure of agreement and all five permanent members of the Security Council agreed a number of resolutions condemning the invasion, imposing economic sanctions on Iraq, and authorising the use of force when Iraq refused to withdraw.

On the other hand, the various agencies set up by the UN have played a valuable part in world affairs. These agencies included the World Health Organisation (WHO), the Food and Agriculture Organisation (FAO), the International Labour Organisation (ILO), the Educational, Social and Cultural Organisation (UNESCO) and the General Agreement on Tariffs and Trade (GATT) which is an international treaty relating to the rules for conducting trade between nations. There has been criticism that some of these organisations are too bureaucratic and subject to political and ideological manoeuvering. At the time of writing this book the UK has withdrawn its membership of UNESCO for this reason.

Discussion question

1 How do you think the UN could be made more effective?

The North Atlantic Treaty Organisation (NATO)

NATO was created in 1949 as the major defence structure for the Western world. Its initial members were the USA, UK, Belgium, Canada, Denmark, France, Iceland, Italy, Luxembourg, the Netherlands, Norway and Portugal. Spain, Turkey and West Germany joined later whilst France partially withdrew preferring to follow an independent defence strategy. With the unification of the two Germanies, the position of East Germany in relation to NATO is currently under discussion.

The purposes of NATO are to settle disputes by peaceful means, to adopt a common defence strategy and to pool resources for common defence.

From 1949 to 1989 NATO and the Warsaw Pact (created in 1955 by the communist countries as a mutual defence organisation) dominated the politics of Europe. Both blocs regarded an attack on one as being an attack on all. The momentous events in Eastern Europe in 1989 and 1990 and the virtual dissolution of the Warsaw Pact, combined with the progress made by the USA and the USSR in disarmament talks has radically altered the defence strategies in Europe. NATO is now busily engaged in defining its new role in the changing situation. In July 1990 the UK also announced considerable reductions in defence expenditure.

Discussion question

2 Now that the political map of Europe has changed, do you think there is a need for NATO? Should Britain disarm, and if so, to what extent?

The European Community (EC) (formerly known as the Common Market)

In 1871, 1914 and 1939, war with France and Germany on opposing sides had devastated Europe. After the end of the war in 1945 politicians in the western European countries, both victors and vanquished, were determined that this should not happen again. The only way to prevent another war in the future was to secure political and economic integration of the countries of Europe.

The first step was the creation of the Iron and Steel Community (ECSC) in 1950. The member nations were France, West Germany, Italy, Belgium, Holland and the Netherlands. The purpose was to integrate the iron and steel industries (essential war industries) in those six countries.

In 1957 by the Treaty of Rome the same six nations expanded their co-operation and created the European Economic Community (EEC). This was basically an economic union but its founders intended that there should be a political union in due course, although the form that it should take was not specified. Another treaty signed at the same time established the European Atomic Energy Community (Euratom) to develop in a co-ordinated way the use of atomic energy for peaceful purposes. The three bodies ECSC, EEC and Euratom were merged in 1969.

The original objectives of the Treaty of Rome were to get rid of all obstacles to the free movement of people and resources between the member states and to promote economic growth throughout the Community. No customs duties or quotas could be imposed on goods moving from one member state to another. A common tariff was to be imposed on goods imported from the rest of the world. There was to be free movement of people to work inside the Community. Some of these rules were introduced immediately whilst in other cases a transitional period was allowed. The intention to allow the free movement of capital between member states has not yet been fully realised. The early years of the EC were very successful and the growth rate in the six countries exceeded that in most other European countries.

Britain and the EC

Britain decided not to join the then EEC at the outset. The main reason was our reluctance to hand over any powers to a supra-national authority. Also, at that time Britain still had close trading ties with the Commonwealth and did not really regard herself as a European nation. Instead, we combined with other non-EEC European states to form the European Free Trade Association (EFTA). The member nations agreed to abolish customs duties and quota restrictions on manufactured (but not agricultural) goods.

By 1962–3 the EEC had been very successful in promoting economic growth while EFTA had not proved a success. Britain now applied to join the EEC but our admission was vetoed by France much to the annoyance of the other five member countries. A further application was made in 1967 but this was neither formally accepted nor rejected.

In 1970 a new Conservative Government under the leadership of Edward Heath took office. He was a convinced European and was determined to gain entry. At the same time, Denmark, Norway and Ireland applied to join. The French raised fewer difficulties partly because they were afraid of the growing economic power of West Germany and also General de Gaulle, who had exercised the original veto, was no longer there.

After long negotiations agreement was reached. Referenda were held in Ireland, Denmark and Norway and in the case of Norway the people voted by a small majority not to join. In Britain accession was obtained by an Act of Parliament with the normal parliamentary proce-

dures applying. No referendum was held. However, in 1974 a Labour Government won the election and attempts were made to re-negotiate the terms of entry. In June 1975 a referendum was held to decide whether or not Britain should remain in the EEC and 67 per cent of the electorate voted in favour. If there had been a referendum at the time of entry in 1972 it is very doubtful whether a majority would have favoured entry.

The EEC was further expanded when Greece joined in 1981 and Spain and Portugal in 1985. It now represents a total population of over 320 million, larger than the USA or the USSR.

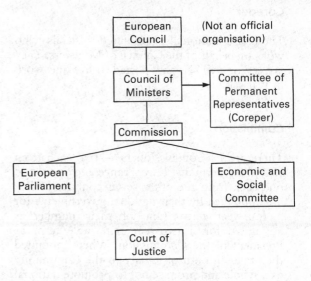

Fig 10.1 Organisation chart for the European Community

The institutions of the EC

The European Council

This is a meeting three or four times each year of the political leaders of the member states. It has no official place in the EC structure and is not mentioned in the Treaty of Rome. The President of the Commission normally attends these meetings. By its nature it is a powerful body and many major decisions are taken at these meetings.

The Council of Ministers

This is the policy-making body within the EC. It consists of one Minister from each of the 12 member states. Which members are there depends on the subject under discussion. Economic matters will be decided by the Finance Ministers, environmental matters by the Environment Ministers. Important decisions are usually made by the Foreign Ministers and in Britain the Foreign Office has overall control of EC matters (*see* Case Study 3). The Presidency of the Council changes every six months, with each member state taking its turn.

Coreper

These are nationally appointed officials who work on behalf of the Council of Ministers. They are senior civil servants posted to live and work in Brussels.

Commission

There are 17 Commissioners — two each from UK, West Germany, Italy, France and Spain and one each from the other seven countries. They are appointed by their national governments for a four-year term. One of their number is appointed for a two-year renewable term as President of the Commission. When appointed they take an oath of loyalty to the Community as a whole and promise not to promote national interests.

Each Commissioner is responsible for a particular area of community work, e.g. economic and financial affairs, agriculture, etc. He will have his own advisers usually called his cabinet. The Commission employs over 10 000 people plus about 1500 translators often working on a freelance basis. Under 3000 of the employees are administrators. The Commission is normally thought of as being a huge bureaucracy but in fact it employs less people than some London Borough Councils. The Commission administers the Common Market, including the Common Agricultural Policy (CAP) but also drafts legislation, is responsible for diplomacy and acts as the Community's 'think-tank'. The Commission is divided into a number of directorates each responsible for a particular area of the Community's activities.

Economic and Social Committee

This is a purely consultative body drawn from three groups of employers, workers and 'various interests', e.g. agriculture, professions, consumers, etc. They are appointed by national governments for a four-year period. All Commission proposals are submitted to them for their comments and these are always sent to the Council of Ministers before a final decision is made.

European Parliament

This consists of 518 members elected for five years by the 12 states in proportion to their populations. The UK has 81 members. Bob Mitchell was a member of the European Parliament from 1975 to 1979 when members were nominated by their national governments and served as both National and Euro MPs. Since then Euro MPs have been directly elected by the people. Britain is the only country that does not use some form of proportional representation (except in Northern Ireland) in its European elections.

The European Parliament does not have legislative power but has to be consulted by the Commission before any proposals are submitted to the Council of Ministers. It has influence and its comments on proposed legislation are taken seriously by the Commission.

It has some control over the Community Budget and can influence spending programmes. It also has the power (not yet used) to dismiss the whole Commission but not individual Commissioners.

There is considerable pressure to make the Community more democratic and give more power to the elected Parliament but this has so far been rejected by the member states through the Council of Ministers. National governments and parliaments are reluctant to hand over power to a European Parliament.

For further details of how the European Parliament operates see Case Study 11.

European Court of Justice

This consists of judges from each of the member states, ruling on Community legislation and giving the final judgement on the interpretation of treaties. It has the task of ensuring that Community legislation is carried out by individuals, companies and national governments. Companies which offend can be fined but only moral pressure can be brought on offending governments. No government has yet refused to implement a decision of the European Court of Justice, although some have used delaying tactics. It may also adjudicate on disputes between the various EC institutions which involve an interpretation of the original treaty.

The European Court of Justice should be distinguished from the European Court of Human Rights which is not part of the EC machinery.

Decision making in the EC

The original demand for legislation on a particular matter may come from a variety of sources: a member government, the Council of Ministers, the European Parliament or the Commission itself. The Commission prepares the draft legislation and then submits it to the Council, Parliament and also the Economic and Social Committee. The latter two will give their opinions and may suggest amendments. The draft submitted to the Council will be discussed by the members of Coreper who will consult their member governments. The Commission may then amend the proposed legislation in the light of representations made to it. The final document will be submitted to the Council of Ministers who take the final decision.

Important decisions have to have unanimity but there is now an agreement to make less important decisions by weighted majority voting. 'Weighted' means that the votes of the larger states carry more weight than the votes of the smaller states. Any decision to enlarge the Community must have a unanimous vote and has to be ratified by the Parliaments of each of the member states.

There are three main types of legislation:

1 **Regulations:** these are binding upon all mem-

ber states and take precedence over national law.
2 **Directives:** these set an objective to be achieved, usually within a certain time limit, and member states then have to introduce national legislation to achieve these objectives.
3 **Decisions:** these settle a particular issue often of some urgency. They are directly binding but are addressed to specific organisations within the member states.

The Common Agricultural Policy (CAP)

The one area where the EC has succeeded in formulating a genuine common market is in agriculture through the CAP and it is this policy which has been most heavily criticised, particularly in Britain.

The basic principles of the policy are set out in Article 39 of the Treaty of Rome. They are:

- to increase productivity through technical progress and the best use of all the factors of production, particularly manpower
- a fair income for the farming population
- the stabilisation of markets
- security of supply
- reasonable prices to consumers.

In fact there has been considerable overproduction with 'wine lakes' and 'butter mountains'. It is also argued that prices are higher than necessary. A large proportion of the Community's budget has been taken up in administering the CAP.

Competition policy

One of the objectives of the EC is to have free and fair competition in trade between member states. Organisations are prevented from engaging in price-fixing and other agreements which distort free competition and also from using a dominant position (monopoly) to distort the market.

Any government wishing to subsidise one of its industries should notify the Commission. In many cases the subsidy may be regarded as reasonable, particularly if temporary. However, if the subsidy is not considered justified it may be referred to the Council of Ministers and in the last resort taken to the European Court.

Regional Development Fund

The Regional Development Fund was established to give help to the poorer regions of the Community. For many years Italy and the UK were the main beneficiaries but since the accession of Greece, Spain and Portugal the emphasis has changed.

All applications for regional aid must come from the member states and aid will normally only be given for areas which also receive regional aid from the national government concerned. Since 1985 there has been a relaxation in this rule as the EC is encouraging financing of programmes as well as individual projects.

Social Fund

This is concerned with training, re-training and job creation schemes. Emphasis is placed on schemes that give help to the young unemployed. Applications for non-repayable grants can be made by organisations in the private and public sectors.

The single market — 1992

In July 1987 the EC took a large step forward when the Single European Act came into force, having been ratified by all the Parliaments of the member states. The Single Act describes the internal market as 'an area without internal frontiers in which the free movement of goods, persons, services and capital is ensured in accordance with the provisions of this Treaty'. The internal market aims to eliminate barriers to free trade such as frontier checks, different national product standards and major differences in indirect taxation and excise duties. The target date for full realisation is 31 December 1992.

At the same time it was agreed that more decisions should be taken by majority voting, although unanimity (and, therefore, the possibility of a veto) was retained for such issues as

indirect taxation, free movement of persons and the rights and interests of employed persons.

There are also proposals to increase the amount of money available in the Regional and Social Funds. The member state governments retain the right to pass national laws to control immigration from non-EC countries and to combat terrorism, crime and drug trafficking.

It is not yet certain whether all the provisions of the Act will be achieved by 1992. For example, Britain strongly opposes Community proposals for harmonised labour laws and company legislation.

Britain's trade figures

Table 10.1 gives Britain's imports and exports to the EC and other countries. These show that over 50 per cent of Britain's trade is now with EC countries. This percentage is likely to increase with the coming of the single market.

Table 10.1 UK imports and exports (May 1990)

	Imports (£m)	Exports (£m)
European Community	5 714.3	4 749.7
Rest of western Europe	1 360.9	851.4
North America	1 650.4	1 276.4
Other developed countries e.g. South Africa, Japan, Australia and New Zealand	856.4	570.2
Oil-exporting countries	225.2	608.7
Other developing countries e.g. Brazil, Egypt, Jamaica, Pakistan, Singapore	1 027.6	899.2
Soviet Union and western Europe	202.1	171.9
Totals	11 036.9	9 127.5

(Source: *HMS Monthly Digest of Statistics*)

European Monetary System

In October 1990 Britain agreed to join the European Exchange Rate Mechanism (ERM), an important part of the European Monetary System (EMS).

The future

It is by no means certain how the EC will develop in the future. There are those who want to proceed rapidly towards a European supra-national government with a common currency, a European Bank and a powerful elected European Parliament with legislative powers. Others are fearful of the loss of national sovereignty which these measures would entail and whilst support-ing greater economic co-operation do not wish to proceed with political integration. The ques-tion for the 1990s and beyond is whether the EC (including possibly some of the former communist states in Eastern Europe) is to become a genuine community or to remain as a community of nation states.

It was the disagreement over Britain's attitude towards future developments in the EC that led to the resignation from the Government of Sir Geoffrey Howe — the first step in the process which ultimately led to the resignation of Mrs Thatcher as Prime Minister.

Discussion question

3   Do you think we should move towards a politically integrated Europe, even if this means a considerable loss of national sovereignty?

Written questions

4   You are the Administrative Assistant to the Managing Director of a local firm making steel containers.
    (a) Your company has recently lost a lucrative order to a company in Spain. You suspect that this firm is only able to quote a lower price because it is receiving a subsidy from the Spanish Government. Write a report for your Managing Director explaining what procedure he should adopt to have this matter investigated by the EC.
    (b) Your company is finding difficulty in recruiting skilled labour locally and has decided to undertake a project of training young unemployed people. The cost of this training is high. Investigate the possibility of obtaining a grant from the European Social Fund. Write a report for your Managing Director summarising your findings and the procedures to be adopted in attempting to obtain a grant.
    (c) Seventy per cent of your company's production is exported mostly to other countries within the EC. Write a report for your Managing Director explaining the likely effects on your company's business now that Britain has joined the European Exchange Rate Mechanism (ERM).

5   Divide into groups of two or three and visit local organisations to find out how they are preparing for the single market in 1992. Each group should prepare a written report on its findings to be followed by a class discussion to determine whether or not these organisations are ready to meet the challenge of 1992.
    Organisations to be covered should include a local authority; a large manufacturing company; a small- or medium-sized manufacturing company; a large retailer; a professional body, e.g. accountants or solicitors; a bank, building society or other financial institution; a university or other institution of higher or further education; a travel agent; a transport undertaking; a trade union and the local chamber of commerce.

6   (a) Referring to the statistics of imports and exports in Table 10.1 calculate the percentage of Britain's total trade with each of the regions and illustrate this data in a pie chart.
    (b) Obtain the equivalent statistics for 1970 or earlier and explain how the direction of British trade has changed since we joined the EC.

CASE STUDY 11 The European Parliament

Introduction

A book of case studies on public administration institutions is incomplete without a case study looking at the organisation of the European Community and questioning the impact it has on the British way of life.

The countries which form the European Community are bound together by three international treaties, of which the most important is the Treaty of Rome. The Treaty of Rome was signed in 1957 by Belgium, France, Italy, Luxembourg, the Netherlands and Germany. They were joined in 1973 by Denmark, Ireland and the UK; in 1981 by Greece and in 1986 by Portugal and Spain.

The principal Community institutions are:

- the Commission
- the Council
- the Parliament
- the Court of Justice.

The Commission

The Commission, i.e. the Executive Civil Service, is headed by 17 Commissioners nominated by the Community governments, including at least one from each member state. It makes proposals for Community laws, monitors compliance with the treaties and administers common policies.

The Council

The Council of Ministers comprises Ministers from each member government and it is responsible for making the final policy decisions, taking the European Parliament's advice into account. Heads of State and government meet as the European Council three or four times a year to discuss major issues and to chart the future course of the Community.

The Parliament

Britain and the other Community countries elect members to the European Parliament (MEPs) every five years. The European Parliament represents 320 million people, more than in the USA, the Soviet Union or Japan. The MEPs sit in party groupings and not by country, e.g. Socialists; European People's Party (Christian Democrats); Liberal, Democratic and Reformist; European Democrats, etc. The Parliament in full session meets in Strasbourg; its committees usually sit in Brussels and its secretariat is based in Luxembourg.

As in national Parliaments, the European Parliament scrutinises draft legislation, questions the Executive (both Ministers and Commissioners), draws attention to the problems of constituents and debates issues of immediate concern to the Community. Much of the detailed work of the European Parliament is dealt with by specialist committees which report and recommend on the following subjects:

- Agriculture, fisheries and food
- Budgetary control
- Budgets
- Development and Co-operation
- Economic and Monetary Affairs and Industrial Policy
- Energy, Research and Technology
- Environment, Public Health and Consumer Protection
- External Economic Relations
- Institutional Affairs
- Legal Affairs and Citizens' Rights
- Petitions
- Political Affairs
- Regional Policy and Regional Planning
- Rules of Procedure, the Verification of Credentials and Immunities
- Social Affairs and Employment
- Transport
- Women's Rights
- Youth, Culture, Education, Information and Sport.

The Court of Justice

The European Court of Justice consists of judges from all Community countries. It adjudicates on disputes arising from the application and interpretation of Community laws which affect member states, institutions, companies or individuals.

Further details of these institutions are given in Chapter 10.

Figure 10.2 shows how the services of the European Parliament are organised in directorates and identifies the position of Helen McAvoy, our contact for this case study, a British subject working for the European Parliament in Brussels. At the time of compiling the case study the European Parliament employed 3483 staff at their headquarters.

Case study situation

Helen McAvoy has worked for the European Parliament since 1979 as a Linguist, Head of the Press Assessment Service and Head of the Documentary Research Service (her present job). She graduated from Glasgow University with a Master of Arts honours degree and then gained experience in the European Commission and elsewhere as a Research Assistant, Product Development Assistant, Linguist, Administrator and Project Manager before joining the European Parliament.

As Head of the Documentary Research Service Helen is responsible for the following:

1 Staff management for 10 employees (listed in Fig 10.2).

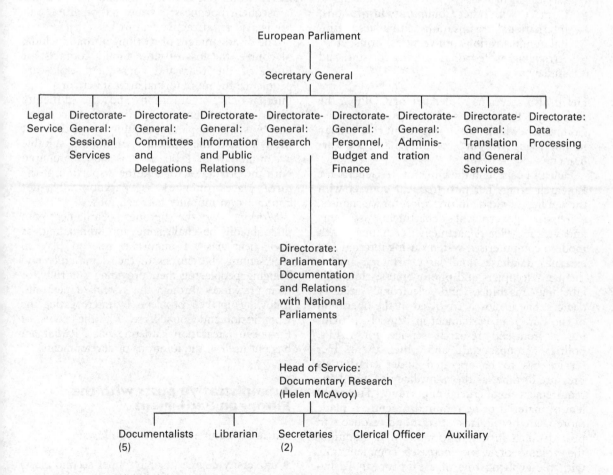

Fig 10.2 Organisation chart for the European Parliament

2   Management and supervision of work in the following sectors:
    - documentation (interrogation of internal and external databases, preparation of subject dossiers, scanning of periodicals)
    - librarianship (cataloguing, acquisitions and subscriptions)
    - microtheque (both microfiche and micro-films)
    - informatics
    - budget
    - security system
    - secretariat (word processing, mail, news-papers, periodicals, official documents, loose-leaf updates, labelling, orders, loans, photocopies, telecopies).
3   Liaison with MEPs and political groups.
4   Liaison with other Director-Generals and services in Brussels.
5   Contacts with other Community institutions, international organisations, embassies, natio-nal administrations, universities, firms, etc.
6   Arranging professional training for staff and students.

Helen also serves as a member of COPEC, the European Parliament's Equal Opportunities Committee, which has an important role to play in improving working conditions for the Parliament's female staff.

Helen's position in the Directorate-General for Research brings her into frequent contact with the public, providing information for journalists, embassies, government departments, students and visitors. Her department is equipped with modern computerised systems using internal and external databases and laser printers; micro-theque; telecopiers and photocopiers; electronic labelling machines and electronic security devices. She is closely involved in the operation of the European Parliament in Brussels, provid-ing a front-end research service for MEPs, political groups, staff and other users. Her service has to be operated under continuous pressure of time, as the immediacy of members' requirements is of crucial importance. The prob-lem of material being required urgently is made more acute by the lack of staff and resources to provide such instant information. In addition, the volume of work increases commensurate with the evolving role of the European Parlia-ment. Another difficulty arises from having to operate the library in two main places of work and the resulting division of resources.

Working abroad

Helen McAvoy has worked abroad for most of her career, and moved to Brussels with her partner, Frank, who works as a Conference Interpreter for the EC Commission. The two have followed roughly the same career pattern as linguists and administrators. Frank is now work-ing as Head of the Parliament's Infrastructure Service in Brussels.

Helen sees the main advantages of working abroad for the EC as being the international, cosmopolitan atmosphere; the interesting mix of different cultures and languages; the ease of travel from one country to another and the consequent openness to other nationalities. Sal-ary is also an attractive feature.

The disadvantages of working abroad include, of course, the loss of close family contacts for much of the year and consequent child-care problems; the more formal atmosphere of a large international organisation and the difficulty experienced by many people in making contacts and by some people in adapting to the different lifestyle; and the difficulty of finding suitable accommodation. Promotion is slow compared with the private sector and the dispersion of the three places of work is, paradoxically, not conducive to mobility between jobs.

Working for the European Parliament can undoubtedly be challenging and stimulating, as Parliament has an important role to play in representing the citizens of the Community and bringing people together, providing a forum for their grievances through the system of petitions, following up their problems by interrogating the Commission and Council, etc. With the process of European integration gathering pace, Parliament has put itself in the forefront of developments.

Administrative posts with the European Parliament

Entrance requirements are as follows:

- university degree (usually upper second class) or equivalent professional experience

- usually a number of years' experience as an administrator in the field described in the advertisement
- a thorough knowledge of English and a very good knowledge of another Community language — knowledge of additional languages is also taken into account
- age limit: usually 35 years but exceptions are granted for child-rearing periods, etc.
- nationality: one of the member states of the Community.

Competition is based on: eliminatory comprehension and logical reasoning tests; essays on Community subjects; précis; and language tests.

As there is an imbalance, i.e. a shortage, in the number of British officials working for the European Parliament compared with other nationalities, efforts are currently being made to encourage British subjects to apply for Community competitions. The Community's equal opportunities policy has focused attention on the need to employ a larger proportion of women.

STUDENT ACTIVITIES FOR INDIVIDUALS

1 Note the current news relating to the EC on TV or in the newspapers and prepare a digest of each item as it would be given to brief the Minister of State at the Foreign Office (Case Study 3).
2 Discuss with representatives of local businesses the effects of the single European market. In a report to your Course Tutor state your findings and suggest what steps you consider traders should now be taking to seize the opportunities and meet the challenges as the trade barriers are removed in Europe.
3 Your company in the UK is planning to set up a branch in France. In a memo to your Manager explain what problems are involved and suggest where you would advise her/him to seek advice.
4 Draft a circular letter in a Community language introducing the products/services of one of your local firms to traders abroad.
5 Write a letter enclosing your cv applying for

an administrative post at an international organisation based abroad.

STUDENT ACTIVITIES FOR GROUP WORK

1 Selected students are to give short talks to the group on the items of EC news extracted for Task 1 above. Discuss the implications of these developments for Britain.
2 In groups, carry out a survey of each of the member states of the EC and prepare illustrative material to show:
   (a) the number of MEPs elected by the country and the number of people they represent
   (b) the political groups in which these members serve
   (c) the name of the EC Commissioner(s) appointed by the country
   (d) the name of the Head of State of the country concerned
   (e) the country's principal imports and exports and details of Britain's trade with it
   (f) any other relevant information concerning the country.
The group should then present their findings to the class.
3 Discuss:
   (a) if you were in Helen McAvoy's position:
      (1) how would you prioritise your work to satisfy the 'immediacy of members' requirements'?
      (2) what new technology methods might be used to share resources when operating the library in two main places of work?
   (b) how does the role of an MEP differ from that of an MP?
   (c) what effects have EC legislation had on Britain, e.g. Single European Act, European Monetary Union, etc.
   (d) 'There's no need to learn a foreign language as everyone speaks English'. What do you think of this attitude? What is your college doing to prepare students and the business community for greater involvement in the EC?

Part F

Accountability and control

11 The judicial system

Every organisation needs rules if it is to function in an orderly manner. There must also be some sanction if the rules are broken. The larger the organisation the more complex the rules become. In the case of a state these rules are known as laws. A law may be defined as 'a rule of human conduct, imposed upon and enforced among, the members of a given state'.

In the English legal system there are three sources of law:

1 **Common law** — formed by the Judges since the twelfth century and originally based on custom. To ensure consistency Judges follow the practice of judicial precedent. In deciding a case a Judge will consider the decisions of Judges in previous cases. Normally a Judge is bound by decisions made previously in higher courts. As a result of this a considerable body of case law has been built up.
2 **Equity** — originally based on principles of fairness and equality and used where the common law was defective or unjust. Today it is applied in all civil courts and takes precedence when there is a conflict with the common law.
3 **Statute law** — based on legislation passed by Parliament. Today it is the main source of English law. As Parliament is supreme the judiciary can only interpret legislation where it is vague; they cannot disregard it or rule that it is invalid.

The rule of law

One of the essentials of a democracy is that people should live under the rule of law. At the end of the nineteenth century Professor A V Dicey in a book called *Introduction to the Study of Law and of Constitution* wrote that there were three features which guaranteed personal freedom under the British Constitution:

1 The absence of arbitrary power. Governments and their representatives must show that they have legal powers to back their actions. If not, the courts will rule their actions to be invalid.
2 No person or organisation is above the law, which shall apply to rich and poor alike.
3 As we have no written constitution individual rights are part of the ordinary law of the land. Since Professor Dicey wrote these words society has become very much more complex and government has much more power. Many people challenge the concept that we live under a rule of law. There have been accusations that government bodies, e.g. the Security Services, have acted in an arbitrary fashion. The excessive secrecy within which government operates (*see* Chapter 13) makes it difficult to discover the facts.

The cost of litigation means that many poor people are unable to pursue their claims through the courts. There is a legal aid system but many believe it to be inadequate. It is no longer universally accepted that the ordinary law of the land is adequate to protect individual rights. Hence the current discussion about the need for a Bill of Rights enshrined in the Constitution (*see* Chapter 13).

Discussion question

1 Do you believe that 'all people are equal in the face of the law'?

Civil and criminal law

Criminal law is that part of law involving offences against the state. An offence against the state is a crime and if convicted results in some form of punishment (imprisonment, a fine, probation, etc.). Crimes range from murder to exceeding the speed limit. It is the function of the police to detect crime and of the Crown Prosecution Service to prosecute the offence in the courts. Ordinary citizens can bring private prosecutions but these are rare.

Civil law is mainly concerned with the rights and duties of individuals towards each other. It includes:

- the law of contract determining whether a promise is legally enforceable
- the law of torts (a tort is defined as a civil wrong) dealing with such matters as nuisance, negligence, trespass and defamation
- the law of property dealing with the rights of individuals over land and property, e.g. landlord-tenant relationships
- the law of succession dealing with such problems as the probate of wills
- family law including divorce and matrimonial disputes.

The penalties in civil cases are usually damages or an injunction, i.e. a process which orders someone to do or to refrain from doing a specified act.

Law courts in England and Wales
(*see* Fig 11.1)

1   Criminal courts

(a) Magistrates' courts
These are mainly concerned with minor criminal offences but also have some jurisdiction in civil matters, e.g. matrimonial. They sit without a jury and are known as a court of summary jurisdiction. The magistrates are lay people and come from a wide variety of backgrounds. They are advised by legally-trained justices' Clerks. In some larger cities there are full-time legally-trained stipendiary magistrates. Some offences can only be tried in a magistrates court, some must be tried in a Crown Court with a jury,

whilst in others the defendant may choose. Because of the overloading of the court system recent legislation has increased the number of offences to be tried summarily, i.e. in the magistrates' court.

Appeals from the decisions of magistrates courts are heard in the crown courts except for some civil appeals which may be heard in the Queen's Bench and Family Divisions of the High Court.

(b) Crown Courts
These try the more serious criminal cases (indictable offences). They are presided over by a Circuit Judge or Recorder (part-time Judge) and sit with a jury. The most serious cases will be heard by a High Court Judge.

(c) Court of Appeal (Criminal Division)
This body hears appeals, on both matters of fact and law, from the decisions of the Crown Courts. It is presided over by the Lord Chief Justice who sits with at least two other High Court Judges.

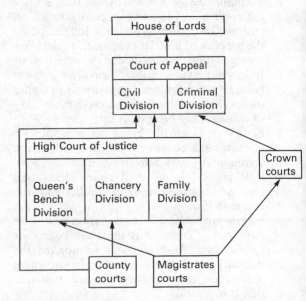

Fig 11.1   Law courts in England and Wales

2 Civil courts

(a) County Courts

These courts hear civil actions for smaller claims. Cases are normally heard by a Judge sitting alone but occasionally there may be a jury. Appeals from the decisions of these courts usually go to the Court of Appeal (Civil Division). County Courts may also have jurisdiction in undefended divorce petitions.

(b) High Court of Justice

The High Court of Justice deals with civil cases where larger sums of money are involved. It is divided into three divisions:

- Queen's Bench Division dealing mainly with contract and tort
- Chancery Division dealing with estates, trusts and bankruptcy
- Family Division concerned with divorce and some probate matters.

Normally cases before the High Court are heard by a single Judge but in some cases (e.g. defamation — libel and slander) there will be a jury as well.

(c) Court of Appeal (Civil Division)

This court hears appeals from the County Courts and the High Courts. It is presided over by the Master of the Rolls assisted by 14 Lord Justices of Appeal. Normally three Judges will hear an appeal but in more important cases there could be five. They operate a majority voting system.

House of Lords

The House of Lords is the final court of appeal for both civil and criminal cases. They only adjudicate where an important point of law is involved. Normally the Court of Appeal will have to give permission for a case to be sent to the House of Lords. In a few cases the House of Lords will hear an appeal direct from the High Court. Its members are the Lord Chancellor, the ten Lords of Appeal in Ordinary (Law Lords) and any former Lord Chancellors or peers who have been Judges.

The Judicial Committee of the Privy Council

This committee consists of all Privy Councillors who hold or have held high judicial office in the UK. It hears appeals from those Commonwealth countries who, after being granted independence, requested it to retain the right of appeal. It also hears appeals from courts in the Colonies, Isle of Man, Channel Islands, ecclesiastical courts, prize courts and tribunals of the medical, dental and optician professions. It sits informally, does not give judgements but instead advises the Monarch who then issues an appropriate Order in Council to deal with the matter.

Coroners courts

The main duty of a Coroner is to investigate sudden deaths. The Coroner may hold an inquest and must summon a jury when there is reason to suspect that death was due to unnatural causes, e.g. murder, road accident, etc. The purpose of the inquest is to find the identity of the deceased person and the place and cause of death. If members of the jury find that death was due to murder or manslaughter they may name the person responsible and the Coroner can issue a warrant of arrest. The Coroner also deals with matters relating to treasure trove, i.e. the discovery of hidden coins or plate.

Small claims courts

In some areas these courts have been established under the jurisdiction of the County Court to deal with civil claims involving small amounts of money. Procedures are informal and presided over by a Registrar. There is no need to employ Solicitors.

Natural justice

All courts of law observe the rules of natural justice. These are:

1 Each side in a dispute should have the opportunity to present its case before a decision is made.

2 Both sides should be entitled to know the reasons why a decision has been made.
3 The decisions should be based only on the evidence presented to the court.
4 No one should be a Judge in their own case.

If any of these rules are broken during the proceedings of a court case the Court of Appeal will normally quash the verdict or order a re-trial.

Jury system

As we have seen juries are used in the more serious criminal cases and in some civil cases. It has always been thought a fundamental right for a person to be tried by a jury of their peers.

All persons between the ages of 18 and 65, with a few exceptions, are liable to be called for jury service. Any person not wishing to serve must provide a very good reason (e.g. a medical certificate) to be exempted. People who have been convicted of a criminal offence resulting in more than three months imprisonment may be disqualified, but those who have received prison sentences of more than five years are permanently disqualified.

In criminal cases juries consist of 12 members. For many years juries had to be unanimous but now majority decisions of at least ten votes to two may be accepted in some cases. Juries in county court cases may have between seven and eleven members.

In recent years there has been some criticism of the jury system. Points of criticism have been that:

- some cases, e.g. complex frauds, are too difficult for jurors to understand
- juries may be too easily influenced by eloquent advocates
- juries are subject to threats of intimidation from outside parties, i.e. jury nobbling
- persons at 18 may be too inexperienced to make rational judgements.

On the other side it is argued that juries represent the common sense views of ordinary people who have a strong sense of justice, e.g. the acquittal of Clive Ponting. They have stood the test of time and in the main there is public confidence in jury trials.

In defamation cases juries not only have the responsibility of giving a verdict but also decide on the amount of damages. There have been criticisms that the damages awarded in some famous libel cases are out of proportion to the offences committed.

Discussion question

2 Does the jury system still have a part to play in British justice? What do you consider should be the minimum age for jurors?

The legal profession

In Britain there are two types of practising Lawyer: Barristers (known as advocates in Scotland) and Solicitors. Solicitors deal directly with the clients and may represent them in the lower courts. Much of their work is involved in such matters as conveyancing and takes place outside the courts.

Barristers mainly concern themselves with advocacy in the courts. They may not deal directly with clients but only through the recommendations from Solicitors. After practising for more than ten years they may apply to 'take silk' and become a Senior Barrister known as a Queen's Counsel. When appearing in court they will be accompanied by a Junior Barrister. Most High Court Judges are recruited from their ranks, although in recent years more Solicitors have been appointed as Recorders (part-time Judges).

There is considerable criticism of the rigid division between Barristers and Solicitors. Very few other countries adopt this system. Recent proposals by the Lord Chancellor to break down this division and to allow Solicitors, in certain circumstances, to represent clients in the higher courts has caused a major controversy. Undoubtedly there are more restrictive practices in the legal profession than in most other professions and those in favour of change believe that the cost of litigation could be substantially reduced if some of them were swept away. Those opposed to change argue that the independence of the bar is a crucial part of the British judicial system.

The judiciary

Lay Magistrates or Justices of the Peace are appointed by the Lord Chancellor. Anyone can recommend someone for appointment as a Magistrate. There is considerable secrecy about the procedures of selection. Some Magistrates serve on Police Committees (*see* Chapter 7).

Judges are appointed by the Crown on the advice of the Prime Minister and the Lord Chancellor. The Prime Minister appoints the Lord Chancellor who is a member of the Cabinet and also recommends the appointments of the Lord Chief Justice, the Master of the Rolls, the President of the Family Division of the High Court and the Law Lords. The Lord Chancellor recommends the appointment of all other Judges and Recorders. There is now a compulsory retiring age of 72 for Circuit Judges and 75 for High Court Judges. The salaries of High Court Judges are paid from the Consolidated Fund (as explained in Chapter 5) and they can only be removed from office by the Crown on an address from both Houses of Parliament. Judges in the lower courts can be removed by the Lord Chancellor for misbehaviour or incapacity. Removals are very rare, but there have been cases where Judges have been persuaded to resign.

The main criticism of the judiciary is that they are drawn from too narrow a social circle and tend to be too conservative and resistant to change. On the other hand, the few Judges who have been innovative are often criticised as producing Judge-made law and usurping the role of Parliament.

Discussion question

3   What changes, if any, would you make in the appointment of magistrates?

The Law Officers

These are the Attorney General and the Solicitor General. Both are MPs and members of the government. They are both Barristers despite their name. Their function is to provide impartial legal advice to the government. On occasions this can produce problems as in the Spycatcher case and the Westland Affair. The Attorney General is responsible for the work of the Director of Public Prosecutions whose consent is needed to bring some cases to court.

Crown Prosecution Service (CPS)

This service is a recent innovation and has taken over the role of the police in deciding whether to prosecute and in presenting cases in the lower courts. There have been considerable early problems and the CPS has been subjected to much criticism from Magistrates and Crown Court Judges mainly involving delays in bringing prosecutions. It is too early to say whether these are teething problems or a defect in the system.

Discussion question

4   Do you think the introduction of the Crown Prosecution Service has improved the administration of justice? If not, what changes would you make?

Legal aid

In criminal proceedings the court has power to order legal aid to be provided where the interests of justice demands it. The amount of legal aid provided depends on the disposable income of the applicant and the amount of their capital. An assessment is carried out by the Department of Social Security (DSS).

In civil cases the applicant should approach the area committee of the Law Society who will decide whether they have a justified case. Again, the DSS will make an assessment and decide the amount of legal aid, if any, to be granted.

Anyone over 16 may obtain legal advice under the 'Green form scheme' which enables a Solicitor to provide advice (but not representation in court) up to a maximum value. Those on very low income may receive this advice free.

There are criticisms that the legal aid system is inadequate and that many people are deprived of pursuing justified claims because of inadequate resources. There are certain areas, e.g. defamation where legal aid is not available.

Judicial review of legislation

As Britain has no written constitution judges cannot declare any law made by Parliament to be unconstitutional. As we saw in an earlier chapter Parliament is supreme. However, they can and do interpret legislation when there is some doubt as to the meaning of the wording in an Act of Parliament. For example, in one statute the words 'cats, dogs and other animals' were written. In this context do the words 'other animals' mean all other animals or only domestic animals? In this case the court ruled in favour of the latter interpretation and there is now an accepted rule that where general words follow particular words then the general words shall be deemed to be of the same category as the particular words.

If there is no ambiguity in the words then the court must interpret them literally even if this leads to an unfair result. However, in recent years courts have endeavoured to find alternative interpretations which produce a reasonable result. In the case of *Daymond* v *SW Water Authority* (1973) the House of Lords ruled that a water authority did not have the power to charge an owner or occupier of premises not connected to the main drainage for sewerage and sewage disposal services even though the Water Act 1973 contained words giving the authority 'power to fix, demand, take and recover such charges for the services performed and facilities provided as they think fit'. This decision was regarded as a great victory for the individual consumer against the large public authority.

Sometimes the judicial interpretation of an Act may mean that new legislation has to be introduced to correct the fault in the original legislation. An example of this was the House of Lords interpretation of the Race Relations Act 1968 in the case of the *Dockers Labour Club and Institute Ltd* v *Race Relations Board* (1974). As a result, a new Race Relations Act was introduced in 1976.

Judicial review of administrative acts

With the complexity of modern legislation it is impossible for the original Act of Parliament to cover all eventualities. Most acts therefore give the Minister power to make orders, regulations or rules which have the force of law. This is known as delegated legislation. Because of lack of time there is often very little parliamentary scrutiny of delegated legislation. Indeed some statutes, e.g. the Health and Safety at Work Act 1974, are really only enabling acts which lay down basic principles but the real 'meat' comes in the subsequent orders made by the Minister. It is important that these ministerial actions should be subject to legal checks. For this reason we have the doctrine of *ultra vires*.

A court may declare an action *ultra vires* if it can be shown that the Minister or civil servant has exceeded the powers given by Parliament and taken an unauthorised action or an authorised action in the wrong way. The doctrine of *ultra vires* also applies to local authorities and other public bodies created by statute. Anyone objecting to what is proposed or what has been done can apply for a High Court Order by the following:

- Prohibition Order preventing a Minister or public body from doing something.
- an Order of Certiorari to quash the decision of an authority which has already been made.

The aggrieved party may apply for a judicial review of a decision and ask the court to make a declaration of their rights and to state what the law is.

It is also possible for an individual to compel a Minister or statutory authority to take an action which it is statutorily obliged to do. An Order of Mandamus will compel an authority to carry out its duties (*see* Chapter 8).

Conclusion

The courts do their best to protect ordinary citizens from the abuse of administrative power. They have strongly resisted attempts in some legislation to exclude their review powers, but the courts are overstretched and litigation is expensive.

In Chapter 13 we shall examine the work of administrative tribunals in settling disputes between government and its citizens. We shall also look at the work of the Ombudsman.

Discussion questions

5   What is meant by 'natural justice'?
6   Do you think the ordinary citizen has adequate protection against the administrative actions of officials? If not, how would you improve the situation?

Written questions

7   You have been called to do jury service. Write a letter to the appropriate person asking to be excused from jury service giving valid reasons why you believe you should be excused.
8   You are stopped by the police when driving, breathalysed and found to be just over the limit. You have not been involved in an accident and have no previous motoring convictions. You are subsequently charged and plead guilty by letter. Write this letter and include a plea of mitigation as to why you should not be banned from driving.
9   Write an article for your local paper explaining how the small claims court procedure operates.
10 Write an article giving the arguments for and against the reintroduction of capital punishment. The concluding part of the article should give your own opinion with reasons.

12 Employment law and industrial relations

Employment law

In the 1960s and 1970s a series of Acts of Parliament laid down the statutory rights and duties of both employers and employees. This culminated in the Employment Protection (Consolidation) Act 1978. Since then, under the Conservative Government, subsequent legislation has modified the 1978 Act in some respects. The stated reason was to relieve the administrative burden on particularly small businesses but the result has been to reduce workers' rights in significant ways.

The 1978 Act only related to full-time workers defined as those working more than 16 hours a week or who have worked continuously for an employer for more than eight hours a week for at least five years. A recent government White Paper suggested that the 16 hours should be increased to 20 hours but this would be in direct conflict with EC proposals to give equal rights to all workers working more than eight hours a week. The 1978 Act does not apply to those classified as independent contractors.

Contract of employment

A contract of employment exists as soon as an employee proves his or her acceptance of an employer's terms and conditions of employment by starting work. Most larger firms, particularly in the public sector, do provide a full written contract of employment but there is no statutory requirement for this to be done, except in the case of a formal apprenticeship.

If a full contract is not provided the employer must, within 13 weeks of the employee starting work, give the employee a written statement which should cover the following points:

- the names of the employer and employee
- the date employment began and whether any previous employment counts as part of the employee's continuous period of employment
- the scale of remuneration and the intervals at which it is paid
- the hours of work, including a definition of normal working hours
- details relating to holiday entitlement and holiday pay
- provisions for sick pay
- details of pensions and pension schemes
- the length of notice of termination of employment which both the employer and employee must give
- the title of the job which the employee is employed to do.

In addition, except in the case of very small employers, details should be given of disciplinary rules and grievance procedures. Instead of giving all the above details the employer can refer the employee to an existing document which is readily available, e.g. a collective bargaining agreement or company rule book.

Implied terms

There are certain duties and responsibilities for both employers and employees which may not be written into the contract but will be implied by the courts in any dispute. For example, the employer has a duty to pay wages on time, to indemnify employees for any expenses or liability incurred in the proper performance of their duties and to take reasonable care of his employees at work (*see* later in this chapter).

The employee has a duty to obey any lawful orders given by his employer which are within the scope of his contract of employment; to exercise care and skill in the performance of his duties; to act reasonably and to act in good faith, e.g. he must not disclose confidential information to third parties.

Employee's statutory rights

These include:

- a right to maternity leave and re-engagement (see later)
- time off for ante-natal care
- reasonable time off for trade union duties (limited by the Employment Act 1989) and for public duties, e.g. councillor or JP
- a right to an itemised pay statement giving gross pay, deductions and net pay
- a right to a written statement on request giving reasons for dismissal providing that he has been employed continuously for over two years
- time off to look for alternative employment if already declared redundant
- a right to payment in periods when health and safety legislation require suspension from work
- limited guaranteed payments where no work is available, e.g. lay offs caused by external strikes, i.e. outside the place of work.

Termination of employment

Contracts of employment are normally ended either by notice or summary termination, i.e. on-the-spot dismissal. The period of notice that either side must give is usually stated in the contract but if not there are statutory minimum requirements. An employee who has been employed for more than four weeks must give at least one week's notice. An employer must give at least one week's notice to an employee who has been employed for up to two years and one additional week for each year of employment above two years to a maximum of 12 weeks.

Unfair dismissal

Any employee who has worked for an employer continuously for over two·years can, if he believes that he has been unfairly dismissed, either summarily or by notice, appeal to an industrial tribunal. Before the tribunal hearing is set, a conciliation officer from the Advisory, Conciliation and Arbitration Service (ACAS) will attempt to mediate (*see* Case Study 13). The tribunal will determine the reason for the dismissal and whether it falls into one of the categories which would constitute a fair dismissal. These include the capability or qualifications of the employee; his conduct; if he is redundant or if the employee could no longer work in that position, e.g. a lorry driver who loses his licence. The tribunal will also consider whether the correct procedures have been followed.

The Employment Act 1990 lays down that an employee cannot claim unfair dismissal if at the time of his dismissal he was engaging in unofficial industrial action. In the case of official strike action the employer can dismiss all his employees but cannot be selective if he wishes to avoid actions for unfair dismissal.

Certain dismissals are regarded as automatically unfair. For example, if a woman is dismissed solely because she is pregnant or an employee is dismissed because he joins or refuses to join a trade union. In the latter case the two-year rule does not apply.

An employee may claim unfair dismissal in certain circumstances even though he has technically not been dismissed. This is known as **constructive dismissal**. It applies where an employer's action is such as to be a significant breach of the employment contract, e.g. where an employer arbitrarily demotes an employee to a lower rank or a poorer paid position. The employee may refuse to accept this and resign and possibly still claim to have been unfairly dismissed.

Remedies

The tribunal, if it finds that the employee has been unfairly dismissed may order one of three remedies:

- re-instatement, i.e. the employee is given back his original job
- re-engagement, i.e. the employer is instructed to re-employ the dismissed employee at an equivalent rank and salary but not necessarily in the same job
- award damages which will consist of a basic award based on the employee's length of employment and a compensatory award to cover loss of earnings, pension rights, etc.

One of the purposes of the industrial tribunal procedure is to ensure good industrial relations so in most cases damages rather than re-instatement or re-engagement will normally be awarded.

Industrial tribunals

An industrial tribunal consists of three members appointed by the Secretary of State. The Chairman is legally qualified whilst the other two members are drawn from lists made in consultation with employers' organisations and trade unions. There is an appeal to the Employment Appeal Tribunal and from there to the Court of Appeal and House of Lords.

Redundancy

Redundancy occurs when an employee is dismissed because his employer has discontinued or intends to discontinue the business for which he was employed or because the need for his particular service has diminished or is expected to diminish. Employers who recognise an independent trade union have a statutory duty to consult with that trade union before redundancy is declared. If the employer fails to consult, an appeal can be made to an industrial tribunal which may order a protective award ordering him to continue to pay the employee's wages for a specified period.

Many large companies have their own redundancy schemes but the state scheme is a minimum award to which all employees made redundant are entitled. The amount of the award depends on the length of service and only applies to those who have worked continuously for more than two years. A person over the age of 65 is not entitled to a redundancy payment. Until the Employment Act 1990 came into force the rule was 65 for men and 60 for women but this has now been extended to 65 to conform with EC sex discrimination regulations. A person may be refused a redundancy payment if it can be shown that he was offered and refused reasonable alternative employment. When the redundancy scheme was originally introduced there was a redundancy fund and employers could claim back a percentage of their payments from the fund but this was finally abolished in the Employment Act 1990.

Discrimination

The Sex Discrimination Act 1975 made it unlawful for an employer to discriminate on sexual grounds in the appointment, training, treatment, promotion and dismissal of his employees. It applies to both men and women and also covers discrimination against a person on grounds of marital status. It also covers contract workers who may be self-employed. The Sex Discrimination Act 1986 brought British law in line with EC rules and it is now unlawful to discriminate with regard to retirement age.

There were some exceptions where the acts did not apply (e.g. Ministers of Religion) but the 1989 Employment Act reduced these categories considerably. It is now possible for women to work underground in the mines. There are still jobs which pregnant women are not allowed to do where there could be a danger to the unborn child.

There are two types of discrimination: direct and indirect. Direct discrimination is where an employer on the grounds of a woman's sex treats her less favourably than he treats a man. Indirect discrimination could take the form of placing a restriction on the work which, whilst not expressly mentioning sex or marital status, would in effect bar many or all of one sex or status from taking up the work. It would be up to the employer to prove that the restriction imposed was necessary.

Complaints of sex discrimination can be made to a tribunal which is empowered to award compensation if the case is proved. Alternatively, the complainant can ask the Equal Opportunities Commission to investigate the alleged discrimination. If it finds the case proved it can issue an order requiring the employer to discontinue the discrimination. The employer then has the right of appeal to the tribunal.

The Race Relations Act 1976 makes it unlawful to discriminate on grounds of colour, race or ethnic origins. It deals with both direct and indirect discrimination and relates to recruitment, terms of employment, opportunities for training and promotion, and dismissal. The remedies and procedures are the same as for sex discrimination. The Commission for Racial Equality has similar functions and powers to those of the Equal Opportunities Commission. A code of practice on racial equality in employment came into force in 1984.

Equal pay

The Equal Pay Act 1970 which came into effect in 1975 is aimed at preventing discrimination between men and women as regards their terms and conditions of employment. It only applies where a contractual relationship already exists between the complainant and his or her employer. The woman must be employed on like work with a man in the same employment or on 'work rated as equivalent' or on 'work of equal value'. There is a considerable amount of case law, sometimes conflicting, on what constitutes 'work of equal value'. European Community law also applies as Article 119 of the Treaty of Rome requires member states to maintain the principle of equal pay for equal work among the sexes. This has been extended by directives to include pay and conditions and to work of equal value.

By 1988 the average women's pay was about 74 per cent of men's pay. This was mainly because in many occupations such as the Civil Service and local government women occupied the lower grades and also a considerable proportion of women work part-time. A recent EC judgement seems to imply that to pay lower rates to part-time workers is itself discriminatory. Complaints concerning equal pay are dealt with by the normal tribunal machinery.

Maternity

There are three statutory rights relating to maternity:

- the right not to be dismissed because of pregnancy
- maternity pay
- the right to return to work after pregnancy.

Since 1987 the employer is responsible for paying maternity pay but recoups it from the Department of Social Security. How much the woman receives will depend on how long she has been employed before the qualifying date, i.e. the 15th week before the expected week of confinement. If she has been employed for more than two years she receives six weeks at 9/10 of her normal pay followed by 12 weeks at a lower rate.

To qualify for the right to be re-employed after pregnancy she must have been employed for at least two years up to the 11th week before confinement. She must inform her employer that she wishes to return after pregnancy and must return before 29 weeks after the birth, having given three weeks prior notice to the employer. If the employer has less than five employees the right to return does not apply providing the employer can show that it is not reasonable to re-employ her in her previous job and there is no suitable alternative employment available for her.

Health and safety

The Health and Safety at Work Act 1974 (HASWA) lays down a number of general duties to which both employers and employees must conform. These are:

1   It is an employer's duty to ensure so far as is reasonably practicable the health, safety and welfare at work of all his employees.
2   It is an employer's duty to conduct his undertaking in such a way that, so far as is practicable, non-employees are not exposed to risk.
3   A duty is imposed on a controller of premises made available to others, not his employees, to take measures to ensure that, as far as is reasonably practicable, the premises, entrances and exits are safe for those using the premises.
4   A duty is imposed on anyone who designs, manufactures, imports or supplies articles for use at work, so far as is reasonably practic-

able, that the article is safe and that adequate information on its use is supplied.

5 A duty is imposed on an employee to take reasonable care at work for the health and safety of himself and others who may be affected by his conduct at work and to co-operate with his employer to enable his employer to carry out his duties.

The act is drawn up in wide terms and the Minister has power to make regulations dealing with specific matters after consultation with the Health and Safety Commission. It is eventually hoped that the act will cover all health, safety and welfare matters but until it does previous legislation such as the Factories Act 1961 and the Offices, Shops and Railway Premises Act 1963 remain in force.

The duty of enforcing the act and previous legislation lies with the Health and Safety Executive who appoint a number of inspectors. Failure to comply with the act is a criminal offence punishable by a fine and in some cases imprisonment. The act applies to all persons at work, including the self-employed. Nothing in the act prevents an employee injured at work from taking a civil action against his employer and claiming damages.

Protection of wages and low pay

The Truck Acts of 1831 and 1896 ensured that manual workers must be paid in coins of the realm and restricted the deductions from pay that an employer could make, e.g. for bad workmanship. The Payment of Wages Act 1960 permitted cashless pay with the employee's written agreement but the agreement could be revoked at any time by a manual worker. These acts were repealed by the Wages Act 1986 and employers can now insist on cashless pay for all new employees.

The 1986 Act stated that the employer should not make deductions from an employee's pay unless:

- authorised by statute, e.g. income tax, National Insurance, attachment of earnings
- authorised by a provision in the contract of employment notified to the employee in writing or
- agreed by the employee in writing prior to making the deduction.

There are certain exceptions including previous overpayment or money deducted because of industrial action.

Where an agreed deduction is made, e.g. for a cash deficiency, it must not amount to more than ten per cent of gross pay for any particular pay day, although it could be carried forward over successive pay days until the whole deficiency has been met. There is no requirement that the deductions are fair and reasonable, only that it has been agreed in writing by the employee.

The Wages Act 1986 also gave the Minister the right by order to abolish any Wages Council. These had been established over the years in areas where trade union organisation was poor, e.g. in retailing and catering, and could set minimum pay levels in these industries. This conflicts with the open market economic policy of the Conservative Government and they have abolished some of the Wages Councils. In particular, they have raised the minimum age for Wage Council operations from 18 to 21. As a result there is no legal protection against low pay for anyone under 21. The Labour Party has announced that if it wins the general election of 1991–2 it will introduce a legally enforceable minimum wage. The trade union movement is divided in its attitude towards a statutory minimum wage. Those representing low paid workers tend to be in favour but others fear that employers will regard the minimum wage as the standard wage.

The trade unions

A brief history

In the early nineteenth century a combination of workers was regarded as a criminal conspiracy (e.g. Tolpuddle Martyrs) and it was not until 1871 that they were recognised at civil law. The 1871 Trade Union Act provided that a trade union was not illegal because it was in restraint of trade and that a registered trade union could own property and bring court actions in its registered name. Another Act of 1875 legalised peaceful picketing and declared that no action of a trade union was illegal unless it was also illegal if committed by an individual.

In the Taff Vale case in 1901 the House of Lords awarded damages against the union for the loss that its strike action had caused to the employer. This decision virtually made all strikes unlawful. In 1906 the new Liberal Government passed the Trade Disputes Act. This stated that trade unions were completely immune from actions in tort and that inducements to break employment contracts were not actionable. This immunity lasted until the Employment Act 1982, except for a brief period from 1971–4 when the ill-fated Industrial Relations Act was in force.

Trade unions may also engage in political activity and many are affiliated to the Labour Party. The Trade Union (Amendment) Act of 1913 permitted political activity providing it was approved by a majority of its members. A separate political fund had to be established and any individual member had the right to contract out of paying the political levy. The Trade Disputes and Trade Union Act of 1927 which closely followed the 1926 General Strike changed this to 'contracting in' whereby members who wished to pay the political levy had to expressly ask to do so. This act was repealed by the Labour Government in 1945 and 'contracting out' was restored. The Employment Acts of 1984 and 1988 provide that every union must hold a secret postal ballot of its members, subject to independent scrutiny, before a political fund can be established and this ballot must be repeated every ten years and there are certain limitations, e.g. preventing a union transferring money from its general fund to the political fund. Every member of the union must be informed of his right to 'contract out'. Most ballots which have been held under this procedure have shown a large majority in favour of a political fund and some unions which previously did not have one have now established a political fund, e.g. NALGO — see Case Study 12.

Trades Union Congress (TUC)

Most trade unions are affiliated to the TUC, an umbrella organisation representing the general interests of trade unionists in discussions with the government. It holds an annual conference which discusses resolutions put forward by individual unions and this provides an opportunity for media coverage of the trade union point of view.

Trade unions and the law

A trade union is defined by the Trade Union and Labour Relations Act 1974 as an organisation, wholly or mainly of workers, whose principal purposes include the regulation of relations between workers and employers or employers' associations. A large proportion of workers in this country are covered by collective bargaining agreements whilst some occupations have special institutionalised pay bargaining procedures such as Whitley Councils for civil servants and local government workers. Trade unions are not corporate bodies but they have the power to own property and make contracts.

We shall now proceed to examine the current law relating to trade unions under the following headings:

1 The closed shop
2 Internal union affairs
3 Industrial action
4 Secondary action
5 Unofficial action
6 Picketing

1 The closed shop

This was an agreement between an employer and one or more trade unions whereby all employees of the company were required to be a member of a trade union (or in some cases one particular trade union).

The 1980 Employment Act extended the permissible grounds for non-membership, created a conscientious objection clause and allowed any employees already in employment when the closed shop came into operation to opt out. The 1982 Employment Act declared that there must be a secret ballot of all employees every five years and in order to inaugurate or retain a closed shop 80 per cent of those entitled to vote or 85 per cent of those voting must approve. The 1988 Employment Act declared that if a person was dismissed for refusing to join a trade union then that was classified as an unfair dismissal whilst the 1990 Employment Act declared that it was unlawful to refuse employment to a person because he is or is not a member of a trade union. As a result the closed shop is now dead and remarkably has been killed off with very little resistance from the trade union movement.

2 Internal union affairs

The declared objective of the Conservative Government was to give more power to the individual union member. The Trade Union Act 1984 declares that every union must hold a secret postal ballot for the election of its General Secretary, President and Executive Committee. Such a ballot must be held at least every five years. Each candidate must be given full facilities to produce and circulate an election address. The government will provide the funds for holding such ballots. Several unions at first refused to accept government money but now most do. The 1988 Employment Act extended the right of individual members to take court action if they felt they had been unfairly disciplined by the union or if they believed union funds have been used in an unlawful way. It also established a Commissioner for the rights of trade union members to assist individual union members in dealing with such complaints.

3 Industrial action

Trade unions still have the right to call a strike or other forms of industrial action but in order to do so they must fulfil stringent conditions:

1 They must establish a trade dispute between the employer and his employees. A trade dispute can be about pay, conditions, disciplinary actions, dismissals, etc.
2 A ballot of all those affected by the proposed action must be held before the action is taken and the ballot must be subject to independent scrutiny. A vote by show of hands is now forbidden.
3 Voting papers must indicate who is authorised to call industrial action.

If these conditions are not met then the union's immunity is lifted and employers can sue. There are limits to the damages that can be obtained. However, employers may seek an injunction and if this is not obeyed the union will be in contempt of court. Then unlimited fines can be imposed and the union's property can be sequestrated. This device was used very effectively during the miners' strike which was called without a ballot.

4 Secondary action

The requirement that a trade dispute must be between an employer and his employees and the strengthening of this in the Employment Act 1990 means that virtually all secondary action is now unlawful, i.e. sympathy strikes or strikes against government policy.

5 Unofficial action

Unions have been made liable for the actions of their officials including shop stewards. If unofficial action is taken the union, to escape liability, must rapidly disassociate itself from the action and individually notify all those who may be taking part in it. The employers, of course, have the right to take legal action against those who unlawfully called the dispute.

6 Picketing

The 1980 Employment Act permits picketing in furtherance of a trade dispute by an individual at his place of work for the purpose of peacefully persuading any person to work or not to work. There is no statutory limit on the number of pickets but a Code of Practice on Picketing suggested a maximum of six at any one entrance. The 1986 Public Order Act gives the police rights to regulate numbers if they fear that serious disorder may occur.

Secondary picketing is unlawful because of the requirement that a person may only picket at his place of work.

Non-peaceful picketing is a normal criminal offence and may be dealt with by the police. The mass picketing used during the miners' strike can now be dealt with under the Public Order Act as it can be clearly shown that the intention is to intimidate others and the organisers are also subject to criminal sanctions.

Conclusions

The power of trade unions has been severely limited by a series of Acts of Parliament during the 1980s. For a number of reasons, including unemployment, the membership of trade unions has declined. If the Labour Party were to win the 1991–2 general election some of the powers may be restored although they have declared that they will not repeal the legislation dealing with strike ballots.

Employers' organisations

The Confederation of British Industries (CBI) and the various trade associations are used as a channel of communication to the government in expressing a collective view of employers on economic and industrial matters. The CBI, like the TUC, now holds an annual conference where issues of importance to employers are discussed and made known to the public and to the government.

Discussion question

1 Discuss the following cases and advise the complainant whether you think they have a complaint to put before an industrial tribunal:

(a) Miss A was half an hour late for work and was sacked on the spot by her employer. Her excuse was that she had had a 17th birthday party the night before and had overslept.

(b) Mr B, who had been employed by a company for five years, was instructed by his Foreman to sweep the factory floor. He refused and punched the Foreman on the nose. He was instantly dismissed.

(c) Mr C, whose normal working hours were 8 to 5, was told at 4 pm that he must work overtime that evening. He refused and when his employer insisted he walked out and told his employer to 'stuff his job'. When he returned to work the next morning he was refused admittance and told that as he had resigned there was no work for him.

(d) Mr D was told that his job had become redundant. He was offered an equivalent job in the company's second factory 25 miles away. He refused and then claimed redundancy pay.

(e) Mr E was appointed to a post working in a children's home. It was later revealed that he was a homosexual. He was then dismissed by the local authority. He had previously worked for the same local authority in another capacity for three years.

(f) Mrs F worked as a Cashier in a self-service petrol station. One evening a customer drove up, filled his car with petrol and drove off without paying. According to her contract of employment Mrs F was responsible for any cash or stock deficiency and the employer deducted the loss from her wages.

(g) Miss G was employed for three years as a University Lecturer. No complaints were made during this period about the quality of her work. When appointed she stated on her application form that she had an honours degree in Economics. After three years it was discovered that she was not a graduate and she was dismissed on the spot.

(h) Mr H was a long distance driver. He was instructed by his employer to make a journey which would have involved him exceeding the legally permitted driving hours. He refused and was then transferred to another job inside the firm which paid less.

Your assessment of the above cases should take into account the law as it stands at the moment. If appropriate refer to similar cases which have previously been discussed by industrial tribunals or the courts.

Written questions

2 Miss Jones has been appointed to the post outlined in the following advertisement. Draw up a suitable contract of employment for Miss Jones.

3 Mrs Smith aged 25 a divorced woman with a two-year-old child applied for the Receptionist post, as illustrated. She was an expert typist and had three years previous experience as a hotel receptionist. She was not interviewed and found out that the successful applicant had had no previous hotel experience. When she made further enquiries she was told that the post was only suitable for a single woman.

Write a report indicating whether you believe she has a case to take before a tribunal on the grounds of sex discrimination.

RECEPTIONIST REQUIRED
for 3-Star Hotel

Aged 20-30

Typing and previous hotel experience essential.
Good telephone manner important.
Shift duties including week-ends.
Accommodation available for single person.
Apply in writing to Manager, Blue Lion Hotel, High Street, Jonesville.

---

4 Miss Andrews is a 16-year-old trainee working in a large office. She recently suffered an injury when using the guillotine in the office. You are the trade union representative and you are to have a meeting with the employer about this accident.

Draw up a checklist of the questions that you wish to put to management referring where necessary to the appropriate legislation.

5 You are an Administrative Assistant in a large construction company. Seven days ago the workers on one of the building sites walked off the job and have subsequently refused to return to work. The workers belong to the Society of Building Workers and you have several times phoned the General Secretary but he has stated that it is an unofficial action and there is nothing that he can do. You have now learned that workers on two other sites belonging to your company have taken unofficial action in sympathy with the original strikers.

Write a report for your Managing Director referring to current trade union legislation and advise him what action, if any, the company can take.

CASE STUDY 12 National and Local Government Officers Association (NALGO)

Introduction

NALGO, the public services trade union, is the third largest TUC-affiliated body and the largest solely 'white-collar' union in the world. It represents more than 750 000 staff — professional, administrative, technical, supervisory and clerical — in local government, the NHS, higher education, new towns, and the electricity, gas, water and transport industries.

Objects

NALGO's objects are contained in the union's Constitution and Rules. Three main areas can be distinguished:

- helping **individual members** in all sorts of situations arising from their work, e.g. grading appeals, redundancy situations, re-organisations, unfair treatment, discipline and providing a range of other services including legal, financial, welfare and educational
- helping **groups of members**, e.g. salary negotiations and improvements in other conditions of service
- concern with **wider social and political issues** which affect members and their families.

Branch organisation

There are over 1200 branches based mainly on employer units. It is the branch that the member has to go first to present views, to get advice or to seek help with individual problems. The main functions of a branch are:

- to protect the interests of members
- to negotiate local improvements to national agreements
- to inform members about NALGO national policies and ensure that members' wishes are known
- to see that other NALGO services are available to members.

The branch meeting is the principal policy-making body at local level and all branch members are entitled to attend. The day-to-day management of the branch is conducted by a branch executive committee. In larger branches departmental stewards committees will form an important part of the branch structure.

District organisation

Every branch has representation on its district council, as indicated in Fig 12.1. The district council's functions are:

- a means of communication between branches and the national bodies in NALGO's policy making processes; the link is two-way, with information and instructions about national policies being passed down to branches via district councils, whilst branches are able to communicate their wishes and proposals for national action up to the relevant national bodies through the district
- to assist and advise the National Executive Council (NEC) and the national committees on general union policy.
- a regional assembly in policy making, bringing NALGO branches in one area together to decide what policies are best to meet particular needs and problems in their part of the country
- to ensure that the various services in the district have NALGO representation on the

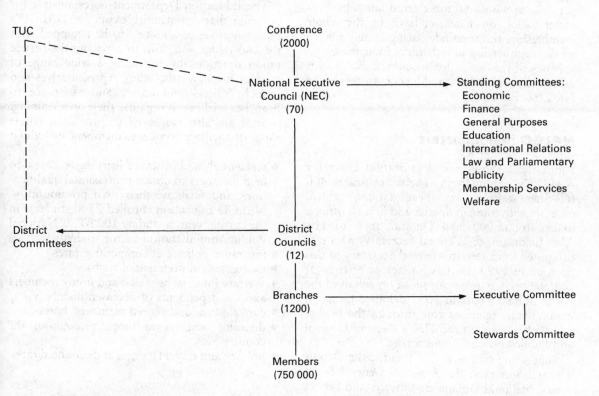

Fig 12.1 Organisation chart for NALGO committees

staff sides of regional/provincial negotiating bodies
- to oversee branch organisation, recruitment levels within the district, and to see that ancillary services are available locally.

National organisation

There are two major policy making bodies at national level — conference and the NEC. The conference is NALGO's 'Parliament' serving as the union's supreme policy making body and it meets for a week in June each year to direct the union's general policy. Over 2000 people attend the conference — every branch is entitled to one representative per 500 members. The NEC, the district councils and professional associations are also represented. Each representative should have been briefed by their branch before attending the conference and all are accountable to their branches when they return.

The NEC is responsible throughout the year for policy matters. It consists of about 70 persons, of whom 60 are elected annually by a secret ballot, on a district basis by the whole membership, the remainder being largely elected by the membership in individual industries.

Much of the detailed work at national level is delegated to specialist standing committees of the NEC (see Fig 12.1).

NALGO headquarters

Figure 12.2 shows the organisation chart for NALGO's headquarters. There are nearly 400 full-time staff at the headquarters, which, together with those in district and branch offices, makes around 900 in all. The staff are headed by Alan Jinkinson, the General Secretary, who was promoted from Deputy General Secretary to this position in 1990. He has a place as of right at conferences, where he can speak on behalf of the NEC; he takes part in NEC debates; he has a major public relations role through the media; and he has seats on the TUC's General Council and Public Service Committee.

Supporting him is David Prentis, the Deputy General Secretary, the Assistant General Secretaries, National Organising Officers and Service Conditions staff (providing professional advice on service conditions matters, preparing the detail and arguments in favour of claims for improvements in salaries and other conditions of service of NALGO members, as well as bringing professional expertise to the staff sides of national negotiating bodies). Further support is given by research staff, who provide information on a whole range of topics, such as current economic trends, pay movements in various sectors of the economy, health and safety, changing technology, equal rights, etc.

A publicity department keeps members informed about NALGO and current issues affecting their employment, controls recruitment efforts, and advises branches on local publicity and production of their own magazines. It produces NALGO's monthly newspaper *Public Service* which is distributed to all members and its weekly newssheet *NALGO News* sent to all stewards.

The legal department contains qualified solicitors able to give advice and support to members on legal issues and problems arising from their employment.

The Education Department is responsible for ensuring that opportunity exists for NALGO's representatives at all levels to be equipped with the knowledge and skills to carry out their trade union functions by providing a wide range of courses for stewards, safety representatives and branch officers and advice and assistance to branches wishing to organise their own training.

Staff are also employed to provide a whole range of ancillary services to members, including:

- residential and distance-learning courses to help members to obtain professional qualifications and facilitate their own promotion — NALGO Education enrolled 2500 students in the current year, including 100 BTEC National Public Administration Sector students
- insurance policies at competitive rates
- mortgages on preferential terms
- Welfare Fund to help sick and needy members and the dependents of deceased members
- convalescent and retired members' homes
- discount schemes in shops throughout the country
- holiday and travel facilities at discounted rates.

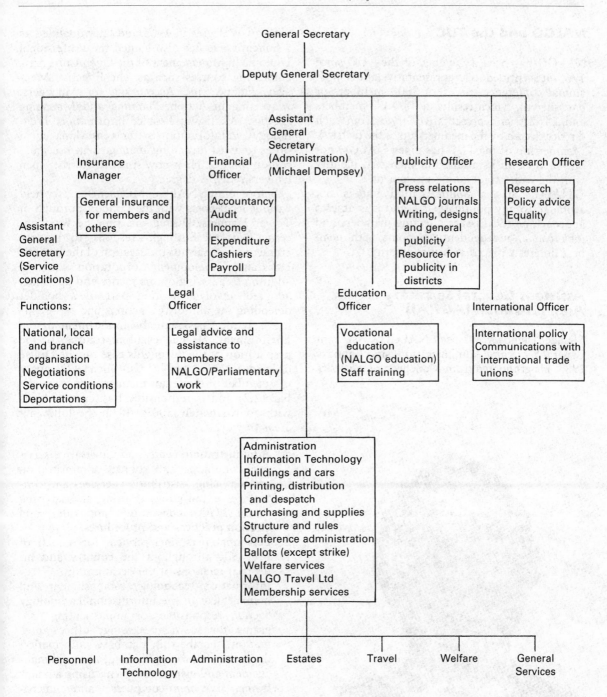

Fig 12.2 Organisation chart for NALGO's headquarters

NALGO and the TUC

NALGO has been a member of the TUC since 1965. It is entitled to a representative at the TUC annual conference for every 5000 members or part thereof, which results in 48 NEC members and 24 district representatives (two from each district elected by the membership of the district). Membership of the TUC has given NALGO not only a voice in its affairs but increased identity with the wider trade union movement.

NALGO has a political fund but is not affiliated to any political party and it is able to approach political issues affecting members and jobs from an independent viewpoint, with members' interests placed as a first priority.

Assistant General Secretary for Administration (AGS(A))

Michael Dempsey has been NALGO's Assistant General Secretary (Administration) since January 1985. He graduated from Manchester University

Fig 12.3 Michael Dempsey, Assistant General Secretary (Administration) of NALGO

with a law degree in 1965 and later qualified as a Solicitor. He has also gained the Professional Diploma in Management of the Open University, embracing courses such as The Effective Manager, Finance and Accounting for Managers, Marketing in Action, Planning and Managing Change, Managing People, Information Technology and Information Systems for Managers in order to assist him in his management roles and responsibilities. He is now studying for the Open University MBA degree.

Before joining NALGO Michael Dempsey held various legal posts with the London Borough of Tower Hamlets. During this time he was concerned with the Borough's response to the government proposals for the creation of the London Docklands Development Corporation which, in addition to advising on the tactics and approach adopted, involved writing part of a booklet defending the authority's actions and representing it at meetings with the Department of the Environment. He had eventual conduct of the preparation of the Borough's case for the House of Lords Enquiry. At NALGO Michael Dempsey is a member of the senior management team (*see* Fig 12.2) and is responsible for seven sections with approximately 300 staff, in the following areas of work:

1 **Administration:** central administrative services; committee and council administration and servicing; distribution services and conference organisation; drafting and advising on NALGO's constitution and rules; and election practices and procedures.
2 **Personnel:** personnel services for a staff of over 900 throughout the country and industrial relations of the organisation.
3 **Information technology:** establishment and management of the Information Technology Section responsible for implementing programs for word processing; office automation; membership database; information database; desktop publishing; financial management and insurance systems using a mainframe, a mini-computer and microcomputers.
4 **Estates:** management and purchase of buildings; headquarters maintenance; and the control of a 150 unit car fleet.
5 **General services:** purchasing and supplies; printing; and headquarters office services such as post and reception.

6 **Welfare:** administration of NALGO's Welfare Fund; and management of four convalescent homes and two old people's homes.
7 **Travel:** management of NALGO Travel Ltd, a hotel and a holiday centre.

Michael Dempsey is a member of a Working Party of the TUC which negotiated the 'Union-law' scheme with the Law Society. The principal feature of this scheme is the adherence by Solicitors to a code of practice embodying professional standards. He has also been appointed by the Lord Chancellor as a Member of the Council on Tribunals.

The principal duties and responsibilities for the post of AGS(A) are:

- responsibility, under the general direction of the General Secretary/Deputy General Secretary, for the overall administrative functions relating to the union and its ancillaries
- responsibility, on behalf of the General Secretary, for the administrative functions relating to the NALGO annual conference; the NEC and its staff (excluding major aspects of staff policy, which remains with the General Secretary)
- to co-ordinate the functioning of all departments and sections at headquarters and district offices in the administrative aspects of their work
- responsibility for the servicing of the General Purposes, Welfare and Membership Services Committees and of the Staff Whitley Council, together with appropriate *ad hoc* working parties.
- management of the seven sections which form the Administration and General Services Department.

Office services

Michael Dempsey's main difficulty in administering office services throughout an organisation as large and complex as NALGO is in controlling and maintaining standards across the various departmental and district boundaries of the organisation. He has recently appointed a new Head of Administration to tackle the problem of integrating administrative activities in the corporate interest. The new head has been asked to prepare for the Assistant General Secretary and the NEC, in full consultation with the staff concerned, proposals for the organisation of an administration section containing the following services:

1 Central Committee Services, and in consultation with the Personnel Officer, service to the Staff Whitley Council and its committees; in addition, service to the National Retired Members' Committee and conference and to retired members.
2 Any typing services which are recommended for central provision.
3 Headquarters distribution services, including:

- despatch
- addressing
- postal services
- messenger services

together with any other services where benefit might be obtained by rationalisation.

Administrative and clerical posts

The following are examples of the duties and responsibilities of three of the staff employed in the General Secretary's Department at NALGO:

1 Administrative Assistant
- assists with Rules Revisions Sub-Committee work, including preparation of agenda, minutes and executive action
- assists with the National Women's Rights Committee and support work
- checks branch rule amendments and maintenance of filing system; liaison with the Service Conditions Department
- assists with work related to appeals panels, including expulsions and suspensions
- administers the system concerned with the transfer of members between branches; liaison with the Service Conditions Department
- registers new branches and passes appropriate information to the Service Conditions Department, Finance Department and District Organisation Officers.

2 Administrative Secretary
- controls the office of the AGS(A), dealing with work arising as the postholder thinks appropriate, in consultation with the AGS(A)
- deals with incoming and outgoing correspondence, as required, including drafting and despatching replies to correspondence
- arranges for dictation and word processing to be undertaken, either directly or by the use of the typing pool
- deals with telephone enquiries and initiates work on the telephone as required
- maintains and enhances the filing system and controls the diary of the AGS(A)
- deals with administrative work relating to meetings and conferences.
- operates the Claire Call Management System, analysing (in conjunction with Information Technology Staff) the information produced and reporting to the AGS(A) any incidence of over or under utilisation of resources on the telephone system
- assists at annual conference, as required.

3 Clerk
- filing
- photocopying
- routine administration of a circular system to branches covering members who have been disciplined
- routine telephone enquiries
- daily headquarters mail opening
- assists with despatch from General Secretary
- arranges Appeals Panel hearings
- despatches standard letters in disciplinary cases and makes up new files
- collates and despatches National Women's Rights Committee agendas and other material
- maintains register to show progress of appeals through the system.

Elections

Michael Dempsey and his staff are particularly busy when postal ballots have to be organised for elections. The following are some of the tasks which have to be undertaken for an election:

- regulations for the acceptance of nominations are published

- forms for nominations are printed and members are invited to apply from districts with their election addresses
- ballot forms and election addresses are printed and distributed to individual members
- a telephone 'helpline' is set up for people who did not receive their ballot papers
- ballot papers are returned to a scrutineer for the votes to be counted
- the election results are notified to members in the monthly newspaper *Public Service*.

Budgetary control

Individual managers have responsibility for their own department's budgets and these are prepared on a committee basis within an allocation decided by the Finance Committee. The major difficulty which is experienced by managers in controlling their budgets is the lack of information readily available concerning current spending levels but steps are currently in hand to set up a system which will provide them with this information.

STUDENT ACTIVITIES FOR INDIVIDUALS

1 Prepare a leaflet for new employees outlining the role of NALGO (or another trade union) and stating how to join; the role of its local branch and how the views of members are made known to the national council; the union's role in negotiating pay and conditions and the facilities it offers to members.
2 In a memo to the Assistant General Secretary explain how you consider a new computerised budgetary control system should be organised and how it might affect the decisions of the Finance Committee and the performance of Managers.
3 Draw the administrative organisation chart for NALGO (Fig 12.2) and indicate examples of Michael Dempsey's functional, line, staff and lateral relationships.
4 Construct a job description and a personnel specification for one of the administrative or clerical posts in the General Secretary's Department of NALGO.
5 Draw up a checklist which Michael Dempsey's staff could use for organising NALGO's Annual Conference.

1 Examine a recent submission by a trade union relating to wages and conditions, prepare arguments for and against and role play a wage bargaining session.
2 Discuss:
(a) the effects of TUC membership on a trade union, such as NALGO
(b) the reasons for the growth of white-collar trade unionism
(c) the problems of 'administering office services throughout an organisation as large and complex as NALGO'. Would decentralisation of some functions prove to be beneficial and, if so, which functions would you suggest and how would you endeavour to maintain standards in them throughout the organisation?
(d) the means by which the Administrative Assistant could liaise with the Service Conditions Department, Finance Department and District Organisation Officers
(e) the role of the National Women's Rights Committee. Are women given equal opportunities in your own organisation? If not, why do you think they lack such opportunities?
(f) why you think public service manual workers are generally excluded from NALGO? What advantages and disadvantages would be gained if NALGO and NUPE were to form a joint union?

CASE STUDY 13 Advisory, Conciliation and Arbitration Service (ACAS)

During our visit to the London and South East Regional Office of ACAS we met Gordon Ifill, an Administrative Officer dealing with public enquiries. A graduate in chemistry from the City of London Polytechnic, Gordon joined ACAS three years ago, first of all working in its administrative support division and later at the enquiry point. The internal organisation of ACAS and Gordon's position in the regional office is given in Fig 12.5.

The role and services of ACAS

ACAS is an independent body charged with the duty of promoting the improvement of industrial relations. It seeks to discharge this responsibility through the voluntary co-operation of employers, employees and their representatives and it has no powers of compulsion. Its approach in all matters is impartial and confidential. The services it provides are free.

ACAS is directed by a council consisting of a Chairman and nine members — three nominated by the Confederation of British Industry, three by the TUC and three independent members.

Fig 12.4 Gordon Ifill, Administrative Officer at ACAS

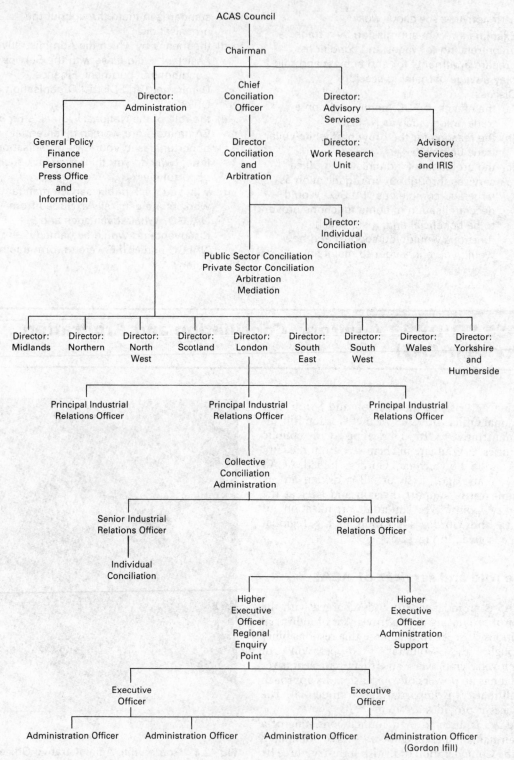

Fig 12.5 Organisation chart for ACAS

Advice and information is available to everyone concerned with employment — employers, employees and their representatives — in organisations of all sizes in every sector of commerce and industry on matters such as:

- management of change
- communications, consultation and participation at work
- personnel policies and manpower planning
- pay systems, productivity and related matters
- job evaluation and equal pay
- negotiating arrangements
- absence and labour turnover
- job design and work organisation
- introduction and employment implications of new technology
- motivation, morale and stress at work
- trade union recognition
- disciplinary, grievance and disputes procedures
- industrial relations and employment legislation
- training in industrial relations.

Advisers will, where practicable, seek to secure the involvement of employees and their trade unions together with management in a joint examination of their employment and industrial relations problems.

Industrial stoppages

The number of days lost in industrial disputes has declined rapidly in the 1980s. The following are the number of working days lost through stoppages for the period 1983 to 1988:

1983	3 754 000
1984	27 135 000
1985	6 402 000
1986	1 920 000
1987	3 546 000
1988	3 702 000

(Source: *HMSO Annual Digest of Statistics*)

Conciliation in trade disputes

Conciliation is a means of enabling the parties in a dispute to reach their own agreements through discussion and negotiation. Conciliation is voluntary. Agreements are reached by the joint decision of both parties. ACAS Conciliators have no power to impose, or even recommend, settlements.

Arbitration services

An independent arbitrator or board of arbitrators examines the case for each side and makes an award. Arbitration awards are not legally binding but since arbitration is chosen voluntarily by both parties as a means of settlement such awards are binding in honour. Before seeking arbitration efforts should normally be made to settle a dispute by conciliation.

Mediation

ACAS may be involved in appointing a mediator. For example, the parties to a dispute may ask for the help of an independent third party to mediate and make recommendations for a settlement or to suggest a basis for further discussion.

Conciliation in individual cases of complaint

ACAS has a duty to promote a voluntary settlement of certain complaints from individuals arising from alleged unfair dismissal and other infringements of individual rights under the Employment Protection (Consolidation) Act, the Equal Pay Act, the Sex Discrimination Acts, the Race Relations Act, the various Employment Acts, Transfer of Undertakings Regulations and the Wages Act 1986.

Procedure for seeking help from ACAS

Requests for assistance should be made by letter or telephone to the local ACAS regional office. Employers, employers' associations, trade unions or individuals can approach ACAS separately or jointly. If the problem is a collective dispute the employer and union concerned may approach ACAS jointly or the individual parties may make separate approaches. Shop stewards and workers' representatives involved should seek the advice of their full-time union official in the first instance. Before considering requests for conciliation, arbitration or mediation ACAS takes account of any disputes procedure agreed between employers and unions and whether it has been fully used. Individuals with a complaint in respect of the following matters should complete a form of complaint and send it to the Central Office of Industrial Tribunals:

- unfair dismissal
- equal pay
- sex discrimination
- racial discrimination
- guarantee payments
- suspension on medical grounds
- maternity grants
- time off for ante-natal care
- time off for public duties and for trade union membership activities
- time off in the event of redundancy to look for work or arrange for training
- written statement of reasons for dismissal
- itemised pay statements
- certain matters concerning redundancy
- trade union membership and activities (action short of dismissal)
- exclusion or expulsion from trade union membership
- certain matters concerning the transfer of undertakings.
- certain matters regarding unlawful deduction from pay.

The forms of complaint and explanatory leaflets are available at job centres, local employment offices, unemployment benefit offices and from some trade unions. On receipt of the form the Central Office of Industrial Tribunals will send a copy to ACAS and a conciliation officer will try to settle the complaint without the need for a tribunal hearing.

Publications

ACAS publishes a wide range of information leaflets, advisory handbooks and booklets, codes of practice, discussion papers and occasional papers to provide information on all aspects of its work.

Enquiry point

Gordon Ifill's primary task is to act as a helpful and efficient point of contact between the public and other interested parties to provide advice on ACAS services. Gordon and his colleagues at the regional public enquiry point answer some 84 000 enquiries every year mainly over the telephone but some in writing and some in person when people call at the office. The staff have to be prepared for the unpredictable nature of the enquiries; some are simple with clear-cut solutions but others involve far-reaching industrial relations issues. A call queuing system is in operation which ensures that calls are answered in strict rotation. Members of the ACAS staff are sworn to secrecy by the signing of a declaration under the Official Secrets Act. The service provided is confidential and impartial. No information can be divulged to others and no attempt is made to identify the names of callers.

Typical enquiries received at the enquiry point are:

1 An employer telephones concerning an employee who has been employed for two years and drinks alcohol at work. What steps can be taken to discipline or dismiss the employee?
2 An employee complains that his employer intends to pay his wages by credit transfer. The employee has received his wages in cash for 30 years and cannot see why he should have to change now.
3 An employee asks if there is a statutory right for the length of holidays and amount of holiday pay.
4 An employer wishes to know if there is a limit to the amount of time which an employee can take off for trade union duties. One of their employees is away from work for at least five hours every week and it severely disrupts the work schedule.
5 An employee telephones to ask if they are entitled to receive sick pay when they are ill.
6 An employee seeks advice concerning the job she is being required to do to infill for another employee who is on maternity leave. She considers that her job is less favourable than the job undertaken by the absent employee.

Correspondence

Gordon replies to letters of enquiry either by writing them in longhand for typing or simply selecting standard paragraphs from an index of commonly-used paragraphs for the secretarial staff to call up on their word processors and print them out automatically in letter form. The following is an example of a standard paragraph used for this purpose:

An employee who has the necessary qualifying period may ask the employer for a written statement of the reasons for dismissal. If the employer refuses or fails to provide a written statement, and the employee considers that the refusal or failure is unreasonable, the employee may complain to an industrial tribunal. A complaint may also be made by an employee, if given a statement which he or she considers to be inadequate or untrue, by completing form IT1 available from the local job centre, employment office or unemployment benefit office. I have enclosed leaflet No 14 'Rights to notice and reasons for dismissal' and refer you to page 9.

The staff at the enquiry point have to be well informed about the latest developments and changes in all aspects of employment law and personnel practice. They attend weekly departmental meetings to discuss developments in case law; read cases reported in the media (an Administrative Assistant has responsibility for monitoring all media reports) and they receive the in-house publication *ACAS News* which is a useful source of information for staff.

1 Assume that you are working at the Regional Public Enquiry Point at ACAS. What would you say in reply to each of the typical enquiries on p. 168?
2 Prepare standard paragraphs which could be used on the word processing system at ACAS for replying to letters on the following matters:
(a) equal pay

(b) time off in the event of redundancy to look for work or arrange for training
(c) contracts of employment.
3 The following are the numbers of individual conciliation cases received and analysed by the London and South East regions of ACAS in a recent year:

	London	South East
Unfair dismissal	9 727	6 335
Equal Pay Act	34	69
Sex Discrimination Act	173	163
Race Relations Act	400	100
Other employment protection provisions	650	571

Prepare suitable diagrams to illustrate this data for a brochure showing the percentages for each type of case.
4 Students each study different matters from the list of those dealt with by ACAS (p. 168) and present their findings to the class in five minute talks.

STUDENT ACTIVITIES FOR GROUP WORK

1 Prepare a leaflet to be issued to new employees setting out the basic employment rights for staff. Each group should prepare different topics selected from the list relating to individual complaints given on p. 168.
2 Visit an industrial tribunal and prepare a report on a case heard giving the arguments for and against and the decision reached.
3 Discuss the introduction and employment implications of new technology, e.g. the computerisation of an office procedure in one of your local organisations.
4 At present ACAS has no powers of compulsion. Discuss whether you think it should have greater statutory powers when dealing with industrial disputes.
5 Refer to the statistics relating to industrial stoppages on p. 167 and (a) suggest why there was a substantial increase in 1984 and (b) explain why the legislation introduced since 1980 has been instrumental in reducing the number of strikes and stoppages.

13 Accountability

Introduction

In theory the government (the executive) is responsible for its actions to the people through the democratically elected Parliament. As we have seen in previous chapters this may at times be a myth rather than a reality. To exercise effective control, Parliament, as the representatives of the people, must know what the government is doing. It is often claimed that British government is one of the most secretive of all the democratic nations. For example, the decision to make the 'H' bomb and the radiation leak at Winfrith were withheld from Parliament — and indeed from many members of the government — for many years.

The 30 year rule

Decisions and minutes of Cabinet meetings are kept secret for 30 years whilst some decisions are not even revealed then. This rule has been partially breached by the publication of the diaries of former Cabinet Ministers, e.g. Richard Crossman, Barbara Castle and Tony Benn. In 1975 the Attorney General sought an injunction to prevent the publication of the first volume of the Crossman Diaries. This was refused by the courts. The Prime Minister then appointed a Committee of Privy Councillors under the chairmanship of Lord Radcliffe to look into the matter. They recommended that ministerial authors should be precluded for 15 years from publishing information in the following categories:

1 The author must not reveal anything that contravenes the requirements of national security operative at the time of the proposed publication.
2 He or she must not make disclosures that would be injurious to his or her country's relations with other nations.
3 He or she must not publish information destructive of the confidential relationship upon which the system of government is based, i.e. relationship between Ministers and advisers in the Civil Service or outside bodies. New legislation was not proposed but it should be left to the former Minister as an obligation of honour. Any manuscript must also be submitted to the Secretary of the Cabinet before publication. Civil servants and serving and former military officers are required to submit manuscripts for security vetting.

Both the Castle and Benn Diaries seem to have breached recommendation (3) of the Radcliffe Report whilst recent revelations by a former diplomat breached recommendation (2) and caused problems between Britain and Saudi Arabia.

The Wright case

Publication of the book *Spycatcher* by Peter Wright, a former member of the security services, caused a furore. The government made determined efforts to prevent its publication either in this or other countries. Injunctions were served on newspapers to prevent them from publishing extracts. The government took the view that no member or ex-member of the security services should ever be allowed to reveal information obtained in the course of his or her duties.

Discussion question

1 Do you think the British government was right to try to prevent publication of the book *Spycatcher*?

Official Secrets Act 1911

This act formed the basis of British secrecy legislation for nearly 80 years. Section 1 dealt with espionage and was generally accepted but there was considerable criticism of Section 2 which was all-embracing and in effect says that any crown servant who communicates any information obtained in the course of his duties to an unauthorised person is guilty of a criminal offence. It follows that, in theory, a civil servant who reveals the colour of his Minister's carpet could be guilty of an offence. Section 2 was often criticised by the Courts and the Franks Committee, set up in 1972, said it should be replaced on the grounds that 'a government which operates in greater secrecy than the effective conduct of its proper function requires . . . will lose the trust of the people'.

In 1984 Sarah Tisdall, a junior civil servant, was prosecuted under the act for sending information about the arrival of Cruise Missiles in Britain to a national newspaper. She was found guilty and sentenced to six months imprisonment. However, in 1985 Clive Ponting, a civil servant at the Ministry of Defence, sent information about the Falklands War to an MP. He was charged under the Official Secrets Act and in his defence argued that an MP was a proper person to whom information could be disclosed. Despite the trial Judge's rejection of this argument, he was acquitted by the jury (*see also* Chapter 4).

Clearly the days of Section 2 were numbered and the Official Secrets Act 1989 replaced the discredited Section 2 of the 1911 Act. It narrowed the range of material that it is a criminal offence to reveal, making special reference to security matters, defence, international relations, crime and special investigations. It made it clear that if a person or a newspaper to whom the information was revealed then published it they would also be guilty of an offence. There was no 'public interest' defence.

Access to official records

Should individuals have access to their own records held by public authorities? The main argument for access is that individuals have a right to know what official files say about them. They then have the opportunity to correct any errors which could cause them problems at a later date. The argument against is that doctors, teachers, social workers, etc. will be reluctant to put frank assessments on paper if they know that their clients have access to their files.

The Data Protection Act 1984 provides that any computer system which processes personal, name-linked data (except those concerned with national security and crime investigation) has to be registered and citizens have a right of access to the records held on them. Manual records are, however, excluded from this provision.

The Access to Personal Files Act 1987, Access to Medical Reports Act 1988 and the Access to Health Records Act 1990 allow the public more access to records. Education and social service departments do allow access by individuals but they usually require that a period of notice be given. This gives time for sensitive material to be removed from the file.

Some countries allow much greater access to individual records than has been the custom in Britain. For example, in some Scandinavian countries every person's tax return is open for public inspection.

Discussion question

2 Do you think individuals should have open access to the files on them (or their children) kept by public authorities?

Freedom of Information Act

The controversy over secrecy has led to a demand for Britain to have a Freedom of Information Act similar to that existing in the USA and other countries. In 1978 the Labour Government announced that it intended to introduce such legislation but before it could do so it was defeated in the 1979 general election. The Westland Affair in 1986 and several other leaks of official information have revived the demand. Less secrecy would mean less leaks. It would be better if government information was presumed open unless judged otherwise rather than presumed secret unless judged otherwise, as at present.

Individual rights

Most democratic countries have a Bill of Rights guaranteeing certain basic individual rights such as freedom of speech, freedom of religion, etc. It is usually either incorporated in a written constitution or published as a separate document associated with it. There is then some form of Supreme Court which has the power to declare invalid any legislation which infringes these basic rights.

Britain has no written constitution and no Supreme Court. Our judges can only interpret legislation and have no power to declare it invalid. Parliament is held to be supreme. Those in favour of an entrenched Bill of Rights in Britain argue that the power of the executive has grown too strong and must be curbed. For example, if there had been an entrenched right to freedom of assembly then the government would have been unable to ban workers at GCHQ Cheltenham from belonging to a trade union. Those opposed to a Bill of Rights argue that most of these decisions are political in nature and it would be wrong to take power away from Parliament and pass it into the hands of unelected judges.

Britain is a signatory to the European Convention of Human Rights. Individuals can petition the European Court of Human Rights in Strasbourg and a number of British citizens have done so in recent years. Britain has been found in breach of the Convention on several occasions, e.g. immigration rules, caning in schools. The British Government is bound by international law to recognise these judgements and has on occasions introduced new legislation, e.g. the Mental Health Amendment Act 1982, to conform to its rulings.

One possible compromise would be to incorporate the European Convention on Human Rights into British law. We would then have an enforceable statement of individual rights defining the relationship between state power and individual freedom.

Redress of grievances

We have seen in Chapter 11 how administrative actions can be challenged in the courts but litigation is expensive and often beyond the reach of the ordinary citizen. Alternative methods have had to be devised to settle disputes between government and members of the public.

Planning legislation has provided for appeals by individuals against planning decisions of local authorities. In some cases a public enquiry will be held, conducted by an Inspector appointed by the Secretary of State for the Environment. The Inspector reports to the Minister who may accept or reject his recommendations. Disputes between officials and members of the public may also be settled by administrative tribunals. These operate as informal courts and operate on the basis of fairness and impartiality. Examples include social security and industrial injuries tribunals. There is usually an appeal procedure to the High Court. Tribunals may also settle disputes between individuals, e.g. rent tribunals in landlord and tenant legislation.

Ombudsman

In 1967 the office of Parliamentary Commissioner for Administration (PCA) was established to investigate complaints of maladministration by government departments. He was appointed by the crown, his salary paid out of the Consolidated Fund and he reports each year to Parliament.

Complaints to the PCA must be channelled through an MP who, with the consent of the complainant, forwards the complaint to the Commissioner. He then decides whether or not the complaint falls within his jurisdiction. If he decides to investigate the complaint he has the power to call for all relevant papers and to interview any officials involved. He issues a report and may recommend an *ex gratia* payment to be made to the complainant if he has suffered a financial loss. In other cases an apology will be sufficient. It must be stressed, however, that he can only investigate allegations of maladministration. He cannot challenge the legislation itself.

In 1973 NHS Commissioners were established to investigate complaints of maladministration in the NHS. Complainants have direct access to them but they will only investigate if they are satisfied that the health authority has had a reasonable opportunity to investigate the complaint and make a reply. They have no power to investigate complaints about the clinical judgement of doctors and other staff. This is a weakness in the system, to which the Commissioners have referred in their annual report.

In 1974 The Commission for Local Administration was set up to investigate complaints of maladministration by local (and certain other) authorities. There are three Local Commissioners, known as Local Ombudsmen, each covering a particular part of the country.

Before taking a complaint to the Local Ombudsman, complainants should give the local authority an opportunity to investigate their complaint and also approach their local Councillor. If the Local Ombudsman finds the complaint justified he or she issues a report suggesting remedies for the grievance. This must be considered by the local authority concerned but they cannot be compelled to accept the recommendations.

None of the Commissioners has powers to investigate complaints against the nationalised industries. Most of them do have their own consumer councils but these have not proved an effective method of dealing with complaints. Many people believe that the powers of the various Ombudsmen need to be widened and this view was endorsed by the Widdicombe Report in 1986.

Discussion question

3   Do you think the Local Ombudsman should have the power to compel a local authority to take appropriate action when maladministration has been proved?

Financial accountability

The Comptroller and Auditor General supported by the National Audit Office, as referred to in Chapter 5, monitors national government expenditure, whilst in the case of local government expenditure this task is undertaken by the Audit Commission which was mentioned in Chapter 8 and is the subject of Case Study 14.

Complaints against the police

Another area of controversy is how to deal with complaints against the police. Until recently, complaints were investigated by the police themselves under the supervision of the Chief Constable. This still applies to a large number of minor complaints. However, it was felt that with regard to more serious complaints the public could only be re-assured if an independent investigation machinery was introduced. The Police and Criminal Evidence Act 1984 set up a Police Complaints Authority consisting of 14 lay members appointed by the Home Secretary to supervise police investigations into more serious complaints defined as those involving death or serious injury. The Authority has investigating officers to assist the police and issues a statement saying that the investigations have been held in a proper manner. It has the power to overrule the Chief Constable as to whether disciplinary action should be taken.

If a criminal offence is involved the papers are sent to the Director of Public Prosecutions who decides whether or not to prosecute. The Chief Constable can institute internal disciplinary proceedings and penalties may include dismissal, reduced rank, fine, reprimand or caution.

There is still some public concern about the way investigations into complaints are carried out and some organisations, notably the National Council for Civil Liberties, have called for a completely independent complaints procedure and an end to the police investigating complaints against themselves.

Discussion questions

4   How do you think complaints against the police should be handled?
5   Discuss which of the following complaints would be eligible for investigation by one of the Ombudsmen (national, health service or local). In each case say which is the relevant Ombudsman and suggest what action you would advise for those complaints over which they have no jurisdiction.
   (a) A delay in making payments for housing benefits.

(b) A taxpayer complaining that he had been unfairly charged interest on income tax which had been paid late through no fault of his.

(c) An excessive amount set by a district council for its community charge.

(d) A patient attending the Casualty Department of his local hospital having to wait three hours before being seen by a doctor.

(e) A householder complaining that she had been overcharged on her electricity bill.

(f) A youth complaining that the police assaulted him in the local police station.

(g) A patient claiming that a hospital surgeon had removed her appendix unnecessarily.

(h) The refusal to grant an attendance allowance to a sick relative.

6 Should the right to silence for defendants in criminal trials be maintained?

Written questions

7 List the basic freedoms that could be included in a British Bill of Rights.

8 Find out details of the US Freedom of Information Act. State, with reasons, whether you think it provides a safeguard against corruption. Would a Watergate-type scandal in Britain ever be uncovered?

9 A friend has asked for your assistance in taking up a complaint with the Local Ombudsman concerning the county council's refusal, after appeal, to allow his daughter, Joanne Barker, to attend the school of their choice — the Francis Cross Comprehensive School. Your friend maintains that insufficient time was allowed by the Appeals Committee to hear his case. The matter has been raised with Mrs M G Brown, the local County Councillor, but she was unable to persuade the Education Officer to review the case. Write a letter for your friend to send to the Local Ombudsman.

10 Examine in detail any case brought by a British citizen before the European Court of Human Rights. What action, if any, did the British Government take as a result of the court decision?

CASE STUDY 14 The Audit Commission

Case study situation

Patricia Church is the Administration Manager at the London headquarters of the Audit Commission. She joined John Banham (Director of the CBI), the first Controller of the Audit Commission, when it was formed in 1983. The Audit Commission was established by the Local Government Finance Act of 1982 to bring local authority auditing in England and Wales under the control of a single independent body. The Audit Commission should not be confused with the National Audit Office, formerly the Exchequer and Audit Department, which is the public auditor for central government.

Patricia Church, having gained GCE 'O' Levels and RSA Shorthand and Typewriting qualifications at a grammar school, began her career as a Secretary at the London Borough of Islington.

Further career progression came from employment within marketing, manufacturing and entrepreneurial private companies which, combined with the knowledge gained from various management courses, developed her administrative skills and experience.

The organisation and role of the Audit Commission

The Audit Commission has a Chairman, Deputy Chairman and 15 members drawn from — but not representing — a wide range of interests including industry, local government, the accountancy profession and the trade unions. Members are appointed by the Secretary of State for the Environment and the Secretary of State for Wales. The Chief Executive, who has the title of Controller of Audit, reports to the Commission and is appointed by them, although this is subject to ministerial approval. Howard Davies, the current Controller, was appointed in March 1987 to succeed John Banham. The organisation structure of the Audit Commission is illustrated in Fig 13.2. The headquarters operates from two sites: one in London and the other in Bristol. London is concerned with policy-making and the special studies, whereas Bristol undertakes finance, personnel, computing and serves as the headquarters for the District Auditors. The Commission is required to be self-financing with its income coming almost entirely from the fees charged to local government for audit work. It receives no government grant or subsidy. The Commission's main duties are to appoint Auditors to all local authorities in England and Wales and to promote studies to encourage economy, efficiency and effectiveness in local

Fig 13.1 Patricia Church, Administration Manager of the Audit Commission

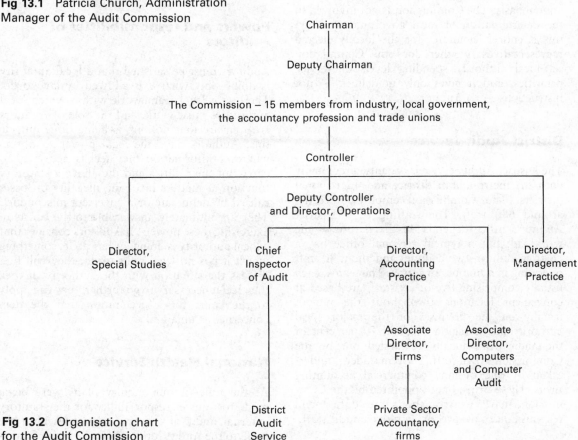

Fig 13.2 Organisation chart for the Audit Commission

government. The Commission and its auditors have two major roles:

1 They must ensure that local authorities are spending money and reporting their financial situation in accordance with the law, and that there are safeguards against fraud and corruption.
2 They seek to encourage the authorities to help themselves by showing how services can be provided as cost effectively as possible.

Neither the Commission nor its Auditors can force local authorities to save money — local authorities are responsible to their local electors for how money is spent and for assessing local needs and priorities. However, the Commission and its Auditors can, and do, suggest ways in which value for money can be increased. In the first six years of its operation, the Commission has identified opportunities for value improvement totalling more than £900 million on an annual basis. The Commission is not involved in the determination of local government policy; this is entirely a matter for the locally elected representatives. Neither does the Commission set local authority spending levels or service priorities, and it gives only guidelines — not instructions — to Auditors.

District Audit Service

The District Audit Service is organised regionally with the metropolitan district and 12 regional districts. The Commission employs, directly, around 680 staff. The staffing of a District Auditor's office depends on the nature of the workload, but a typical regional office has a District Auditor, two deputies and about 40 staff operating in a number of teams. The teams, each usually comprising five or six staff, are based at convenient locations throughout the region, usually on the premises of the major local authority in the region. Around 70 per cent of the audit work locally is carried out by the Commission's own staff. The remainder is undertaken by one of nine commercial accounting firms. These firms, once appointed by the Commission, have exactly the same duties and responsibilities as directly employed audit staff.

Special studies

The findings of national studies which identify good management practice and performance indicators and lead to the achievement of better value for money are published in reports, copies of which are sent to all local authorities. The topics covered become the subject of particular attention by Auditors in their examination of local authority work.

Some of the subjects dealt with in these special studies include:

- the competitive council
- the role of the chief executive
- better financial management
- obtaining better value from further education
- saving energy in local government buildings
- improving cash flow management in local government
- improving council house maintenance.

Powers and responsibilities of Auditors

Auditors must be satisfied that a local authority is doing only what it is allowed by law to do. There is a legal framework within which local authorities must work, and the role of Auditors is to ensure that nothing is being done outside this. Auditors have the legal power to obtain whatever information they feel is necessary to carry out their duties and they have a statutory function in matters involving illegality or losses caused by deliberate or inadvertent misconduct. They are ultimately answerable to the courts in exercising these powers. If Auditors consider that a local authority is doing, or has done, something which it has no legal right to do, they will first discuss the situation with the authority. If they then feel it necessary to go further, they can apply to the court for a declaration that the item concerned is unlawful.

National Health Service

At the time of our enquiry plans were being made to transfer responsibility for the statutory external audit of the organisations within the NHS to the Audit Commission. A Health Studies directorate was set up in London to undertake research and produce both published reports and material for auditors to use locally. The Commission's staff were planning to visit each region of the NHS to explain the new approach in detail to authority members and senior staff.

Administration Manager's role and responsibilities

Patricia Church's position as Administration Manager at the Audit Commission is given in the organisation chart for the London headquarters in Fig 13.3. Her responsibilities are as follows:

- the overall running of the Controller's private office
- personal assistance to the Controller

- management of the London office, i.e. provision of general support services, office systems and procedures, rent, rates, building maintenance and re-decoration, cleaning, furniture, equipment, stationery and setting and controlling budgets
- staff management relating to support staff in London and secretarial staff throughout the Commission; recruitment and selection of new employees, training, appraisal, promotions and technical skills standards
- special projects which involve organising major conferences, meetings and other functions such as the Commission's fifth birthday conference at the Queen Elizabeth II Centre, a recent lecture at Banqueting House and the Value Improvement Prize Competition and Award Ceremony.

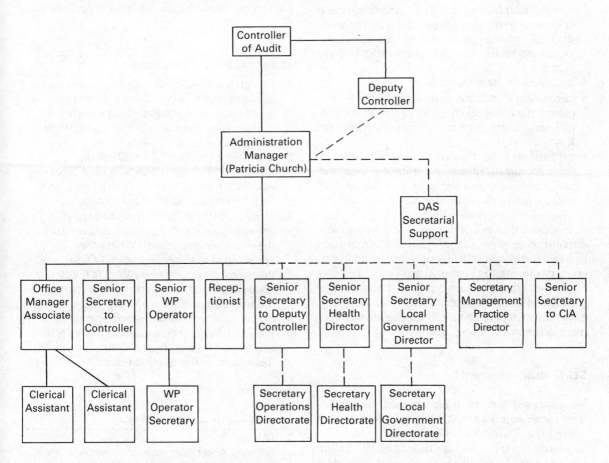

Fig 13.3 Organisation chart for the Audit Commission's London headquarters

Accommodation

At the time of our visit the Commission had recently taken over additional floors of the Vincent Square building to provide much needed accommodation for the expansion of services and Patricia Church was responsible for making the necessary arrangements. These involved:

- negotiations with the property owners regarding the lease and rent
- arrangements for the Surveyor to inspect the property
- appointment of Architects to re-design the floors in conjunction with the Heads of Departments; a computer-aided design program was used in the first place to lay out the floor plans
- consultation with the Computing Department concerning cabling for the computer network system, telephones, etc. (a database network system operates throughout the country to all districts, providing access to the database, electronic mail and a computerised diary system)
- arranging tenders for building works
- purchasing furniture and equipment — the opportunity was taken to change from vertical to lateral filing cabinets because they take up less space
- the final stage in this programme of work was to make arrangements for moving furniture and equipment into the new accommodation and supervise the operation.

Accommodation in London is expensive and it is difficult to recruit suitably qualified administrative and secretarial staff. Consideration had been given to moving the headquarters out of London but it was thought to be essential to retain a presence in London for the regular contacts with government departments and to provide a convenient centre for holding meetings.

Staff management

We discussed aspects of employment and training of staff with Patricia. When people apply for office jobs with the Commission they are required to take an aptitude test including spelling and technical skills. Patricia considers that it is important to make the interview as informal and friendly as possible by arranging it in a room with easy chairs. She looks for staff who will fit into the office and become good members of the team. Applicants are encouraged to talk about themselves and their ambitions and the reason why they have left their previous job or are planning to do so. Once a decision has been made, references are taken up to provide additional information about the applicant. The offer of a position is conditional upon a satisfactory response.

All staff of the Commission take part in a performance appraisal scheme. Forms are completed twice a year by the employee's immediate line Manager and the findings and future targets agreed by both parties.

Internal training courses are arranged for office staff dealing with such matters as time management, prioritising work loads and adapting to new technological equipment and systems.

STUDENT ACTIVITIES FOR INDIVIDUALS

1 Design a leaflet which explains to the public changes made in your own organisation which were designed to increase value for money as a result of 'economy, efficiency and effectiveness'.

2 Draw up a profile of the skills and qualifications required to take up a career in auditing, having regard to the powers and responsibilities outlined in the case study.

3 The Audit Commission has changed from vertical to lateral filing cabinets 'because they take up less space'. What other advantages are there for lateral filing? Are there any disadvantages? Why is it still necessary to have paper-based systems in a modern computerised office?

4 Prepare a checklist of the arrangements Patricia Church would need to make for a lecture to be given by the Chancellor of the Exchequer at Banqueting House.

STUDENT ACTIVITIES FOR GROUP WORK

1 Discuss:
   (a) why Audit Commission members are drawn from, *but do not represent*

industry, local government, the accounting profession and the trade unions

(b) the 'legal framework within which local authorities must work' the doctrine of *ultra vires* and the role of the courts

(c) the problems of administering the Audit Commission from headquarters split between different locations. How can new technology assist in solving some of these problems?

(d) what is meant by 'providing districts with access to a database'?

2 Consider Patricia Church's techniques of interviewing and how you would encourage applicants to talk about themselves. Role play, with video if possible, a staff interview for a vacancy in one of your organisations to demonstrate your group's ideas.

Comparisons and conclusions

Tasks

1 For each of the case study organisations state:
   (a) their main objectives
   (b) those responsible for making major decisions
   (c) the ways in which members of the public can influence their work
   (d) the sources of their finance and what control government exercises over their expenditure
   (e) which of the organisations employ civil servants and which of them employ local government officers
   (f) what parliamentary control and/or scrutiny there is over their activities
   (g) what judicial control exists over their activities.

2 Draw an organisation chart showing the inter-relationships of the public sector organisations depicted in the case studies, with the British Parliament and relevant government departments as the starting point.

3 Compare the management structure of British Gas plc with one of the public sector organisations.

4 Explain the relationship and involvement of your own organisation or your college with one or more of the case study organisations.

5 State which of the case study organisations would deal with each of the following matters:
   (a) organising public sports and leisure centres
   (b) selecting parliamentary candidates
   (c) managing doctor and dental services
   (d) controlling expenditure for the internal maintenance of school buildings
   (e) ensuring that local authorities spend money in accordance with the law
   (f) protecting British interests overseas
   (g) controlling Network TV
   (h) organising the home help service
   (i) scrutinising draft European legislation
   (j) approving new taxation proposals
   (k) developing sources of energy
   (l) campaigning for better homes
   (m) providing a conciliation service in trade disputes
   (n) negotiating salaries for local government employees.

6 Discuss the involvement of the case study organisations in any of the current events reported in the local, national and international news during recent weeks.

7 Discuss the effects of legislation introduced in the past three years on each of the case study organisations.

8 What changes do you foresee over the next five years in each of the case study organisations and to what extent do these depend on which political party is in power?

List of relevant statutes

Abolition of Death Penalty Act	1965	Education Reform Act	1988
Abolition of Domestic Rates (Scotland) Act	1987	Education (Student Loans) Act	1990
Abortion (Amendment) Act	1990	Emergency Powers Act	1939
Abortion Reform Act	1967	Employers Liability (Compulsory Insurance) Act	1969
Access to Health Records Act	1990	Employment Act	1980
Access to Medical Reports Act	1988	Employment Act	1982
Access to Personal Files Act	1987	Employment Act	1988
Act of Settlement	1701	Employment Act	1990
Act of Union	1707	Employment Protection Act	1975
Administration of Justice Act	1960	Employment Protection (Consolidation) Act	1978
Administration of Justice Act	1964	Equal Pay Act	1970
Administration of Justice Act	1969	European Communities Act	1972
Administration of Justice Act	1970	European Communities (Amendment) Act	1986
Administration of Justice Act	1985		
Appropriation Act	annually	Factories Act	1961
		Finance Act	annually
Bill of Rights	1689	Food and Drugs Act	1955
British Museums Act	1964		
British Nationality Act	1981	Geneva Convention Act	1957
British Nationality (Hong Kong) Act	1990		
Broadcasting Act	1990	Habeus Corpus Act	1679
		Habeus Corpus Act	1816
Chronically Sick and Disabled Persons Act	1970	Health and Medicines Act	1988
Commons Disqualification Act	1957	Health and Safety at Work Act	1974
Companies Act	1985	Health Services Act	1982
Consumer Protection Act	1987	Housing Act	1988
Contracts of Employment Act	1963	Housing (Scotland) Act	1987
Contracts of Employment Act	1972	Housing (Scotland) Act	1988
County Courts Act	1959		
County Courts Act	1984	Immigration Act	1971
Courts and Legal Services Act	1990	Industrial Relations Act	1971
Criminal Justice Act	1967	Industrial Training Act	1982
Criminal Justice Act	1972	Interception of Communications Act	1985
Criminal Justice Act	1987		
Criminal Law Act	1977	Juries Act	1974
		Juries (Disqualification) Act	1974
Data Protection Act	1984		
Defence of the Realm Act	1914	Legal Aid Act	1982
Diplomatic Privileges Act	1964	Legal Aid Act	1988
Diplomatic Privileges Act	1971	Legal Aid (Scotland) Act	1986
Diplomatic and Consular Premises Act	1987	Life Peerage Act	1958
		Local Government Act	1894
Education Act	1944	Local Government Act	1948
Education Act	1987	Local Government Act	1949
Education Act	1988	Local Government Act	1958
		Local Government Act	1972

Index